# TROUBLE BREWIN

# TROUBLE BREWIN

## A TRUE STORY OF SEX, MURDER, LOVE AND BETRAYAL

## BELINDA BREWIN

metro

Published by Metro Publishing Ltd,
3, Bramber Court, 2 Bramber Road,
London W14 9PB, England

www.blake.co.uk

First published in hardback in 2005

ISBN 1 84358 140 X

British Library Cataloguing-in-Publication Data:

A catalogue record for this book is available from the British Library.

Design by www.envydesign.co.uk

Printed in Great Britain by Creative Print & Design (Wales)

1 3 5 7 9 10 8 6 4 2

Papers used by Metro Publishing are natural, recyclable products made
from wood grown in sustainable forests. The manufacturing processes
conform to the environmental regulations of the country of origin.

Pictures from the author's collection, except:
p1, top Fairfax Photos/Robert Pearce; p4, bottom © National Pictures;
p7, main © Rex Features; p11 © Alpha Press;
p14, top © www.apexnewspix.com; p16 © Empics / PA

Every attempt has been made to contact the relevant copyright-holders,
but some were unobtainable. We would be grateful if the appropriate
people could contact us.

*For my children Montana and Indiana.*

*For my mother Anne and in memory
of my dearest friend Paula*

# ACKNOWLEDGEMENTS

I would also like to thank the following people:

My father Charles and his wife Laura for their support, advice and the peace of their home which enabled me to write some of this book.

My brother Tobey and his girlfriend Alex Lyons, who must have wondered when the trial would end and when they could have their house to themselves again. Their love and support helped me through the ordeal of giving evidence.

My sisters Nicola, Miranda and Julia... just for being there, always.

Charlie King who has truly enriched my life and, if I lived to be 150, I could never repay the gratitude I feel I owe him. Anyone who has a friend like Charlie is truly blessed. Thank you from the bottom of my heart.

Christo Lefroy Brooks, whose kindness and generosity cannot be put into words. I will never be able to thank you enough.

Mark Cook for being the rudest most irreverent friend I have and for making me look good when I felt like the back of a bus. He was a true and loyal friend to Paula as he is to me.

Geoff Weedon, whose help, encouragement and friendship throughout the writing of this book was unwavering and often hilarious. Thanks to him I can now do joined-up words!

The Breakfast Club Girls: Diana Breitmeyer, Mel Waldron, Andy Weedon, Corinna Knowles and Diana Rossiter. who have been my lifeblood and whose unquestioning support is the main reason I am still standing today. Diana B comes in for a special mention for not kidnapping my cats whilst I was away and Mel who looked after my daughter, Indiana, for such long periods I would have forgiven her for thinking she must have adopted her.

Rose and Trevor Downing, who have been firm friends since I came to Devon. Rose for always standing up for me and for giving me a piece of her mind when I needed it and for looking after my dog Boom-Boom for what must have seemed like weeks on end.

Tony Bishop, who had the unenviable task of interviewing me for hours on end and who I hope will become a good friend. Everyone should know one policeman like Bish, he's a top man.

Catherine Mayer for being a friend to me when I needed one. Thank you.

Mel and Anton for their astounding kindness, loyalty, generosity and many a fantastic drunken night and without whom the world would be a much duller place. (PS: thanks for introducing me to Rose and Dot!)

My lawyer Keith Dolan for working so hard on my case all those years ago and my barristers Peter Guest and Jerome Lynch QC.

Anthony Burton, a wonderful friend and an excellent lawyer whose huge kindnesses and help never went unnoticed.

Sue and Rick for being such good listeners and Sue for letting me flirt with her handsome husband.

David Chambers, the Bursar at Blundells School for his patience!

Colin and Evie Diamond, who though far away, are very close to my heart. A huge thank-you from myself and my girls.

Andrew Young, a brilliant barrister and Lisa Pannucci, a fantastic lawyer who worked hard and were unerring in their support of myself, Paula and Tiger. I will always appreciate that and you know how much you mean to me.

Natalia Jedlinski for being my friend and standing by me for the last 30 years, especially when it really mattered.

Davo and Cossi Edwards for being my friends and making me wish I lived in Sydney, just to be near them.

Susie Jackson for dressing me in beautiful clothes when I had no money.

Kevin Hanley, who I can't wait to buy a drink for and who I know was as thrilled as me to hear the news. See you soon.

Susie Aplin, just for being a top girl and because I love her Maria and Anton for being such good friends and Maria for lending me her apartment, it was the best week I spent in years! And also because she has the best tits I've ever seen and I just love her.

Andy Rowell, Russell Ferris, Dick Langdon, and even Graham Thurlow who all helped make a very traumatic time a lot easier ... Well, all except Graham who made me cry and I am still waiting for the written apology and flowers!

To all at Blake Publishing, but especially John and Rosie for seeing the bigger picture and, of course, Michelle and Adam, as this book would not read as well without their efforts. Also Lucian who had to put up with me being grumpy ... only once!

And most importantly to the two juries in this book for making the right decision both times. I am eternally grateful to them.

# CONTENTS

# PART ONE

PART ONE

# CHAPTER ONE

Paula was dead.

I was standing in Sainsbury's car park in Chelmsford, Essex. The phone felt like a lead weight in my hand. 'Tell me it's not true,' I whispered to Jo Fairley, Paula's oldest friend. It couldn't be: I had spent three hours with her the night before making sure she was OK. She clearly hadn't been.

My head was spinning and my first thoughts were for Tiger, my goddaughter. Michael's sister and mother had tried so many times to get custody of her; with Paula gone, who was going to stop them? I had to get her out of that house and somewhere safe, but what chance would I have against blood relations? I knew I had to get back to London, and even in those first few moments a little inkling of the horror of the next few days and months was beginning to dawn on me ...

My eldest sister Nicola and my younger daughter Indiana emerged from the supermarket. We were on our way to visit my elder daughter Montana at her new boarding school. I had woken up at seven o'clock that morning – far too early to call Paula – but as we travelled across London my mobile phone had constantly sounded the tune of 'Waltzing Matilda'. It meant that Paula's number was calling, but I was still angry at her from the night before, and in no mood to listen to some feeble excuse or gushing apology.

Moreover, I had my daughter in the car and was in no position to use the kind of language I thought was fitting. I would call her when we got to the school, and then we could work out what time I was going to pick her and Tiger up to go to Bob's for Pixie's party. But 'Waltzing Matilda' kept ringing and, when we stopped at the supermarket to stock up on tuck for Montana, I gave in and answered the persistent phone call. It wasn't Paula at all, but Jo telling me the terrible news.

In a state of shock, I explained to Jo that I was visiting Monty. As soon as I had seen her and explained the situation, I would be heading back to London. Tiger was safe and with her sisters at Bob's, which was a relief – I had visions of the Social Services taking her into care until some legal requirements had been satisfied. I didn't think anyone would remove her from there, at least not immediately.

I called Bob. I told him how sorry I was, and asked how Tiger and the other girls were. He told me that Pixie's party was still going ahead, as he did not want the girls to sit around and be morose. He asked me if I was OK, but like me he sounded devastated. There was a silence. I said I'd see him later and hung up. I then switched my phone off.

The school looked daunting from a distance. Henry VIII had built the main building as a home for Anne Boleyn, and it was magnificent and imposing. As I drove down the drive, I wanted to cry so badly, but I had to remain calm. I thought how Paula would never again be able to do what I was doing now – just a daily routine of going to school to see her children. I was early and the school was at Mass. I met a nun and explained the situation, and she had my daughter taken from the chapel. She was so happy to see me and ran down the corridor with outstretched arms – something Paula's children would never be able to do to her again. I took her in my arms and hugged her tight, then pulled Indiana into our embrace. The tears welled up in my eyes, but I still didn't cry.

I didn't word it very well. I said I had to leave because of Paula. 'Not again,' complained Monty. 'She always ruins everything.' I suppose she was right, but this time she had ruined things forever – for herself and for her children rather than anyone else. Four-year-old Tiger, ten-year-old Pixie, eleven-year-old Peaches and seventeen-year-old Fifi would never be able to hold their mother again. I explained what had happened. Monty cried and wanted to come home. She wanted to see Pixie and Peaches and wanted to know if Tiger was going to be staying with us. I couldn't answer any of her questions; she seemed very distressed and I hated to leave her there. Nicola was an angel and stayed at the school all day. The nuns said they would make sure she was fine and said they would mention us in prayers that evening. As I walked back to the car, I couldn't help but see things differently. I was suddenly aware how fragile life was, and it was scary. I ran back to kiss Monty again, and to tell her that I loved her.

With Indiana in the car with me, I started the journey home. I switched my phone back on and it buzzed constantly with text messages and voicemails. Many of them were from the press wanting me to confirm whether or not what they had heard was true, and if I could give a statement or enlighten them on how this tragedy had occurred. I remember speaking to Andy Coulson – now the editor of the *News of the World* – who was absolutely charming and sweet; even though he was a journalist, he had also rung in the capacity of a friend. When I told him that something had occurred between Paula and me the evening before, he advised me not to say a word to anybody about it. It was advice well given and well taken. Along with whatever else they were bound to drag up, no one needed the papers to be full of the fact that I'd had a huge row with her the night she died.

As I approached London, I could see Canary Wharf. I thought of all the meetings Paula and I had had there. The feeling of desolation that it inspired must have been obvious, because every now and again a little hand would reach over and stroke my arm or my cheek, and a little voice would say, 'Mummy, are you OK?' or 'Please, Mummy, don't be sad.' But how could I not be? Half of me wished I hadn't been so cross with Paula the night before; half of me thought I should have been more cross. But I knew that I would even miss those times when she was being a complete pain in the arse.

Suddenly, I was snapped out of my self-pity.

'Why didn't her friend help her?' Indiana asked.

I was confused. She must mean Jo. 'Jo couldn't have helped her, darling. Paula was already dead when she arrived.'

Indy looked baffled. 'No,' she said, 'not Jo. The girl who was in the house.'

'What girl?'

'The girl you don't like.'

I was totally flummoxed. 'What's her name?' I asked.

My daughter couldn't remember. 'You shouted at her once,' she said.

Well, that was no kind of clue – I shout at a lot of people! I simply couldn't think who else could have been in the house that night. I didn't feel up to a 'guess who' conversation, so, as I wound my way through London, we tried together to piece together the events of the previous day …

Paula and I had first spoken over toast and a cigarette that morning – she had the toast, I had the cigarette. She wanted to know if I would go down to Portobello Market with her to pick up Pixie's dress, which was a present for her birthday. Pixie, as talented as ever, had designed a very beautiful, slinky evening dress that Paula had had made up for her by a seamstress she knew. Paula loved Portobello, and everyone there seemed to love her. She was going for lunch at 192, a nice restaurant just off the market, and asked if I would join her. I couldn't as I'd promised Indiana I would go for a bike ride, but I agreed to meet her later that afternoon so that Indy and Tiger could go to the park. Paula was in better spirits than she had been for a long time; she was worrying about her weight, as she always did, but she seemed optimistic about the future and was looking forward to working again.

Around four o'clock, Indy and I went over to St Luke's Mews. I knocked, then let myself in with my key. The front door opens directly into the living room, and the kitchen is beyond that at the back of the house. The stairs from the living room led directly into Pixie and Tiger's bedroom, and to the right of that was the bathroom. Peaches's room was next to the bathroom, and a further set of stairs led up to Paula's bedroom and a little roof garden. Her bedroom was decorated with Ralph Lauren wallpaper that we had bought on one of our many shopping trips, and on the balcony hung her treasured Australian flag. Whenever she and Michael had a row and he thought he was losing the battle, he used to retaliate by saying, 'Why don't you get off my fucking flag?' It was a reference to the Union Jack being part of the Australian flag. I could never see where he was coming from, but it never failed to make Paula laugh. The argument would be over, they would fall back into bed and the big love would yet again be in full swing.

I loved Paula's house – it was like stepping into a Moroccan kasbah. Paula was sitting among a pile of wrapping paper and birthday cards. She was absolutely thrilled with how fabulous Pixie's dress looked. Paula doted on Pixie, and she just couldn't wait to see her face when she gave her the dress. We chatted for a while. It was at the time of the petrol shortage, and Paula said she would look after Indy while I scoured the city and motorways for fuel. She seemed perfectly happy, and I certainly did not get the impression that she was trying to get me out of the house; in fact, as I was leaving, her next-door neighbour was in the mews and Paula invited her daughter in to play with our girls.

Two hours later, and with a full tank of petrol, I headed back into town feeling quite pleased with myself. Every petrol station I passed was either roped off or had queues of cars lined up causing havoc with the rest of the traffic. I parked right outside the brightly painted house and knocked on the door. As I went to unlock it with my key, the door opened. I couldn't believe my eyes: the Paula that greeted me was not the Paula I had left two hours before. At first I thought she was drunk, but I had seen her drunk many times and I soon realised that it wasn't alcohol. Then it dawned on me what the problem was, and I was shocked. It had been a very long time since I had seen her in this state – probably two years, maybe more – and my blood started to boil. I was furious. She stood there in her green dress with what looked like tea stains down the front, swaying and looking like she was going to faint. She started to mumble something, but she was completely incoherent.

I told her to sit down and that I would be right back. I certainly didn't want the children coming downstairs with Paula in such a state. They were ensconced in Paula's bedroom on the top floor, watching – ironically – *Sleeping Beauty* on the huge Bang & Olufsen television that had been a gift from Finlay Quaye, and surrounded by the enormous array of Barbie dolls that both Tiger and Indiana adored. They would play for hours with them. They had even made their own hairdressing salon that the dolls attended, changing the name of one of their Ken dolls to Nicky – because even Barbie should only ever have her hair done by Nicky Clarke! Luckily, the two of them were totally engrossed in each other, and it took them a few seconds to acknowledge that I was even there. They had eaten, they were very happy and they were totally oblivious to Paula's state, which was a relief.

I came downstairs with a heavy heart and asked her what she had done – not that I really needed to. I have never quite understood why anybody would want to take a drug that just makes you fall asleep and vomit. Heroin is evil and insidious and, though I make no claim to being an angel myself, I could never understand why anybody would go near it. Paula was sitting in a chair with her head in her hands. I knelt in front of her and put my arms around the back of her neck. She was very sweaty and her hair was damp and limp against her head. I kissed the side of her cheek and felt so sad for her, but also angry. She had to pull herself together, so I told her to get up as we were going to go for a walk. I tried to get her to stand up but she was like a dead weight, and I certainly couldn't carry her around the block.

I have never drunk tea or coffee, but they seem to be a cure-all for most people so I made my way to the kitchen – tripping over a pile of extremely badly wrapped presents on the way. I put the kettle on and was amazed by the devastation. It was as if in a few short hours Paula's house had been burgled and hit by a hurricane both at the same time. There were remnants of the food that the children had had, and pots and pans everywhere. A pile of magazines that had been stacked on a chair were now strewn across the floor, and the chair itself had been overturned. The place stank, and I noticed that Paula had been sick. I took her a glass of water and some sweet tea and told her to drink them. I then headed back into the kitchen to try to bring some semblance of order to the chaos. Under the sink was an enormous array of cleaning products – Paula, the complete antithesis to me, was an avid cleaner, and she had to have every new cleaning product that appeared on the market.

An enormous amount of disinfectant later, I felt I was finally getting somewhere. I went back to the living room to check on Paula. She was holding the mug of tea very precariously in her hand and looked as if she was about to nod off. 'That's it,' I said, 'we're going outside.' She seemed to come to and appeared a little startled, as if she didn't remember me arriving. I put her arm around my shoulder and helped her up.

'I don't want to go out,' she mumbled. 'What if somebody sees me?'

'You should have thought about that before you got yourself into this state,' I told her.

We walked to the end of the mews and on to All Saints Road. There were people still making their way back from the huge Saturday antique market, but nobody gave us a second glance, and I doubted that anybody would have recognised this shuffling woman as the radiant Paula Yates. She wanted to sit down as she didn't feel well, and her eyes were rolling, but I had to keep her walking. It was either that, I told her, or call an ambulance, which I knew to be pointless, as she wouldn't get in it. I also knew from past experience that calling an ambulance would result in yet more press headlines about Paula's mental state. Considering what followed, I clearly had my priorities wrong ...

We carried on walking, and Paula seemed to be becoming more lucid. We walked around the block a few times, unable to take a different route as I had left the children in the house and I didn't want to be more than a shout away. It started to get cold and I noticed that the tea stains on her dress were looking more like the mess I had cleared up in the kitchen, so we headed back to the house. Paula kept telling me she was sorry and asking me if I was cross with her. I wasn't cross as such, just very disappointed and slightly confused as to what had triggered this major relapse when things were looking better for her and we had been through so much worse. I also wondered where she had got the drugs from, as she certainly would not have known herself where to get them. I wondered whom she had met for lunch, and if they were the source of the heroin. Still, the walk had helped, and I thought that Paula would feel like a new person after a good night's sleep.

Once inside the house, Paula wanted to start her usual routine of washing up and cleaning. I suggested that I run her a bath first so that she could freshen up. She couldn't remember if she had eaten anything, which meant that she probably hadn't, so I suggested she have some soup that was in the kitchen. I still had vague suspicions that she had been drinking, so, while I continued tidying up and running a bath, I searched the cupboards and drawers for any alcohol. There was none. I asked her if she had any in the house and she assured me that she didn't. There weren't any empties in the bin. I know because I checked.

The bath was run and full of whatever concoctions and potions I could find. Paula's bathroom reminded me of the toiletry department in Harrods, still full of items that she had received when she was doing her beauty column for *OK!*. She got in the bath. I washed her hair for her and she seemed to be getting a lot better. I asked Paula where the hairdryer was. She said she didn't know, so I went to go into Peaches's room to have a look. She shouted to me that it wasn't there and not to go in, as she had been sick there earlier. She said she had cleared it up, and as I'd seen quite enough sick stains for one day I took her word for it and didn't even open the door to the room.

In hindsight, it was odd that the door was closed at all.

Paula got out of the bath and she and I sat on the bottom of the steps leading to her bedroom. I asked her why she had done this to herself. She said it was the pressure of being in London, having spent the summer in Hastings. She had a house there and had been hanging out on the beach with the girls, including her long-term friend Jo Fairley who lived close by. She said she felt free and herself in Hastings – she loved the sea – and yet in London she felt trapped and isolated. She also said that I had not come down to see her the weekend before, and that she had been hurt by that. It was feeble and ludicrous. I told her she was selfish and that there was really no point in the conversation as her arguments were pathetic and she wouldn't remember anything in the morning, so it was best we all saved our breath for the next day. We also needed to talk about work, and had agreed previously that we would discuss it today, but that would have been futile. She and I were professionally going to go in different directions and I had already taken another job, so I could no longer act as her unofficial manager.

Indiana and Tiger appeared at the top of the stairs and announced they were hungry. Indy helped Tiger get ready for bed, while I cooked some pasta for the two of them. Tiger wanted Indy to stay the night, but that was not possible because she was coming with me the next morning to see her sister. At one point, I was going to take Tiger home with me, and I was still in two minds about it – she could have come to school with us, and Monty would have been thrilled; but it was Pixie's birthday, and Tiger certainly didn't want to miss out on any part of the day. She hero-worshipped Pixie. I asked Paula if she wanted to come and stay, but she said she would be fine at home, and that she wanted to wake up in her own bed. I wish now, more than anything, that I had insisted ...

The girls ate their food while I helped Paula get dressed. She was quiet, and every now and again would look up ruefully and tell me how sorry she was. Indy went upstairs with Tiger for one last play with Barbie before going home. I asked Paula if she would be OK, and told her to get into bed and have an early night. I went upstairs and said goodnight to Tiger, who was sitting on Paula's bed. It may as well have been hers for the amount of time she ever slept in her own bed.

As I got into the car, Paula opened the door to wave goodbye. 'Please, don't be cross with me,' she begged. I blew her a kiss and drove off.

My heart felt heavy. I wasn't sure if I had done the right thing, and wondered if I should have taken Tiger with me. I drove to the end of the mews and on to the same road that I had walked with Paula an hour before, but something was niggling at me. Was she going to go out and buy alcohol? Did she have any in the house? I crossed Portobello Road and turned into Ladbroke Grove. Only a couple more blocks and I would be home; but the niggling feeling wouldn't go away. I got to Lansdowne Crescent where I turned around and went back. I knew what I was going to do: they would both come and stay the night with me. I would insist, and stuff the disruption it might cause in the morning. Indy was thrilled, as it meant she wouldn't have to go to bed straight away and she had another chance to play with Barbie. So I found myself pulling up outside Paula's house once more.

It must have been around nine o'clock – maybe a little after – that I knocked on the door (my house keys were with my car keys and I had left the car running). 'Grab some stuff,' I told her when she opened the door. 'You guys can come and stay at my house.'

'No,' she replied. 'Tiger's already asleep, and I'm tired and want to go to bed.'

'It's no bother,' I told her. 'We can just hang out and watch crap TV.' Then I saw how drowsy she looked. 'But if you're sure you're going to be OK, and you really are going to get some sleep …'

Paula gave me a hug. I kissed her cheek, and I felt reassured. She was going to be fine …

The events of the previous evening were going round and round in my head. We were now approaching Tower Bridge, and Indiana was adamant that she was right and that there had definitely been someone in Paula's house when I had been there. It just didn't seem possible, but Indiana certainly would not make something like that up. Who would have not made their presence known, and why would Paula have hidden them from me? I kept thinking who I might have shouted at – the list of suspects was infinite – but I couldn't think of anybody that I actively disliked.

I couldn't dwell on it for too long, though, as I had my mind on other things. I needed to get home and call Australia. I wanted to speak to Michael's father Kell and his wife Susie to put their minds at rest, and I needed to speak to Colin Diamond, whom Michael had appointed as Tiger's guardian in his will, and who was also executor of the will. He was one of Michael's best friends, certainly his most trusted, and he would know the best way to protect Tiger. Despite the accounts in the press, mainly fuelled by Michael's mother and half-sister, he had always and still does have Tiger's best interests at heart.

Suddenly, my thoughts were once more interrupted by a small voice in the back. 'You must remember the girl, Mummy,' said Indy, 'because you were going to call the police on her.' It was like a body blow. Suddenly, I knew exactly who my daughter meant. It all fell into place – why she had hidden from me, and why Paula would certainly not have wanted me to see her.

Former heroin addict Charlotte Korshak had been in the Priory at the same time as Paula. She came from a wealthy family, and her parents were funding her treatment. I had seen her at Paula's house a couple of times and she was definitely not my cup of tea – no backbone. I arrived one day to find a whole gang of Charlotte's friends playing computer games and smoking joints – normal adolescent behaviour these days, it seems. Paula and Charlotte, however, were ensconced in the upstairs bedroom. I told Charlotte to leave and never come back to the house. I said she had better move quickly, otherwise I would personally kick her all the way down the stairs, out the front door and down the entire length of the mews. I told her, if I ever caught her in this house again, I would call the police. As Charlotte was leaving, I suggested to the rest of the group that now was an ideal time for them to do the same. Paula thought I had been much too harsh on all of them, but as she had just come out of the Priory I felt it was way too soon for her to be taking drugs even on a recreational basis; and I have a real problem with anyone taking heroin at any time. As far as I was concerned, there was no room for compromise.

I dropped Indiana off with some friends of mine, went home, rang Australia and spoke to a business acquaintance of Colin Diamond. He said he would track down Colin and get him to call. I spoke to Kell and said I would speak to him later when I had more details, and assured him that Tiger was being well looked after. He said how sorry he was and that both he and Susie sent their love. They were good people, and I was sorry that Paula had felt the need to fight them so much; after a shaky beginning, they had proved to be staunch supporters of what was right and fair, and they certainly loved their little granddaughter. I also spoke to Catherine Mayer, another good friend of Paula's and part of what I affectionately called the Gang of Three – myself, Jo Fairley and her.

At that point, we all believed that I was the last person to have seen her alive. Because of this, my presence was required, along with Jo Fairley, at Notting Hill Police Station to be interviewed by one of the detectives involved in the inquiry. The police station was halfway between my house and Paula's. I had taken the same route every day for two years, so it was no surprise that I drove straight past the station as if on autopilot. I parked outside in a police bay, hoping I wouldn't get a ticket, or worse still get towed away. The reception area was small and dark. There were a couple of people waiting and only one duty police officer dealing with their queries, one involving the loss of a mobile phone. I waited politely for a few moments, and then the grimness of the station made me feel totally overwhelmed and I went back outside. I sat on the steps and smoked what seemed like my fortieth cigarette of the day. I would wait on the steps for Jo to arrive; but then I was unsure whether she was already there, so I made my way back in. The duty sergeant looked up from what he was doing and, slightly bemused by my reappearance, asked if he could help me. I certainly did not want to blurt out that I was here in connection with the death of Paula Yates, so I said that I had been asked to come here in relation to an incident that had occurred in St Luke's Mews earlier that morning. He gave me a look of acknowledgement, stopped what he was doing and asked the person he was dealing with to give him a minute. He asked my name and went to the phone. He told me to take a seat and somebody would be down immediately. Having not wanted to be crass, I couldn't believe that I had just described the death of my dearest friend as an 'incident'; but before I could cry a rather big guy with a firm handshake introduced himself to me as Detective Inspector Mike Christensen.

He and another gentleman asked me to accompany them to a private room off to one side of the reception area. I had the most bizarre feeling of déjà vu: I had been in a similar situation not too long before, albeit on the other side of the world in Sydney. They were not antagonistic, but, given that I was the last person to see her alive and she was now dead, I expect they viewed me with some suspicion. As I was beginning to explain the events of the previous evening, Jo Fairley appeared accompanied by her husband Craig – a wonderfully handsome, gentle man with whom Paula had spent many an hour flirting. Jo, Craig and I hugged each other. There were few words spoken. Anthony Burton of solicitors Simons Muirhead & Burton arrived shortly after. Another handsome and wonderfully kind man (and another man with whom Paula delighted in flirting), he had not only been Michael's lawyer and friend, but also had become both to Paula. He was one of the first people to come to Paula's the night of Michael's death; now he had that same ashen look that he bore that night.

Jo and Craig were taken by some other police officers to another room as they had to give statements, especially as it was Jo who had discovered her body. I ran through the exact details of what had happened. I then told the police what my daughter had told me on the journey home, and said I had no reason to doubt her but that I could not substantiate it. I also explained the reasons Charlotte would have had for not making herself known to me. They were obviously very interested in contacting her, and asked me if I had a telephone number for her, which I did not. I thought Sam Robinson-Horley, Paula's ex-boyfriend, would have, but he was living abroad when Paula died; when he heard the news, he had got on the first available plane and so was not contactable. I told the police Charlotte had been at the Priory and they would undoubtedly have her details.

Having told the police everything I could, I asked them how she had died. Until they had the pathologist's report, they said, they wouldn't like to hazard a guess. I wondered if she had choked; not that it really mattered – it wasn't going to bring her back.

And for what seemed like the millionth time that day my mobile rang. It was Pixie. 'Will you do me a favour?' she asked me.

'Anything,' I replied. All I wanted was to be able to do something to make her feel better.

'Will you go to my mum's house and pick up the dress for me?'

'I'll see what I can do. I'll call you back as soon as I can.'

The police didn't seem sure whether I was going to be able to go, as technically the house was a crime scene. I told them that the dress was hanging up in the kitchen downstairs, nowhere near the bedroom where Paula had died; it was decided that I would go with two police officers, go straight to the kitchen, retrieve the dress and shoes and leave immediately.

Jo appeared in the waiting area. She wanted to tell me something and seemed a little nervous. She said she did not want to upset me but she had been asked by the police if there had been anything worrying Paula, anything playing on her mind. She had told them that she thought Paula was worried about talking to me about her future work plans which did not involve me. Of course, this was nothing that I didn't know about, but it was sweet of Jo to consider my feelings at that time, and it was very indicative of her kindness and friendship to Paula over many years.

A policewoman touched me on the shoulder and said that they were ready to go whenever I was. Craig, Jo and I said our goodbyes, knowing that we would see each other later at Bob's house. It was a strange feeling getting into a police car to go the short distance to Paula's house. As we drove into St Luke's Mews, I was completely taken aback by the huge number of press and television crews. For some reason, I hadn't envisaged this. 'Are you going to be OK?' asked the policewoman.

I didn't know. 'Is Paula still inside?'

She seemed horrified by the idea. 'Of course not,' she answered. I had naively thought that, if Paula was no longer in the house, the press would have decamped elsewhere – Bob's place, maybe. But, having been through all this when Michael died, I should have realised that they were there awaiting confirmation of the cause of death, and to monitor police involvement in and out of the house.

We got out of the car to the clicking of cameras and to the shouts of journalists' questions, none of which was audible and which sounded like one amalgamated, disjointed reverberation. I had my key and let myself and the two officers into the house. It felt so strange, and even in the short space of time since the previous night the house seemed eerily cold, as if it had been empty for a long time. The living room and the kitchen were very much as I had left them, except that there were two glasses on the table. I found the dress immediately, along with Pixie's other presents, but could not find the shoes. I called Pixie to ask her if she had any idea where they might be. She didn't know, but said they might be upstairs. She also asked if I would bring some clothes for Tiger, as she had left the house that morning with only what she was wearing. I didn't want to tell her that I was confined to the kitchen and the rest of the house was out of bounds – today was not a day for explanations of that nature.

I found a pair of little black shoes behind the door in the kitchen which I knew to be Pixie's; they would do, but they were not the pair she had wanted. I asked the police how long the house would be out of bounds and they were unable to say. I explained the clothing situation to them, and, though we could have gone out and bought Tiger an entire new wardrobe, I felt she needed some familiarity and some things around her that she knew. She had never stayed at Bob's house before, and needed something to help her feel comfortable and safe. I explained that Tiger's clothes were not in Paula's bedroom but on the landing on the first floor. The policewoman seemed visibly moved – I didn't ask but I am sure by her reaction that she had children of her own. The two officers, after a small discussion and a telephone call, said that I could return late the following afternoon with them or some other officers and pick up whatever I felt was necessary.

I put everything in a black bin liner – I didn't really think Pixie's birthday presents should be emblazoned across the front pages – and opened the door to the sound of camera fire. We made our way to the police car and drove back to the station. As we approached it, one of the officers muttered, 'Some arsehole has parked in our bay.'

'Shit,' I admitted. 'That arsehole is me.' We burst out laughing – it was our way of relieving the tension.

I felt exhausted, but this already long day wasn't over yet. As I headed home, I wondered how Bob had coped with the day. I couldn't imagine how he must have felt when he had to break the news to his girls. It was one big mess. I sank into a hot bath and thought about how strange it had been talking about Paula to the police in such a removed and emotionless way. It didn't seem right; it didn't seem respectful. I so badly wanted to call her, to see her. If only I had made her come back with me last night. Today could have been so different …

But no. I couldn't and wouldn't blame myself. At the end of the day, Paula had no one to blame but herself. It didn't make it any easier, though.

I seemed to have spent the whole day since leaving my daughter at school making my way to places that I was dreading arriving at; my next journey – to Pixie's party at Bob's – was worse than any of the others. I didn't know what to expect, and I was worried that one of the girls would ask me a question I couldn't answer. When I arrived, Bob gave me a kiss and, for the first time ever, a big hug. 'Are you OK, big girl?' he asked me.

'Yes,' I replied. 'I'm fine. How are you?' But I needn't have asked. He looked washed out.

Walking into the house was like walking into a different world: the children were getting ready for the party, and there were a few of their friends there already. Pixie rushed out of her bedroom and was delighted to have her dress. She didn't seem too concerned that the shoes weren't the right ones. She took them from me and turned to go, but then she suddenly stopped. 'Thank you,' she said, and put her arms around my neck. I gave her a big hug and held her for just that moment longer. Then she was off. A few moments later, she emerged, looking ravishing and so like her mum.

How could Paula have done what she did and missed all this? You stupid, stupid girl, I thought. One of Pixie's presents that I had brought from the house was marked 'From Tiger', so I gave it to her to give to Pixie. She seemed quite oblivious to what had happened that morning and had had a great day hanging out with her sisters in a new environment. I knew from that moment that, as long as Bob would have her, that was where she belonged – with her sisters who loved her so much, and whom she loved desperately. Paula would have reacted with horror, I'm sure, but she'd lost the chance to vote on this one. Peaches was there – a very cool kid. She has her mother's wit and ability to cut to the quick. Fifi was not at home. She had taken solace with her friends. I gave her a call and left a message. I was – and still am – very fond of her, and we often have a laugh together.

I found Bob's house quite a respite after the madness of the day: at least one place seemed on the surface to be functioning normally. It wasn't what I had expected, but it was good and made me feel a little more tranquil than I had felt since hearing the news. I stayed for a while and then decided to go home – after all, Pixie wasn't a baby, and I was sure that the last thing she wanted was a bunch of grown-ups standing around watching to see she was enjoying herself. As I said my farewells, Tiger asked me if Indy was coming to the party. Only then did I remember that I had left her with my friends. I had promised to call and let them know what was going on, and that was God knows how many hours before. I told Bob I would call him in the morning; he put his hand on my arm, and in that moment I really felt for him.

I called Indy from the car. She was fine, and asked to stay the night, even though it was school the next day. That was OK with me – school seemed an irrelevancy at that moment in time. I realised I was starving, as I hadn't eaten all day. I stopped to buy some food at a kebab place Paula and I used to go to all the time, and then headed home once and for all, mentally exhausted.

As I closed my front door behind me, I left the world on the other side. I sank into my sofa and lit yet another cigarette. I'd take a few moments before seeing what messages I had. I needed to make a couple of calls myself, first, to see if my daughter Monty was all right and, second, to check my sister had got back on the train. I also wanted to see if I could track down Charlotte's telephone number. Nobody I called had Charlotte's number, but I knew a friend of hers whose parents lived round the corner from me, and I decided to pay them a visit in the morning. Then I waded through the messages. There was one from a detective at Notting Hill Police Station asking me to return his call, which I did immediately. He asked me if I knew any friend of Paula's who drove a Porsche, a Maserati or anything similar. Apparently, there had been a lot of noise and raised voices outside Paula's in the early hours, and then someone had driven off boy-racer style. It certainly didn't ring any bells with me, but I promised that, if I thought of anything or anybody, he would be the first to know. It was very puzzling.

Never being one to be able to relax for more than a couple of minutes at a time I started worrying about other things, like Paula's will. I knew she would not want her current will implemented, as it had been written under strained and difficult circumstances and there had been discussion recently of changing it. I could see where the difficulties might lie and it would seem prudent to act quickly. Then I thought about her houses and how I must change the locks. But it was late, it had been a long day and there was nothing I could do now until the morning.

Suddenly, the phone rang. It was Colin Diamond. It was lovely to hear his voice – he has an ability to make you feel that things will be OK. He sounded shocked, but also very businesslike, and his main concern was Tiger whom he looked after and loved like one of his own children. He said we had a lot to discuss and he would be coming over to England hopefully in the next week. I was glad of that. We wished each other goodnight and said we would speak in the morning.

I disconnected the phone, turned off yet another image of Paula on the television and climbed into bed. Paula wasn't going to be coming round tonight; I wasn't going to wake up in the morning to find my shoes straightened, and her and Tiger asleep in bed next to me. That was never ever going to happen again, and for a small moment I could only think about myself and how dreadfully sad I was.

Tomorrow was another day, and a good night's sleep always helps. But, then, I had said exactly that to Paula only twenty-four hours earlier.

# CHAPTER TWO

As I opened my eyes the following morning, I had the feeling I was waking up in a place with which I was not familiar, but I soon realised that the unusual feeling came from the knowledge that Paula was dead. I remember thinking how much worse it must be to lose someone whom you roll over and touch every morning; no wonder Paula went mad immediately after Michael died.

As I was brushing my teeth, the phone rang. It was Peaches. She asked if I was going over to her mum's house, and could she come with me to collect some of her things. Having seen the press camped outside the day before, I instantly knew that it wasn't a good idea. I also knew that she couldn't have discussed the idea with Bob, because he would have been dead against it. There was no point bringing her into the firing line. I told her that I had no idea what my movements would be, but I'd do whatever I could. In the meantime, I said she and her sisters should make a list of anything they needed, and I'd call them later.

I found myself walking aimlessly between the bathroom, bedroom and living room. I had no idea what I should sensibly be doing. It was as though I had walked the same path every morning, and then one day I had woken up and the path had disappeared. I decided to take a shower. The water felt good against my face, and I stood there hoping it would wash everything away. I got dressed feeling a new sense of determination. What I needed was a list. Paula had been a great list-writer – pages and pages of them, all unfinished now. I grabbed a pen, some paper and the phone, and called Notting Hill Police Station. I spoke to a detective there who confirmed that I would be able to go to Paula's house, but he couldn't tell me when. We agreed that he would call me when he had any news, then I would go to the station and from there on to Paula's house. I then spoke to Anthony Burton. He said that there were some legal issues we needed to discuss, mainly revolving around the contents of the will. I rang Peaches and spoke to both her and Pixie. The girls gave me their lists, and I couldn't help but smile at how they were so clearly their mother's daughters: 'Not the purple shoes with the pink bow, the purple shoes with the pink *strap*. Remember that – the pink strap, not the pink bow!' How could I forget? Fifi was still with her friends, so I left her a message and sent her a text to check she was OK. As for Tiger, well, she had nothing at Bob's and needed some familiar things around her, especially her Barbie dolls. I called Indiana – she would know which ones were precious and which could be left behind – but she wasn't there.

It was about ten o'clock when I made my way to the newsagent's armed with a need for cigarettes and a morbid curiosity about how the press would finally treat my friend now she was dead. Would they give her the peace she deserved? When I walked into the shop, the newsagent, who had often served Paula and me, gave me a sympathetic smile and said how sorry he was. Then I saw them: the papers, all lined up on the floor, took my breath away. All of them, with the exception of the *Mirror*, carried beautiful, caring and moving pictures of Paula. It was a shame some of them had not printed similar ones when she was alive. The *Mirror*, however, purported to have the last exclusive picture of Paula. It was at least a year old (her hair was short in the picture, but when she died it was long), and it was awful. Her body was barely cold, and they still couldn't treat her with dignity.

Notting Hill Police Station seemed like a home from home when I arrived, and I was greeted warmly by the officers involved. They reiterated that the house was still a crime scene and that strictly speaking no one was supposed to enter the building. They all agreed, however, that these were exceptional circumstances and that, as the death was not being treated as suspicious, I was to be allowed entry with two officers for the sole purpose of collecting the children's immediate possessions. I agreed to all their conditions and said I would follow them to Paula's house. First, though, there were a few more questions that needed answering.

The police had obviously been busy in the past twenty-four hours, and they were still interested in locating Charlotte Korshak. They asked me again if I knew any friends of Paula's who drove a sports car. It seemed that the departure of this car was accompanied by loud voices and what seemed to have been drunken frivolity. I still couldn't shed any light on either of these, but I said that I might be able to find Korshak's number from someone else. They ran through the chain of events as I had recounted them the day before, and the times that I had given them. It later transpired that the noise they were investigating was nothing more than a guest leaving a dinner party at the house next door. It was nothing to do with Paula.

Questions answered, I followed the two officers, one male and one female, to St Luke's Mews. The press pack sprang into action at the sight of a police car. I opened the door and for the second time in less than twenty-four hours I was letting two police officers into Paula's house. I was hit by the silence: no music, no children, no shouts of 'I'm up here!' We all looked at each other as if we weren't sure what we were supposed to be doing.

What we needed were bin liners. I just hoped Paula had some and sure enough – kitchen drawer, left-hand side – she did. With the roll in hand, I climbed the stairs with my two attendants following behind. I explained the layout of the house to them. First of all, I went into Peaches's room, and it was only then that I realised I had left the bloody list at home. So I put plan B into operation: I opened up the drawers and stuffed as much as I could into as many bin liners as possible. Having finished in Peaches's room, I did the same for Pixie and Tiger. The policewoman sat on the bottom of the stairs leading to Paula's room, and I thought about the number of times Paula and I had sat there watching our girls playing.

Suddenly, I remembered Michael's ashes. Jesus, how could I have forgotten them? I told the police I would have to go into her room to collect them, as there was no way that I could leave them here. They seemed a bit bewildered. I assured them that they were on the bed and that was all I would be taking. One radio call later and I was allowed to climb the stairs to her room. I looked at her bed, the place where she had died and the place where once we had shared many secrets and dreams. No one was going to be dreaming there any more. I grabbed the cushion and was gone. I placed Michael rather ignominiously in a bin liner with some of his daughter's clothes, and that was me finished. We hadn't been there more than thirty minutes.

The girls were delighted with the amount of clothes I had brought for them. Tiger was equally delighted to see me, and asked where Indy was. I wasn't even sure if she'd gone to school; what kind of mother was I? Tiger was thrilled with her bag of Barbies, but her look of delight soon turned to dismay when she realised that I had left her most precious ones behind. Of course – she and Indy had been playing with them in Paula's bedroom while they were watching TV. They must still be there. I promised I would retrieve them for her the next day. I hoped it would be a promise I could fulfil, and prayed that I wouldn't be pushing my luck with an already patient police force.

Bob looked like shit. He had his mobile firmly fixed to his ear – no change there, I thought – but this time it was different. He was having to make funeral arrangements for the mother of his children. We all had our own grief and thoughts to attend to, and he was no different from the rest of us. I felt the burden on him must have been huge, and he certainly looked like he was carrying a heavy weight. I kissed the girls goodbye, and Peaches asked me if I was all right. I should have been asking her that question. Paula would have been so proud of her and, though it wasn't really my place, so was I – proud of all of them.

When I left, I took Michael with me, and on the journey home I wondered where he should live. It was appropriate for Paula to keep him in bed with her: he was her big love, the love of her life. He certainly couldn't live on my bed – much more to the point, I'm sure he wouldn't have wanted to! As I came down the Embankment and turned into Tite Street, I felt a wave of emotion surge through me. I drove past the little park where our girls used to go and play, and where Paula, Michael, Tiger and I had had a picnic one glorious summer afternoon. I drove past our old houses and remembered the days when we were neighbours. None of us would ever have envisaged a day like this in our lives. I felt a renewed determination to discover exactly what had happened the night before last, and decided that after returning home I would go round the corner to my friends whose son knew Charlotte. They would give me her number.

I never had to implement that idea. As I arrived home, my mobile rang. It was Charlotte.

She asked me what had happened, and I couldn't believe the gall of the girl. She told me that she had left Paula's house around nine o'clock and Paula was perfectly all right. Perfectly all right? She had to be kidding! My friend, the mother of four children, lay dead. She kept telling me how sorry she was, but by now I had had enough. I told her the police were looking for her and that she ought to contact them. Charlotte informed me that they had been in touch with her father and were coming to see her. She also told me that she had gone to Paula's house on the Sunday morning to pick up a dress that Paula had given her, but had left when she saw police cars outside her house. She asked me if I would pick up the dress for her, and even began to describe it to me. That was it for me: I couldn't listen to her bullshit any more, and I told her so. I felt so angry that her main concern seemed to be the fact that she had forgotten a dress. I asked her why she had not said hello to me that evening, and she said that she did not know I was in the house. I was there for three hours: how was it possible that she was unaware of my presence when I had been there rattling around for all that time? She said that she was drunk and asleep, but also that she left before I did. None of it rang true; none of it *was* true. I felt more confused than ever, and tried to end the conversation. Charlotte said she wanted to meet me to explain exactly what had happened; I agreed I would only once she had spoken to the police and I had checked with them to see that this did not interfere with their enquiries.

I did, in fact, meet with Charlotte some time later. She called me and asked if we could meet at the bar of the Halcyon Hotel in Holland Park. She looked frightened and rather pathetic – I actually felt sorry for her. It wasn't the first time someone had died and she had been in the vicinity. A boyfriend of hers had died in similar circumstances. There was no point in being angry, though. I told her I did not blame her for Paula's death, and she shouldn't blame herself either. Nevertheless, she could not explain herself in a satisfactory way. She maintained that Paula was fine when she left and that she had not seen her taking any drugs, and tried to excuse everything by saying she was drunk and asleep. But traces of cocaine were later found in the house, and she and Paula had made three trips to the corner shop for alcohol; neither substance was found in Paula's body.

I genuinely didn't blame Charlotte for Paula's death. She was just a child, and I hoped she had learned her lesson – next time it could have been her. She gave me a letter to Paula's girls telling them how sorry she was. I never passed it on to them – having read it, I really didn't think it was an appropriate thing for four children whose mother had died to read. I did think, however, and still do, that if Paula had not met up with her that day she would not be dead. Maybe it would have happened another day and with someone else, but it's hard to imagine. Still, Paula was a grown woman who made a very stupid choice that day. Nobody forced her to take drugs, and I'm sure that, if Charlotte's claims that she herself was not using heroin that day are true, then Paula may well have bullied her into getting it for her. Charlotte was not the strongest character.

I couldn't get the phone call from Charlotte out of my head. I placed Michael somewhere safe and then rang Catherine Mayer. She was equally flabbergasted. She told me that Jo was going to be helping Bob with the funeral arrangements, and co-ordinating whatever needed to be done. I had other duties, however. As executor of her estate, I would have to deal with the legal requirements and any other matters relating to her will. Catherine still had to work, but she would help in any way that she could.

Work! I was supposed to have started my new job at Virgin today! I had completely forgotten. I rang Susie Aplin, who had put me forward for the job, and apologised profusely for not showing up on my first day, and worse still for not calling. Susie, who was a friend of Paula's and an absolutely brilliant girl, castigated me for my stupidity and said no one was expecting me and that there was no problem. She was very sad and, along with everyone else who knew Paula, couldn't understand how this had happened just when things were looking up for her. She told me to call her when I was ready, but, if I was honest, I knew then that it was a lost opportunity. How long could they wait?

On my way to Anthony Burton's office, I couldn't help but think of the many days Paula and I had spent there. The hilarity that used to occur while we were discussing deadly serious business was mind-boggling. Poor Anthony would sometimes despair with Paula; whenever he got cross with her, she would use her tactic of trying to sit on his knee. It never worked! Anthony had been a lifesaver to her after Michael died; he fought her corner, and Tiger's, as if the two of them were his own family, and I for one know the amount of time and energy that he put in free of charge. You would be hard-pushed to find a better lawyer, friend or ally.

Anthony looked like he hadn't slept well. He read me the will, although there really was no need, as I was there when he read it to Paula and she had signed it. I can't remember whether I signed it as a witness or in my capacity as executor. The will had been a bone of contention over the previous months, because she had appointed Martha Troup and her husband as Tiger's legal guardians. Martha had been INXS's manager and a friend of Michael's. After Michael died, she swore allegiance to Paula, saying that she would always be there for her; but life moves on. Moreover, Martha and her husband had split up. Paula always wanted Tiger to have a proper family, with a proper mother and father, if anything ever happened to her, so that ruined that. She didn't know what to do. She was concerned that if there was not a secure, caring environment for Tiger then it would be too easy for her to be whisked away to Australia by her relations there, far away from her sisters and anything that she knew. I was an obvious choice of guardian: Tiger knew me, she was happy with me and my girls, and I certainly wasn't going to be going anywhere. The problems were that I was not financially secure, and worse still I was single. I knew that Jo Fairley would have been happy to be Tiger's guardian, but Paula was concerned that, though she was happily married and financially secure, she had no children of her own and Paula did not want that for Tiger, having been an unhappy only child herself.

If Martha decided to take Tiger, she was quite within her right to do so. I spoke to her subsequently and suggested that Tiger should remain in England with her sisters and Bob, and that it would be a good idea for Martha to support Bob in his bid to do the right thing by the little girl. Martha's immediate concern was that Michael had made no secret of hating Bob; she felt a sense of disloyalty by then supporting the one thing Michael would have been dead against. I could see where she was coming from; but equally I felt that there was only one person to consider here, and that was Tiger. Everyone else of any importance was dead. Martha did eventually agree. We spoke a few times after Paula's death.

The will had been written when Paula and Bob were at the height of their dispute in court when Paula was trying to regain custody of the children. Paula was angry at Bob for having had the children removed from her care. In fact, she was angry with everybody – including Michael's family, whom she did not want to have any contact with Tiger.

Anthony and I discussed the inquest that would be opened into Paula's death in two days' time. We arranged to go together. We then called the Coroner's Office and I asked if it was possible for me to come and see her body. I also needed to collect the jewellery that she had been wearing on the night of her death, and any other personal effects. I decided to go to the Coroner's Office before the inquest; that way I would be able to avoid the press, who would be there in force on Wednesday. We decided that I should arrange to have the locks to Paula's house changed. I called a locksmith and they agreed to do it whenever was convenient for me. I decided to wait until the house was no longer a crime scene; hopefully, the press would then leave and I could come and go as I wanted.

I signed some papers and then left Anthony's office wondering how long it would take the press to release details of the will, as it was now a matter of public record.

As I walked back to the car, I received a phone call from the *Sun* newspaper. It was a journalist called Emma Jones. She asked me where Michael's ashes were, and what I was planning to do with them. I was not expecting that question, and I must have sounded a little flummoxed, but I told her it was not her business. She asked me if I had even got them. I told her again that it really was nothing to do with her, and hung up.

Time was moving on and it was nearly time to pick up Indiana. I knew that she would want to see Tiger, but Paula's little girl was with her nanny, Monique. Monique had worked for Paula for quite a long time – a couple of years at least. Monique did not work at weekends, which was why she had not been with Tiger when Paula died. They were planning on heading down to the country to stay at Bob's home where Paula's funeral and wake was to be held the following Saturday, and where she would finally be laid to rest. I also thought that it might not be a bad idea to let them be for a day. There seemed to be a lot of visitors and phone calls, and maybe everybody just needed a bit of peace and quiet. Jo Fairley rang. She wanted Rupert Everett's number in New York, and also told me that I had to think of a code name for myself, my boyfriend and my girls. I asked why and she explained that the police were closing the roads to Bob's house in the country to ensure that the funeral would remain private. Only those who were invited would be able to get through, and each person would have to give the police both their real name and their code name.

It was great to see Indy's friendly little face appear in the playground, and she ran into my arms. It's wonderful to be loved so unconditionally. Even in your saddest moments, your children can make you smile and feel glad to be alive. I wished Monty wasn't at boarding school, and I wondered how she had been coping. She *had* to come home, and soon. I made a mental note to make the arrangements that evening. We went home, and after I had spoken to Monty, and Indy had spoken to Tiger, we switched the phones off, ate Chinese food, watched TV and cuddled up in bed together. I slept well, even with my daughter spread-eagled across my bed and with one of her feet lodged painfully in my ribs!

Tuesday morning: lost school ties and no cereal. Why is it you either have an abundance of milk and no cereal, or copious amounts of cereal and not a drop of milk? Westminster Coroner's Office was not as daunting as I had expected. The staff were friendly, but I still felt very nervous and couldn't help but think of the mortuary in Sydney. I had never seen a dead body before we saw Michael, and now here I was waiting to see the body of my dearest friend. I wasn't sure if I could do it. Dr Paul Knapman, the coroner, came out to see me and explained what he would be doing tomorrow and that the inquest would be just a formality. His assistant gave me a glass of water, and said they were bringing Paula's body up to the room and to wait a few minutes. Her possessions were at the undertakers, I was told, and I could collect them whenever I wanted. I had already had letters of authority typed up at Anthony Burton's office giving me power of attorney.

The coroner put his head round the door; I could go and see my friend for the very last time.

There she lay. Small. Why do people always look small when they are dead? Is it because the thing that makes them 'them' – their spark, their spirit – has gone? She was so cold. I held her hand and I talked to her. I just wanted her to get up and get in the car with me and come home. This joke was far too cruel and had gone on for three days too many. She was dead – really, really dead, and I was really, really sad. I asked her to help me to do the right thing by her and to watch over her girls at all times. I couldn't help but smile at one point when I remembered her saying what she had wanted done with her ashes. Apart from being mixed with Michael's, she had joked once that I must take a handful and throw them into Dolce & Gabbana!

I didn't want to leave her there. I didn't want to leave her full stop. But the more I sat there talking, the more I realised I wanted to remember her as she had been, full of life, a wonderful person to know. I didn't want this body on a trolley to etch out my memories of the person; she was so much bigger than that. Jools Holland later said it was a tragedy that she died, because she really would have made the most fabulously interesting old person. She could only have improved with age, and it is a shame we all missed out on the experience. I would just have to be grateful for the memories, and for having had the most wonderful friend.

I kissed her again, and then remembered something that I had to do. Maybe it was something that everybody did, I didn't know, but I had seen Paula do it in Sydney to Michael, so I opened the door and asked for some scissors. I then cut some locks of her hair. I was very careful where I cut them from, because I knew that if I'd ruined her hair she would have been furious – as would Mark Cook, her long-time friend and make-up artist. (He still knew I'd done it, and still told me off!) I wrapped it in some paper and put it in my bag, then stood next to her, knowing that the time had come to say goodbye. I wasn't going to go to the funeral home to see her. I had done that with Michael and I found it very disturbing.

But I couldn't leave just yet. I sat quietly for a few more minutes and then got up, kissed her forehead and told her that I loved her. That was the last time I ever saw my friend. It really was as final and simple as that. I walked outside and my life carried on. It was most bizarre.

The trip to the funeral home in the Fulham Road seemed completely surreal. I was given a plastic bag with Paula's jewellery in: the diamond Tiffany cross that Michael had given to Paula the day Tiger was born; a couple of rings and a pair of earrings. Was that really all that was left of her? It seemed so very clinical. I signed the papers acknowledging receipt of the goods and then headed over to Kensington High Street. Paula and I banked at the same bank. I had introduced her, and knew most of the people there by name. They were all very sympathetic and had been expecting me, so all the necessary paperwork was waiting. Siriol, a wonderfully kind and helpful girl who had personally looked after Paula and me, seemed visibly upset and gave me a big hug. It was a nice gesture, and over the next few days I was amazed at the number of strangers who stopped me in the street or the supermarket to say how sorry they were.

For now, though, I had another very important task: I needed to retrieve the sacred Barbies from Paula's bedroom in St Luke's Mews.

I called Notting Hill Police Station and was told that I could enter the house freely. They had also contacted and seen Charlotte Korshak. They would not elaborate on any of the details of their questioning of her, or what action they were going to take. I knew it would not be long before she rang me herself, though. I really wanted to get Tiger her things before she left for Bob's house in the country – ironically named The Priory. The house seemed more desolate with each visit. It also smelled a bit musty, so I opened a small ventilation window in the kitchen. I sat in the living room and wondered what on earth I was going to do with all of her possessions. I would have to speak to Bob and the girls and see what they wanted, and the rest we could decide upon later. I went upstairs to Paula's bedroom, sat on the bed and wondered just how unhappy and how totally stupid she must have been that day. I was finding it hard to forgive her for what she had done, especially after she had experienced the heartache Michael's actions had caused. Even if you believe, as I do, that both deaths were accidental, it does not make them any less selfish. I looked for the silver Zippo lighter that Paula had given to Michael; it was always by her bed, but now it was gone. It was engraved with a heart and the initials PY and MH, and on the reverse side it said PLEASE FUCK ME YOU'RE PERFECT. I thought that I would find it later when I went through her things, but I never did. To this day, I have no idea where it went or who took it. I would dearly love to have given that to Tiger later in life, as it was so typical of her mum. I picked up the Barbies from the floor and proceeded downstairs. Then I thought how emotive it would look, me leaving Paula's house three days after her death with a handful of dolls – I could just see the headlines in the paper the next day. I took a pink flowery pillowcase off Pixie's bed and put the dolls inside that.

The girls were watching television when I arrived at Bob's house, and Tiger ran and put her arms around me. Bob was in the kitchen, and I was shocked when I saw him – he looked even rougher than before and didn't appear to have had any sleep. Bob's partner Jeanne looked tired, but beautiful as always, and I thought how difficult this must be for her. Everybody was talking about Paula, and now all the girls would be living there permanently – at least I hoped they would. It was an abrupt and dramatic change to occur in one's life overnight. Bob and Jeanne's apartment was quite spacious and had three bedrooms, but it was certainly not suitable for four girls and three adults – Monique the nanny was to move in too. They would have to move.

It was hard to believe that another day had passed. Tomorrow was the inquest. I rang Montana's school and spoke to her housemistress to say I would be picking her up from school on Friday and she would be staying at home until after the funeral. It had been a long and tiring day, and I felt mentally exhausted. On my return home, I found that Colin and Kell had rung from Australia, as had Colette Dinningan, Michael's friend and one of Paula's favourite fashion designers. Adam Clayton, U2's bass guitarist, had rung and left a very nice message. Freddie Foreman and his wife Jan rang to see if there was anything that they could do. Paula had loved Freddie: far from being this hard-nosed villain and henchman of the Krays as he is often portrayed, he is a kind and very generous man. He was a father figure to Paula, and he had looked out for her and given her advice. Martin Bashir, he of the Princess Diana and Michael Jackson interview fame, also called. I wondered what he wanted. He had tried to interview Paula after Michael had died, but he wouldn't be able to do so with me. My other calls included practically every newspaper looking for a comment or an interview; and of course my family and friends, who were genuinely concerned. They would all have to wait, as I was going to go to bed: I had an early start, and tomorrow would be another emotional day. The image of my friend lying on that trolley dominated my thoughts as I tried to get what proved to be a very fitful night's sleep.

I woke feeling more tired than I had been when I went to bed. Anthony Burton would be at the Coroner's Court early and I didn't want to keep him waiting; nor did I want to arrive late and be greeted by a deluge of reporters.

Inside the court, we sat in an office where we had a discussion with the coroner and another man whom I believed to be the pathologist. Both Anthony and I wanted to know when the time of death was, and whether we could narrow it down from the early hours of Sunday, 17 September. If Paula's death was estimated at between 11 p.m. on 16 September and 2 a.m. on 17 September, I argued that, for the sake of the children and especially Pixie, the date of her death should be officially recorded as 16 September, thus avoiding it falling on Pixie's birthday. It would not bring her mother back, but a small detail like that seemed highly important to me.

The courtroom opened and myself and Anthony sat in the front. Behind us sat an assortment of journalists from all over the world. It was unfortunate that the police had previously described Paula's death as 'inconclusive', giving the impression that there was a possibility of it being suicide. The coroner said he would have preferred it to have said that they were waiting for further test results, which would have been a lot less emotive. The eventual cause of death was determined to be misadventure. The coroner concluded that, had Paula been a habitual drug user, the amount of heroin found in her system would not have killed her. She had, as I had always maintained, been drug-free for two years; but that night she foolishly took what she thought to be a normal dose, and it killed her. He read out a brief statement and closed the inquest. We left the courtroom, Anthony made a brief statement to the press and we were gone. I went back to Paula's house to oversee the locks being changed.

Bob had been to court himself earlier in the week and had got interim care of Tiger. She was made a ward of court so nobody could take her away from his care and the love of her sisters. The news from Australia was that Tina Shorr, Michael's half-sister, and his mother Patricia Glassop would not be fighting for Tiger. I never believed that – I had known them too long and was sure that they were just rounding up the cavalry to fight for custody.

The newspapers were full of the upcoming legal battle for Tiger.

The *Sun* carried a picture of me with an article that made my blood boil. It was the start of my anger with journalist Emma Jones. The *Sun* claimed that I had only remembered to pick up Michael's ashes after they had 'reminded' me, and if it wasn't for them Michael would have been completely forgotten. The nerve of the woman! And the picture didn't show me carrying Michael's ashes, as they said it did; it was a pillowcase full of Barbie dolls!

Well, I thought, they could write what they want, but any more rubbish like that and I would sue.

Thursday was a glorious autumn day, and I decided I would have to make the trip to Hastings. Having secured one house, I needed to do the same with the other, especially as a tabloid had irresponsibly printed a picture of it. I also wanted to make sure everything had been taken care of before the funeral. The road to Hastings can be very slow – it twists and turns, and God forbid you get stuck behind a truck because you could be there forever, which is of course exactly what happened to me. As I sat behind a massive eighteen-wheeler, I began to wonder if it had been such a good idea to come on my own. The feeling of sadness that occasionally welled up from the bottom of my stomach began to rise. Bugger this, I thought, let's get on with it. I peeped round the side of the truck and there was a clear stretch of road ahead, so I pulled out and put my foot down. Then, as I approached Hastings, I saw the blue flashing lights and heard the siren.

I pulled over, hoping they would pass me by. No such luck. An extremely tall and burly policeman stood by my car and asked me to step out of my vehicle. Why do policeman always ask you why they stopped you? Unless you are really thick, you're not going to say, 'Because I've just robbed a bank and have got the proceeds in the boot! Golly, officer, what do you mean you were only stopping me for speeding?'

As I hadn't robbed a bank, I said, 'Sorry, officer, I have no idea.' I had an inkling that I might have exceeded the speed limit, but how could he have clocked my speed with two cars separating us? I certainly wasn't going to admit to it. Unfortunately, though, I had inadvertently overtaken on a double white line. He started to lecture me – quite rightly but very annoyingly – on how when you are driving it really is best to concentrate on the job in hand, and how apart from dangerous driving he was also going to charge me with careless driving. It must have been my day for not saying the right thing, because I apologised some more and said that I had had a very rough week and had hardly slept. I thought I was going to start crying, and the officer said, 'Don't think crying is going to help you, because it's not.' He told me to sit down on the grass verge where he was going to breathalyse me. I could feel the tears welling up when one of the officers in the car got out and started talking to the first officer. I couldn't hear what they were saying but they kept looking round at me. Then they went to the car and took out a newspaper. They looked at the paper, looked up at me, looked at the newspaper again, nodded to each other and then started to walk over to me.

The second officer seemed very concerned and asked me if I was Paula Yates's friend. I nodded, and when he asked me if I was all right I just burst into tears. So there I was on a grass verge by the side of the road, sobbing, with two very bemused officers not knowing what to do next. The tall burly officer sat down and put his arm around me; I put my head on his shoulder and howled. In between crying, my nose running and me wiping it either on my sleeve or on his shoulder, he must have wished he had never stopped me! By this time, the third officer had got out of the car and not one of them could stop me crying – but at least he had some tissues! They had surmised by now that I must be going to Paula's house and, as I was so upset, they said I was in no fit state to drive and they would take me there. I insisted I was fine; they insisted I wasn't. Five minutes later, I was being driven to Paula's house in my car by a police officer, and followed by the remaining two officers in their car.

So, for the third time that week, I found myself letting police officers into another of Paula's houses. The officers were extremely kind and helped me check the doors and windows, gave me a few tips on security and said they would make a special note on their beat to keep an eye on the house, and would mention it to their colleagues. As they left, with me full of apologies and thanks, the first officer gave me a big hug and a kiss on the cheek.

I went from room to room and removed any small personal items. Between the two houses, I was going to have my work cut out – boy, was Paula a hoarder. It was a habit she had picked up from her father. Jo Fairley's house was just around the corner, and so was her brother's. I spoke with him and made sure he had a set of keys in case of an emergency or a burst pipe. It seemed sensible, and he was totally trustworthy. Job done. I headed to the beach.

As I walked along the beach with a pot of jellied eels and a bag of fish and chips, I wondered how my life could have taken such a different direction to the one I had imagined for myself only five years previously. I have often wondered what would have happened if I had not been the one to tell Paula the news about Michael's death. What if I had not got on the plane to Sydney with her? Would my life have altered so dramatically? I doubt it. But, once we stepped on that plane at Heathrow, things would never be the same again. It had been a roller-coaster few years, and this week the carriage had left the rails altogether. I had been thinking about moving out of London for a while, and walking along the beach that day I decided that, for the sake of sanity and peace and quiet, a move to the country was a must. It was another dream that, a few years down the line, would be shattered beyond all recognition.

A seagull swooped overhead in a vain attempt to steal a chip out of my hand, and I realised I had been a million miles away. I had to head home, and this time slowly – I certainly didn't want to upset my newfound friends in blue.

Friday morning saw me retracing the journey to Montana's school. I was so happy to see my little girl's face and hold her in my arms. I so regretted sending her away to school. She was full of questions and news of school, her sporting achievements and the antics of her pals. She didn't understand what had happened with Paula, and it was difficult for me to explain, as I couldn't fully comprehend it either. She was worried about Tiger and the girls and, even though it was a sad occasion, she was excited to be seeing them all again.

Indiana, Montana and I spent the afternoon in Harrods and,

much to the disgust of my children, I bought them something smart to wear to the funeral. Monty insisted that Peaches would be wearing jeans so why couldn't she? Maybe I'm an old-fashioned girl at heart, but I was insistent. While in Harrods, I rang Bob's best friend Howard, who had been helping him with the arrangements, to make it quite clear that some of Paula's ashes would come to me. I was mindful of the children's wishes, but Paula had been adamant that her ashes would be mixed with Michael's. Howard told me that he was sure that would be fine. I really did not want to have to tell them that there was no choice, because her body was part of her estate, and as executor of that estate I was in charge of what happened to it. I couldn't foresee any problems, though, and certainly did not want to be heavy-handed in such a delicate situation. I also spoke to Jo Fairley to give her our code names for the funeral. There has been a lot of nonsense written about these code names, especially by Gerry Agar in *Paula, Michael and Bob* – a poor book by a woman who didn't know Paula at all well. It is not true that the code name for the funeral was, in true rock and roll style, 'bollocks'. In fact, everybody had their own individual code names, otherwise security could easily have been breached. I had decided upon Minnie Mouse for myself, and my boyfriend's was Mickey Mouse, and the children were Chip 'n' Dale. It seemed that everything that could have been done had been; I knew that Bob and Jo had worked their socks off to make sure that every detail of the funeral would be perfect and something that Paula would have been proud of. Now all we had to do was get up the next day and say our final goodbyes.

Saturday morning, and the girls were still trying to persuade me that they should wear jeans to Paula's funeral. Peaches would be – Monty had asked her – and, more to the point, Paula wouldn't have minded. I wasn't going to win this argument on any logical basis, so it was just a matter of 'I'm your mother and you will do as you are told'. I had decided on a black embroidered Voyage top which both Paula and I had argued over, until I pointed out that she wouldn't fit *one* of her boobs in it, never mind both. I matched this with a silk Prada skirt and shoes and a Colette Dinningan cardigan. The girls looked smart, and I was proud of them. My boyfriend looked immaculate in his suit.

I felt nervous and had butterflies in my stomach. I had a sweet call from Mark Warren whom I had met with Paula one crazy night at Chinawhite – and all three of us became very good friends. He sent his love and told me to blow her a kiss from him. I was so happy to see him on every billboard and TV show promoting the series *Hustle* which he starred in a few years later. He so deserved his success, and I for one knew it would make Paula smile. Finlay Quaye had wanted to come to the funeral, as had Sam Robinson-Horley, but it wasn't my decision and the church was small so numbers were limited.

It was a glorious sunny day, the kind that makes you glad to be alive. It didn't feel like we were on our way to a funeral – more like we were going to a barbecue at a mate's house, albeit a little overdressed for the occasion. The road to The Priory was a sea of well-wishers and press. The people of the village had come out to pay their respects to a past resident who had often allowed the village fîte to take place in her garden, and who had so loved living there. The barriers were up and we were stopped by a police officer who had his clipboard with the guest list. First, he asked for the code names, and when I told him he smiled and said that they found my names very funny. I asked why, and it transpired that most people attending the funeral had used their middle names – and I don't know anyone who named their child 'bollocks'. Perhaps that woman Agar's parents should have – she certainly knows how to write it.

We parked in the field in front of the house and, as the Bentleys and Mercedes pulled up, I thought how Paula would have enjoyed this. She couldn't resist a rock star, and they couldn't resist her. She would have been in her element, and they were all here for her. Monty and Indy were greeted with screeches of delight from Pixie and Peaches. That was all I saw of them for the next hour, except the odd glimpse of them talking and playing happily. The lawn was laid out with flowers for Paula, and some very beautiful and touching messages, including ones from Robbie Williams and George Michael. Bob had laid out the entrance hall with a bar, and what a good job he'd done. There were barrels of beer, and even Guinness – to the delight of a lot of the men and especially the Irish contingent. Bob gave me a hug, and gave my boyfriend a cigar.

There were so many people to say hello to; it was such a shame it wasn't a party. Linda Plentl, Paula's half-sister, was there with her husband Rene. She was a wonderfully kind woman who was devastated by Paula's death. Yasmin Le Bon looked beautiful as ever; she had come on her own because Simon was touring. It was nice to see Bono and his wife Ali, who has a generosity of spirit that is a delight to see in anybody. I had spent a wonderful weekend staying at their magical house in Dublin. I saw Tiger and Indy talking to Nicky Clarke, and wondered if they were picking up tips for Barbie's hair. Jasper Conran arrived in his open-top Rolls, and looked every bit the wonderfully camp fashion designer. Paula and I used to see him in a little Italian restaurant that lay between Michael's house and his office on the King's Road. He never failed to make Paula hoot with laughter, and had been a great friend to her over many years.

I met Rupert Everett in the passageway to the kitchen and stopped to say hello. I wasn't sure how much he wanted to speak to me. The last time I had seen him he had screamed and shouted at me about the state Paula was in at his and Madonna's film premiere. He could not believe that I had allowed her to go. It's always best to know your facts first before venting your anger, but I understood and know that he only ever had her best intentions at heart, and he truly loved Paula. He had paid for her to stay in the Priory on many occasions, and only ever wanted to see his old friend restored to her former self, as we all did. I was pleased to see Nick Cave: in this setting, which was very much Bob's domain, it was nice to see a face that reminded me of the life that she had had with Michael. Michael adored Nick, almost hero-worshipped him. The two of them would hang out at Nick's flat in Notting Hill and on the night that Michael died he had left a message on Nick's answering machine, which later I had to retrieve for the police as Nick was touring in Australia. I took a lawyer with me as I felt it would be best to have an independent observer, and we must have listened to that message about twenty times. Michael was totally incoherent, and we could not understand a word of it. When Nick got back to London, however, he listened to the message and understood it perfectly – they had spent many an evening in that state together, so perhaps he was accustomed to that mode of speech! Michael said that he had heard Nick was going to be in Australia and that he was going to come to the gig, sit in the front row and throw bananas at him. He then said he was looking forward to seeing him in a few days. It was hardly a suicide message.

Nick was heading to the chapel via a doorway from Bob's house to check on the musical arrangements, so I went with him. The church is small and gothic, and I wondered how we would all fit in. Jools Holland was standing by the piano and was making some adjustments to a microphone. Kevin Godley, of 10cc fame, was looking at some sheet music and Nick started tinkering on the piano. I left the lads to it. On the way out I kissed promoter Harvey Goldsmith and Paul McGuinness, U2's manager whom I always seem to meet at funerals. The Kemp brothers were there, as were Annie Lennox and Dave Stewart. It became a bit of a blur after a while.

The peal of the church bells echoed across the garden and it was time to make our way to the church where Paula and Bob had married and their children had been baptised. I sat on the right in the church; there were no formal seating arrangements. Bob and the girls sat in the front row on the left. Paula's mother, whom I had spoken to in the sitting room earlier, sat in front of me. I thought how awful it must be to bury a child, and how much worse when you had been estranged. I don't really know the woman, but had spoken to her on a few occasions on the phone and could not understand some of the heartache she had put her daughter through.

I sat with my boyfriend and my two children. Montana held my hand in hers and in her other hand held that of Mark Cook. The priest said a few prayers and I could feel the tears welling in my eyes. Bono, accompanied by Jools Holland on piano, gave a wonderful and heart-rending rendition of 'Blue Skies'. Rupert Everett read Keats, and his voice resonated deeply round the church and into my heart. And to think that I had asked Bob if I could do a reading! It was perfect. Kevin Godley sang 'True Love' from *High Society* and I started to shake. You couldn't have hoped for a better celebration of a life than this: she would have loved to have been there in person and not just in spirit. Monty gripped my hand tighter.

The priest lit some incense and began shaking it around the church. This was too much for Indiana and she asked if she could go outside as the smell was making her feel sick. Tiger, who had been sitting on Fifi's knee, had the same idea and she and Indy went outside to play. Paul Gambaccini gave the most fantastic eulogy: he went through the entire gamut of Paula's life, and boy it was some life; but oddly, I thought, he barely made mention of Michael. In fact, Michael only appeared as a small footnote in the entire ceremony; but then it wasn't his funeral. Jo Fairley also gave a eulogy that related more to the more private side of Paula. But for me the most poignant moment of the whole funeral was Nick Cave singing 'Into My Arms'. It was Michael and Paula's song, and it swept me back to days in Redburn Street when I had first heard it. Nick had played it at Michael's funeral in Sydney.

Hymns at funerals are so emotive, and none more so than 'Jerusalem'. As the final hymn was sung and the priest closed the ceremony with his blessing, Paula's coffin, covered in scarlet lilies – the same colour as her wedding dress that had adorned the same church all those years earlier – was carried out to her recording of 'These Boots Were Made For Walking'. Much to the amusement and surprise of most of the guests, it was a wonderful way to end. Yet again, she had made us all smile.

We emerged to bright sunlight and beautiful blue skies. Family and close friends were going to accompany Paula's body to the crematorium for a short service some fifteen miles away and then we would be returning. I went with a very tearful Fifi, and Monty went in a separate car with Peaches and Pixie. The ceremony was short, and in no time it was all over.

Back at The Priory, I remember sitting talking to Catherine Mayer and her husband Andy and watching, along with many of the other guests, a little impromptu play that Peaches was directing and organising on the front lawn. By late afternoon, people were beginning to leave; though it seems odd to say it, it really had been a most delightful day. But it had been a long day, and I felt I should take my children home. We said our goodbyes and, with a few people still milling around, we got into our car and headed off.

On the way home, I considered how funerals make you think not only of the life of the person who has died, but also of your own life. They remind you of your own mortality, of the sacredness of life and those that you love. Once we were home and everyone was ready for bed, I hugged my girls and snuggled up with them as they fell asleep. Words cannot describe the love I felt for them that day. And, as I climbed into my own bed, I thought about the trauma that Paula had gone through in her early life and beyond. All she had wanted was to protect her children from any feelings of loneliness, and to make them feel happy, secure and, above all, loved.

# PART TWO

# CHAPTER THREE

I was born on 5 June 1962 in St John's Wood, London, in the middle of a heatwave. To this day, there is a dispute over whether I was named after my great-aunt Belinda or my grandfather's Old English sheepdog. I became affectionately known as the 'string bean', because I was so tall and scrawny.

My family is an eclectic mix of Austrians, Americans, Jews, Protestants and a later smattering of Catholics – the latter being due to my grandmother's well-documented affair with the great writer Graham Greene. My maternal great-grandfather, David Crompton, was an accomplished and well-educated man who ran the English end of the Booth Shipping Line. His brother, Paul, ran the American end. Their mother was English and one summer Paul decided to take his wife and six children to England. With great excitement, an enormous amount of luggage and a few servants, they boarded the ill-fated *Lusitania* and made themselves at home in their first-class cabins. On Friday, 7 May 1915, twenty-five miles off the south coast of Ireland, a German U-boat launched a torpedo attack that sank the ship. The *Lusitania* was listed as being an armed merchant cruiser. The dead numbered 1,201, and included my relatives.

The disaster caused my great-grandfather to move to America. War was still raging in England, and he could quite easily take over the running of the American end of the shipping line. He later met a wealthy, beautiful debutante by the name of Lillian McDonald, and they were soon married. The couple lived happily in Boston and had three daughters and a son: Bonte the eldest, my grandmother Catherine, David, who was better known as Buzzy, and my namesake Belinda.

My other maternal great-grandfather, Sir Charles Waldstein, was an eminent archaeologist and a professor of Greek Art at Cambridge. Not only was he a brilliant scholar, but he was also a sporting man who represented England in the men's military rifle in the first modern Olympics of 1896. He married a formidable and dominant woman by the name of Florence (one in the line of many in our family – you should meet my mother!). Florence had been married previously to a Mr Seligman. He died leaving her widowed with three daughters, though not without funds. It seems that what Florence wanted, Florence got. Family history has it that she reported to her daughters that she was going to marry the professor, and her eldest daughter retorted, 'Does he know this yet, Mama?' They went on to have a son and a daughter: Harry, my grandfather, and his sister Evelyn. They lived in Newton Hall, an extremely splendid house just outside Cambridge. My great-grandfather owned a substantial amount of land and was something of a gentleman farmer. It was his son, my grandfather, who would build up the farm to be the large and profitable business it became.

I know less about my father's side of the family. My paternal great-grandfather on his father's side was also a very brilliant scholar, firstly at Winchester and then at New College, Oxford. He was also a deeply religious man and left scholastic life to pursue a vocation in the Church. He married Emily Jane Darby in 1891 and had three children. The youngest, my grandfather, was christened Clement Noel Brewin, after his father. Clement Senior was a man of great feeling and humanity and in 1900 took his Christianity and his family to America where he spent some time in Brooklyn at the Church of the Holy Spirit. Eventually, Clement Senior returned to England and he died on Ascension Day in 1947; quite an appropriate day to go, I have always thought, for a man of the cloth.

I don't seem to have inherited any of his religious fervour, or the discipline for a scholastic life from any of my predecessors. I could never quite understand where the rebellious side of my nature came from; then I started reading Evelyn Waugh's diaries and I came across my grandmother getting stoned in an opium den in China. Both my sets of grandparents were quite extraordinary people. My paternal grandfather, Noel, went out drinking one night with a bunch of his army colleagues and, as the evening drew to a close, he changed his name to Peter and was known as such from then until the day he died. Like his father, he was also a scholar at Winchester and then went on to the Royal Military Academy at Woolwich. He was one of the youngest majors in World War I, and married my grandmother, Mary Annesley, in 1935. My father, Charles, was born in 1937.

Mary was something of an enigma and, on her death, it came to light that not everything in her life was quite as we had all thought. For a start, she was ten years older than she had always claimed to be. It is difficult to imagine taking ten years off your life and no one being the wiser. She must have been a hell of a good-looking woman to get away with it. Even her place of birth did not match what she had told us all. It is believed now that she was probably the illegitimate daughter of the then Baron Annesley of Castlewellan.

My maternal grandparents Lord and Lady Walston, or Harry and Catherine to you and me, were a fascinating combination. To listen to my grandmother, you would never in your life have met somebody as uninterested in sex as her husband. She, on the other hand, carried on a torrid and passionate affair for about twelve years with Graham Greene, and he wrote *The End of the Affair* about their relationship, much to the disgust of some of the family. It was later made into a film, and Julianne Moore played my grandmother.

I loved my grandmother and, even as a child, I was fascinated by her. She would wear brightly coloured Capri trousers and had been known to entertain in a mink coat and bare feet – very daring in her day. She had an amazing effect on men: she was absolutely stunning and had a dignified air of rebellion about her. Catherine had many bohemian friends including Picasso, Henry Moore and Charlie Chaplin; she was a great socialite who loved a party. In fact, my grandparents held fantastic parties at their home, and Evelyn Waugh described one of them as decadence as never seen before. Many of my family tell me that I am very similar to my grandmother; personally, I could never see it, but while reading about her life I came across a very interesting passage in Norman Sherry's excellent biography of Graham Greene. It transpires that, when my grandparents arrived in England, accompanied by Catherine's family, my very formidable great-grandmother Lady Florence held a party to introduce her son's fiancée. The lawn was awash with women in their finery and floppy hats, and it was by all accounts a very proper and staid affair. Bobs, as my grandmother was nicknamed by her family and friends, appeared on the lawn in a bathing suit and proceeded to do handstands and cartwheels. This absolutely horrified not only her mother, but also her future mother-in-law, but Bobs couldn't have cared less and certainly didn't give two hoots for the thoughts of any of the lords, ladies, earls or dukes who happened to be present.

My grandfather must have had *some* interest in sex – or maybe it was just down to my grandmother's Catholicism that they ended up with six children. My mother Anne was the eldest. She had four brothers – David, Oliver, Bill and James – and a sister, my godmother and friend Susan. David died in a car accident shortly after getting married, and I remember being told the news of his death when I was at boarding school. I hated to hear my mother so sad and, though I was young and hardly knew him, it was the anguish in my mother's voice that gave me my first feeling of loss.

I would hate to give the impression that my grandfather was nothing more than a cuckolded husband who sat at home waiting for his errant wife to return. Nothing could be further from the truth. He was a very brilliant man who achieved many things in his life. He was a great philanthropist and an avid supporter of race relations. He had a great sense of humour and a diversity of friends that would make a dinner party at his house one of the most enjoyable you could ever attend – if you were lucky enough to be asked. There is a wonderful photograph of my grandfather trying to show Fidel Castro how to call in the cattle on the farm by blowing grass through his thumbs. The shah of Iran and his wife once came to stay, and she arrived in a leopard-skin coat and hat with matching bag and shoes, which is always a good look on a farm in Cambridge. During their stay they went to the local pub, The Green Man, and the locals were lucky to get away with their lives, as they thrashed the shah at darts!

In the late forties, in the aftermath of the war, my grandfather was appointed director of agriculture to the British zone in Germany, and following that was agricultural adviser to the Foreign Office. He contested a few seats in the general elections during the fifties, always for the Labour Party, but he never won and so in 1961 Harold Wilson appointed him junior minister in the House of Lords. He held different posts in the government during the mid-sixties, the longest being undersecretary at the Foreign Office, a post he held for three years. Following that he was on the Board of Trade. He then seemed to take a different perspective on life and took the post of Crown Estate Commissioner. Harry held this post for eight years and, when he stepped down in 1976, the Queen rewarded him with the CVO.

His next post was also very close to his heart and I can imagine that as chairman of the Institute of Race Relations he brought compassion, vision and an awful lot of wisdom to his duties. He was instrumental in the talks with Ian Smith when Rhodesia became Zimbabwe, and was a great friend of Mugabe's. I know he would turn in his grave at the atrocities now being committed by Mugabe. He really was a very fine man and one whom I respected and loved immensely, as he loved all his grandchildren.

Up until the age of nine, my life is pretty much a blur, only peppered with the odd memory here and there. My sister Nicola, on the other hand, seems to remember everything as if it happened yesterday. I think it is a sign that she didn't take enough drugs in her youth, or doesn't drink enough alcohol now. Maybe she just makes it up because she knows that I don't have a clue! I don't remember leaving London for Wales, on account of my father's job with Costain. Nothing much happened in Wales, apart from me falling in love with a boy called Bim-Bim and my sister Miranda being born. After a couple of years of unrequited Welsh love, my parents moved me broken-hearted to Yorkshire. Twins, the last addition to our family, were born there and I had yet another little sister, Julia, and finally a brother, Tobey. I didn't like Yorkshire and I hated school even more, especially as I was mercilessly teased for my Welsh accent. We lived in Denbigh Dale at the top of a very steep hill, and the school was at the bottom. More or less on a daily basis, or as often as I could get away with it, I would encourage our black Labrador puppy, Ben, to follow me to school so that I would have to take him home again – ensuring that I missed at least half of the morning's lessons. Once I lost my dinner money in the snow and took so long in finding it that by the time I got to school it really didn't matter as lunch was over. I was already showing my rather lackadaisical attitude to authority and school.

Eventually, we moved to a child's paradise: the family home Newton Hall in Cambridgeshire. It was everything you could dream of as a child – a house with twenty bedrooms. My siblings and I firstly had rooms in the servants' wing, and then we were given the run of the entire third floor. The pranks and naughtiness that we got up to undetected were frightening. Nicola and I attended the village school. There were only about ten of us at the school, and there was only one room and one teacher, so it was going to be impossible to play truant, but I didn't care. If I had to endure school just to live here, so be it. If the weather was fine, I used to go down to the farm after school and watch the huge bull with a ring through his nose in his pen, touch the metal bars in an act of defiance and then run away screaming if it even looked round at me. I used to tell my sisters that I got in the pen with him, but I never did. On the way home, I would sometimes stop at the beehives and help myself to some honeycomb. As I knew absolutely nothing about bees, it was quite extraordinary that I didn't get stung. Nicola, Miranda and I once stole an entire tray from the hive and ate the lot. I was so sick that I have never eaten honey since!

My sisters and I would often dress up in the cowboy and Indian outfits that my grandmother had had made for her children, and we would have amazing battles all over the house. When I grew up, I was going to marry a Comanche Indian and ride horses for the rest of my life. Some days I wish I had. I loved my bedroom. I would lie in bed listening to the wood pigeons and watching the shadows of the trees dance against my walls and ceiling. The sound of wood pigeons today always takes me back to those days of my youth and gives me a warm feeling inside. I also loved the kitchen. It was a heavenly place, and the cooks would always have a treat for us kids. Mrs O'Malley was the best. How could you not love someone who made fish pie like she made fish pie? And as for her treacle tart ... Her husband was a lovely man who always had a magic trick or two for us. He could cut his thumb in half and allow coins to pass magically through the enormous kitchen table. If you ever got lonely, the kitchen was the place to go. Mrs O'Malley would greet you with a hug that was a mixture of flour and sweat, and that warm smell stayed with you for the rest of the day.

Then, of course, there was the Long Room, which as a child I thought was as big as a football pitch, although when I went back to the house as an adult it wasn't nearly as big as I had remembered it. This was primarily my grandfather's room, and it housed everything that a gentleman could wish for while sipping brandy and smoking cigars. The house also accommodated a small chapel that the farm workers and villagers would attend on a Sunday. We could enter it from a door in the house, and no one ever went in there apart from on Sundays – or so we thought. Nicola, Miranda and I would sneak in and pretend to be the Pope giving his people a blessing from the papal balcony in St Peter's Square. We used to get the Communion hosts out and pretend to give Mass. I liked giving the sermons, and my sisters laughed when I castigated the 'congregation' for making their children come to Mass on sunny days, when their time could be better spent outside. It was on one of these occasions when I was dressed in the priest's vestments and playing with the Communion hosts – not the small ones that the priest handed to his congregation, but the big ones that he broke and ate – that the door opened and in came one of the servants. I had just started eating the host and it was glued to the roof of my mouth, which felt as if it was stuck together with Velcro. I couldn't articulate properly, but I knew we were going to be in trouble. My mother was furious, my grandmother livid. I had to apologise to the priest personally and was severely punished; apart from very contritely on a Sunday, I never entered the chapel again. Years later, and with the telling-off and the lecture on blasphemy from my grandmother still ringing in my ears, my great-aunt Belinda told me a story of how my grandmother had been taken to church by her nanny and had stolen two Communion cups. Well, I ask you, which one of us committed the greater sin?

One day, a miracle happened. It started as just another normal school day with all of us in attendance. Our teacher turned to explain something that she had written on the blackboard. Suddenly, there was an almighty crash and she slipped and fell off the small raised platform that held her desk and enabled us to look up her nostrils and her to glare down on us from a place of superiority. She couldn't get up and, when we tried to help her, she screamed in pain. I remember thinking she was going to die. In fact, she had broken her hip and was taken to hospital. She recovered fully – but that's not the miracle. What made us feel that God was smiling on us was the fact that it was halfway through the summer term and most of the class, apart from my sister and me who were going to go to boarding school, were due to go to the secondary school in Cambridge. Our little school, according to the council, was uneconomical to run and was to be closed. The last half of the summer term became a sabbatical. Heaven.

I found out many years later that the reason that I was not sent to a junior school in Cambridge was that my parents had already decided to move to Henley-on-Thames and, as I was starting a new school when we moved, it seemed unnecessary to start another one for the space of a few weeks. So, for a few a brief moments in time, I thought I was the luckiest child alive. My sisters and I hung out, keeping out of the grown-ups' way and trying to get Catalos, my grandmother's African grey parrot, to say more than 'Down with the Pope' and 'Have another drink, James'. The plan for the summer was going full-speed ahead with plenty of fun and lots of mischief. That was all about to change.

Maybe there is a time in everybody's life when you realise that it's quite a scary world and you have to take responsibility for your own actions. One day that summer was just like any other, and yet it ended so differently and haunted me for years afterwards. As a special treat, my wonderfully wild and eccentric aunt Hilary decided to take my sister Nicola and I into Cambridge to go shopping. She was going to the hairdresser's, and Nicola and I would be allowed to venture around the market square and its surroundings on our own. It was very exciting and very grown up. Before we left, we had been given some pocket money, and I had announced that I was going to buy some lipstick and some eyeshadow. My mother thought this was an appalling idea and a total waste of money. Well, she would, as she had never worn make-up in her life. So here I was being allowed to go shopping on my own and then being told what I could buy. Being ten was wholly unfair.

The train journey just added to the excitement. We found an empty compartment with rather worn red seats and trundled into Cambridge Station. Nicola and I accompanied Hilary to the hairdresser's, and she instructed us to return there in an hour. She also told me to buy my mother a bunch of flowers in the market for being so cheeky to her before we left. Another person telling me how to spend my money! But Hilary is quite a formidable woman: if she tells you to buy flowers, you buy flowers. I bought a bunch of carnations – they were pretty and cheap – and then headed off to the market square. I spotted Woolworths amid the multitude of different shops, and Nicola and I made our way there so that we could buy some pick 'n' mix sweets. The fudge ones and the purple Quality Street were my favourites.

I entered the store and saw not the sweet counter, but the make-up counter. It was beckoning to me, and every item seemed to call my name. I didn't have enough money now because I'd had to buy those damn flowers; but I decided that, whatever my mother said, I was going to have some make-up. I chose a lipstick and an eyeshadow, looked carefully around the store and placed the lipstick inside the bunch of flowers and the eyeshadow in my hand, called to my sister and left the store without paying for them. I walked three paces and then felt a hand on my shoulder: it was a store detective asking me – no, *telling* me – to come with him. My sister looked scared. I was terrified. Before the store detective could open the large glass door, I managed to throw the eyeshadow, unseen, from my hand on to the pavement. As he rather briskly escorted me down the aisles to the back of the shop, I made a last-ditch attempt to rid myself of the remaining piece of contraband, the lipstick. I had been holding the flowers upright, and now I let them fall by my side. I gave a small shake of the wrist, and then there was a huge clatter as the stolen item bounced its way down the aisle, landing squarely by the foot of an employee who kindly returned it to my captor. I was done for.

My sister and I were bundled into a small office in the back of the store that had a mirrored glass panel, enabling you to see out but not in. My jailer placed the lipstick on the table and then began to search my other bags and those of my sister. My sister would not stop crying; once it had been ascertained that not only had she not stolen anything but also that she was not an accomplice to my crime, she was allowed to leave to go and fetch my aunt. I was asked my parents' name and address, and I said that I was staying with my grandparents. Stupidly, and very naively, I thought that the detective would be suitably impressed and would let me go, so I said Lord and Lady Walston, Newton Hall, Newton. It certainly did not have the desired effect; on the contrary, he went ballistic. He said if I had been from a council estate he could understand it, but I obviously had a privileged upbringing and therefore needed to be taught a lesson. He asked where I went to school; I explained that I didn't as I was about to start at a new one. He asked me how I thought they would feel if they knew that I had stolen something. He then told me he was going to call the police and they would deal with me.

My entire world was crashing down around my ears. I would never be allowed home again, and I wasn't going to be able to go to my new school. My life was finished. Then the door swung open and there stood Hilary in all her glory. With her hair in curlers, a headscarf and a face like thunder, she let rip. How *dare* I bring the family name into disrepute? I should be ashamed of myself. When

I got home I was going to get the beating of my life and it would not stop there. I thought the blood vessels on her neck were about to burst, and the store detective himself looked terrified. 'I was going to call the police,' he informed Hilary.

'Good idea. Let her rot in the police station overnight.'

'No,' said the man, who up until a couple of minutes earlier had seemed the scariest person in the world. 'I *was* going to call the police, but it looks like the situation will be dealt with adequately at home.'

By now, I was wishing he *would* call the police. As Hilary continued to spit blood, she hoisted me by the straps of my dungarees, reassuring the whole of Woolworths that I would be lucky to see another day; she then marched me out of the shop. She dragged me across the market square until we were well out of sight of the scene of my first major crime, stopped – and started laughing. 'Well done,' she told me, 'we got out of that one, didn't we? That fooled them!'

By now, I needed hospital treatment for shock. We returned to her hairdresser's where she *did* tell me off. She said how stupid I had been and that I would have to be punished. We then went to Boots and Hilary bought the biggest packet of heavy-duty sanitary towels. In those days, they didn't have wings. Fly? You're kidding – they could have built the Hoover dam with them! When the shop assistant asked her if she would like a bag for them, she declined. 'There,' she said, turning to me. 'You can carry them as a punishment.' And what a punishment – this pre-pubescent child being forced to carry these things around Cambridge for the next hour. I had to sit with them on my knee on the train back, and my aunt made me sit in the busiest carriage. To this day, I can feel the shame, first, for stealing, second, for not being very good at it and, third, for the sanitary towels!

As we got off the train, Hilary sat me and my sister on a bench on the platform, put her arm around me and told me not to worry. She said she would not tell anybody what had happened and that, as long as I had learned my lesson, it would always remain our secret and no one would ever know. I certainly had learned a lesson. I remember when I started at boarding school and they read my name out on the first day in assembly, I was sure the headmistress was going to say that she had just had a phone call from Woolworths to say that I was a thief. I dreaded it.

I spent a contented few weeks playing croquet and hanging out. Under normal conditions, my parents' move would have left me devastated, but now it seemed best to move on and have a clean slate somewhere where no one would know me as the lipstick thief. Clearly, I would never be able to go into Cambridge again for fear of being recognised, so a move to Henley-on-Thames seemed ideal.

Middle Culham Farm was situated a couple of miles outside Henley, near Remenham. It was here that I spent the rest of my childhood until I left home. It was a lovely, rambling six-bedroom farmhouse, surrounded by a few hundred acres, and I spent most of the time when I wasn't at school riding, walking, swimming in the river, messing around on the farm and generally getting up to mischief. There are certain things that I remember vividly about my time at that house: one is that my parents separated. I can visualise that day in my mind as if it was yesterday. It was a sunny day and I was playing in one of the barns. I heard my father's car coming up the lane. I waved to him and he stopped. He was driving his silver Porsche – at least I remember thinking at the time that it was a Porsche. Years later, I discovered it was actually a Ford Capri! The car was stuffed full of clothes, and I remember a huge puddle separating his car from where I stood, so I had to lean over and place my hands on the open window. I asked him where he was going and he told me he was taking his clothes to the dry-cleaner's! I never doubted his word – why wouldn't you take every item you ever owned to be cleaned? And off he drove. He never lived with us again. We saw him every weekend, though, and he bought a house in Windsor to be near us and never shirked his duties. I don't have any real memories now of him ever living with us, which is sad; he was and is an excellent father whom I love very much.

My father had an affair with one of my mother's best friends and eventually left to be with her. Laura had four children of her own, and my father five, so it must have been quite some decision; but thirty years later they are still together, which is testimony to how they must have felt for each other, and still do. I am very proud of them both for having had the courage of their convictions.

My mother is the most wonderful woman, and it saddens me that she never found the kind of love that she deserves in life. But she is happy, and really is one of life's unique people. Some days I wish that I had the kind of guts, determination and sheer love of life that she has. I must have made her life hell; even when she sent me to boarding school at great personal expense, I just made her life hell from further away.

On one occasion, I decided to run away from home and then just hid in the summerhouse in the middle of the farmyard. Through a crack in one of the planks, I could see and hear my mother calling me from the yard, but I never made a sound. As it got darker, and my mother became more frantic, I must have fallen asleep. At some point in the night, I heard a car arrive. It was a police car, and my mother was beside herself with worry. I never moved and fell back to sleep. When I woke up hungry in the morning, I decided to walk the twenty yards to the house and have breakfast – completely forgetting that I had run away from home and the events of the evening before! My mother was sitting at the kitchen table and was so happy to see me. Then I made a stupid mistake. When she told me that she had called the police, I told her I knew this as I had seen them. It's funny how you remember the incidents, but the punishments – and there must have been many – fade away ...

The older I got, the more the boys in blue seemed to crop up. In fact, my whole life seems to be punctuated with policemen.

I loved boarding school, and was very happy there, but I do regret the manner in which I left. Had I stayed, however, I would have had a whole different life to the one I have now. I went to a Catholic boarding school, and it was something of a family tradition to go there. I am sure that one of the reasons the school was so lenient with my behaviour was that some of the nuns who taught me had actually been at school with my mother. I was very good at sport. I played centre in lacrosse for East Anglia and ran the four hundred metres for Essex. I was also exceptionally badly behaved, and at times very rude. I would have hated to be either my mother or anyone who had to teach me. There was a little gang of us who were all in the same house: another Belinda, aka Bin, Margaret, Bridget and my best friend Toraun. We were always getting into some kind of mischief – midnight-feast stuff really, nothing too serious. That was until I got suspended from school, first for smoking and then for missing church on a Sunday. Having been caught hiding in my wardrobe in the dormitory, I was sent to the headmistress who told me that I was an ungrateful child. 'Jesus died on the cross for you, and you can't even be bothered to go to church on Sunday to give thanks.'

My reply didn't go down well. 'I'm sure Jesus didn't die on the cross so that I'd be bored for an hour every Sunday.' I was promptly returned to my mother on the instructions that I was not to return until I was repentant – in other words, two weeks.

I did well at school, getting nine O levels, despite being suspended twice – or it might have even been three times. I ran away once and hitchhiked from school to London wearing my friend Jill Hennessy's jeans, and not a bean in the pockets! I eventually made it to my grandfather's London apartment in Albany, Piccadilly. When I arrived, it was late and pouring with rain. The doorman thought I was some street urchin and refused to let me in. Eventually, my mother and my ever-patient housemistress Sister Mary Dismas arrived. I was taken back to school in the dead of night and put back in my bed in the hope that no one would know I had left and there would be nothing more said about it. One of the sisters said that she couldn't wait to see the back of me and that when I left the school she would willingly hold the front door open and then slam it behind me when I'd gone. No wonder I never joined the church! She arranged a very public reprimand for me: I was castigated in assembly, and as a punishment was sent to the infirmary for a week's isolation while she reminded the school of the dangers of being associated with the likes of me. It was a miserable week and I vowed to get my revenge on her.

About a month later, the opportunity landed right in my lap, and the beauty was that I hadn't planned it. In fact, it was not even of my making, but it was sweet to see the look on that old harridan's face and to know there was nothing that she could do or say to me about it. It all started and finished on my birthday. It used to be a school tradition that on your birthday your friends and classmates would put a birthday card or a little present on your place setting at breakfast. Presents were restricted to what you could buy in the school shop – Mars bars or slabs of toffee, that kind of thing. It was also tradition to go to early-morning Mass on your birthday which meant that you arrived at breakfast after it had started and were greeted enthusiastically by the rest of your table, while you tried to look modestly surprised that anyone had remembered your birthday at all. So on the eve of mine, I placed a shoe outside my bedroom door to indicate that I wished to be woken early to attend Mass. Mass was dull, and finally I and a couple of others, who probably went for more honourable reasons, made our way into the dining room. I could see her and she was looking at me as if this really was going to be my last breakfast. Didn't she know it was my birthday? She looked serious. In fact, I was so busy concentrating on her that I had not noticed my table and the stunned look on the faces of everyone there. The table was full of presents and overflowing with cards. I thought it was a joke: nearly everyone in the school had given me a card. It took eight of us to carry my gifts back to my dormitory. The next day, it was announced in assembly that this practice would no longer continue. It seemed as if almost the entire school approved of my behaviour. I was delighted.

If you are slightly rebellious, or good at sports, then you tend to be more popular. I managed both. When I got to the fifth form, which is when I left, I rather excelled myself in the daring stakes, and I think my next trick goes down as one of my better-executed moves. By this stage, I had found myself a boyfriend – a real one, not one that I had made up to impress my friends, not one who gave you mysterious love bites on your biceps because your own lips couldn't physically reach your neck. He was French, looked like a member of some unwholesome rock band, and was very sexy and totally cool. The only problem was that his name was Bruno, which was totally uncool. I had lost my virginity to him in the summer, after which my mother quite remarkably allowed him to live at our house. I hated going back to school and being parted from him, because I was in love and was going to spend the rest of my life with this man. Well, I *was* only fifteen.

My year was going to the Victoria and Albert Museum for some exhibition or other, and it seemed like the perfect opportunity for Bruno and I to meet up. We arranged to meet at the museum, and our original plan was that I would sneak out and we would spend the day together in London. Then, horror of horrors, we were told that we all had to wear our uniforms – a bright red skirt and white shirt. I was going to stick out like a sore thumb, and it was too late to ring and ask Bruno to bring a pair of jeans with him. When we arrived, there he was on the steps of the museum and I was the envy of the entire class, or so I thought. I stayed with the pack, idled towards the back and then just plain stood still. Everyone else continued walking, and Bruno and I started to make our way to the exit when a large booming voice asked me where I thought I was going. Teachers, like mothers, are always in the wrong place at the wrong time. I was stunned. 'I've just been to the loo,' I blurted, 'and I was trying to help this French student who has lost his group.' How kind of me! The teacher said he could join us, and that it would not be long before he was reunited with his group.

So now I had permission from a teacher to hang out with my boyfriend. During lunch, we went 'to look for the rest of his group', and while doing so we managed to slip behind a long burgundy curtain. I remember holding on to it while we were having sex, hoping to God that it wouldn't fall down: it would have clashed terribly with my school uniform, which was hitched somewhere up around my armpits. God knows what the poor people at the museum would have thought; and, as for the nuns, I shudder to think.

I kissed Bruno goodbye and went back to the group announcing proudly that this poor, poor Frenchman had now been reunited with his group and was eternally grateful for the hospitable welcome he had received.

I left school shortly before I was going to be expelled and shortly before I was to sit my O levels. I had finished all the coursework, so I just sat the exams at a different school. I hung out with Bruno for most of the summer and then he announced he was going back to France. I was still only fifteen, but I was determined I was going to go with him. My mother, of course, refused to allow this. There was no doubt in my mind that she had now definitely and irreversibly ruined my life. I would never speak to her again. I continued the rest of the summer hanging out with my friends, pining for Bruno and taking an inordinate amount of drugs. I went to a few music festivals and wondered whether I should just go to France and see if I could find Bruno. Looking back on it, I don't think he wanted to be found, as I don't remember him leaving an address or trying to contact me. Maybe my school trip wasn't as memorable for him as it was for me.

My relationship with my mother deteriorated to such a point that I flatly refused to speak to her. I spent a bit of time at Reading University reading up on what my legal rights were, and realising that I really didn't have any until I reached the age of sixteen. I was going to have to bide my time. I also became a vegetarian around this time, just to annoy my mother. I hardly spent any time at home, and certainly never had the decency to tell her where I might be. Well, she had ruined my life and I was going to do the same to her! I used to spend a lot of time at a pub in Henley which was in those days quite a druggy hangout. When I wasn't there at the weekends, I would go to the golf club to dance.

Around this time, I met my dear friends Robert and Julia Cain and a friend of theirs Terry Doran. Terry was from Liverpool, went to school with the Beatles and was a great friend of George Harrison's – he even lived in his house. We would hang out and at one point I was practically living in the Middle Lodge at Friar Park, George's Henley home. It was a beautiful house, and the gardens are breathtaking; even as a mad fifteen-year-old, I loved the sanctuary and peace of that place. The first time I met George he was shocked to see me wearing leather trousers and said that he had once worn them in Hamburg and it was considered very daring. He was a very special man, and, though I don't pretend to have known him well, whenever I saw him even years later he would always stop and ask me how I was. He would call me Blin', and apart from Terry no one had or has ever called me that. I met him at a party when I was a lot older and he asked me how I was. 'Fine,' I told him.

He took my hand. 'No,' he said, 'how are you *really*? In your heart and your soul?'

I said I really was fine, and he said he was glad and gave me a big hug which was very touching.

It was when I had started hanging out at Friar Park that John Lennon died. I was on my way back from Reading College where I was studying my for A levels and I saw Terry in town. He was driving and, as he sat at the traffic lights, I tapped on the window. He looked dreadful, as if he had been crying, and I asked him what the matter was. He could barely speak and asked me if I had seen the news. Of course I hadn't – I'd been at college all day. And then he told me.

It was a strange time. Security was increased at George's house, and then some nutcase was arrested at Heathrow as he threatened to 'finish off' the job that Chapman had started and murder the rest of the Beatles. I was only seven when the Beatles split up, so it wasn't as if they had had a great influence on my life, but even I could appreciate the appalling waste of life and the real sadness of my friends. A little while after Lennon's death, the postman arrived with a package that needed to be signed for. As there was no one else there, I obliged. I gave the package to George: it was a Christmas present, a silver cigarette box engraved WITH LOVE FROM JOHN AND YOKO.

I had another of those life-changing moments at George's house, one that still makes me cringe with both shame and embarrassment. One day, we were sitting happily in the garden when a friend, John Ward, better known as Magnet, appeared. Magnet had been tour manager for Led Zeppelin and Deep Purple. He was great friends with two of the band members, Jon Lord and Ian Paice – in fact, he lived in the grounds of Ian's house. He would often come over, and though I didn't know him very well then, we were on friendly terms. On one occasion, he left his Filofax in the bathroom. I couldn't believe the telephone numbers he had in it: they included David Bowie and Bob Dylan. Now *that* was cool – Dylan was my hero. I took a piece of paper and started copying numbers down. What was I thinking of? I was only a teenager, but it's still hard to excuse, and I could hardly have rung them up: 'Hi,

Bob! I'm Belinda, I don't know you, but I stole your number from someone's address book who does!' Maybe I just wanted to show off; I certainly didn't think about anyone's privacy. Magnet realised that he had left his book behind and came back for it. He wasn't at all concerned. Why should he be? He was at George Harrison's property, among friends.

Needless to say, I had left the piece of paper in his address book. He found it and was quite rightly furious. Soon everybody knew, and George was advised not to let me on his property, let alone into his home. He came to speak to me. 'Why did you do this?' he asked me quietly.

'I don't know.' I felt totally ashamed.

'Will you ever do something like this again?'

'No,' I replied. 'I wish I hadn't done it the first time.'

George was very kind, and I have never forgotten what he told me next. 'We've all done stupid things,' he said, 'but some of us never got caught. Don't worry what people say or think – it's what's in your heart that really matters.'

It took me months to get over it, but to this day I have never read anything that belongs to someone else. Even after Paula died and I was executor of her will, it didn't feel right looking through her diary and private papers.

One day, while sitting in the garden of Friar Park, George drove down the drive in his Porsche with his wife Olivia by his side and they stopped to speak to me and said they would see me later. I presumed that they meant on their return home and took no further notice. Terry was pottering around the house and he asked me what George and Olivia had wanted. I told him our conversation and he wondered where they were going. About an hour later, the penny must have dropped and I could hear Terry swearing and shouting. 'Fuck! Fuck! Ringo's getting married today!' He had forgotten. How could you forget an invite like that, I wondered. It was a secret and had been kept under wraps and, though I had never met either Ringo or Barbara, Terry invited me along. I had nothing to wear and Terry couldn't even find a clean shirt. Major panic set in. The wedding was at Marylebone Registry Office and then afterwards at Rags in Mayfair. We were in Henley and the ceremony was in an hour. Terry rang a men's shop in Marlow looking for a shirt and we headed down there, me a little bit grumpy as I didn't have anything suitable to wear and no time to go and get something. When we arrived at the shop, I decided to hire a boy's dress suit and tails. I looked a little like I was on half-term break from Eton, but Ringo was polite enough to say that after his wife I was the best-dressed girl there.

We missed the actual ceremony but arrived at Rags with everybody else. I was a little star-struck, and I remember at one point George saying to me across the table, 'Close your mouth!' I must have been sitting there gawping. We sat at the head table with George, Olivia, Paul and Linda – who was so nice to me and very witty. Harry Nilsson was sitting opposite me, and I kept hoping he would start singing 'Without You', but he didn't. Percussionist Ray Cooper winked at me, and I winked back. Barbara's sister had on the best shoes I had ever seen, but I'd never heard of Manolo Blahnik or Jimmy Choo then – even if I had, I would never have been able to afford a pair.

We had photos taken around the cake, and then the fun started. Someone sent out for guitars. They arrived, and with Ray Cooper in place with a few ice buckets, the rhythm section was in full flow. I remember singing 'She'll Be Coming Round the Mountain' and 'Sweet Sixteen'. It was a jolly good sing-song, and I was honoured to have been there. As the evening drew to a close, Terry and I said our goodbyes and left the gang to sing yet another song. We decided not to go straight back to Henley; instead, we drove across London to a recording studio. Mick Fleetwood was in town to record a solo album, and Terry went by to say hello. We stayed for a few hours and listened to him tinker around. I chatted to his wife Sarah.

One New Year's Eve, Terry and I had been invited to a party at Dave Gilmour's of Pink Floyd. I was in two minds about going, as the fallout from my stupidity with the address book had not fully subsided. In the end, I decided to go, so I dressed in a very slinky evening dress that was slit practically to the waist and held up by little spaghetti straps, and waited for my carriage. Terry was late – very late, in fact. Eventually, I got a phone call from him telling me that Viv Stanshall from the Bonzo Dog Doo Dah Band had tried to commit suicide and that we should go to see him. I had never met Viv, although I did know his bandmate 'Legs' Larry Smith, a wonderfully funny man who was designing an album cover for George at the time. So, in the middle of the night, and with me in high heels, we stumbled on to his houseboat. Viv was very depressed, but OK, and Terry agreed to come and see him the next day. We eventually got to Dave's house and the party was in full swing. I remember standing with a cigarette in my hand, acting as cool as a teenager can. A gentleman on the sofa offered me a light, so I bent over and my entire dress fell off my shoulders and on to the floor. I was mortified! Years later, when Pink Floyd were playing Wembley, I went along and while I was backstage a friend of Dave's asked me if I was from Henley. For a moment, I thought the address book was coming back to haunt me. I was almost relieved when he said, 'Your tits haven't grown much!'

# CHAPTER FOUR

After a while, Terry moved to America. Magnet and I were friends again, but the situation at home – and my inability and unwillingness to speak to my mother, or even act like a civilised human being when I was there – needed immediate attention. I rarely came home, and with Terry in America I spent more and more time in the pub, hanging out with my friends and taking drugs.

On one occasion, I had been given some LSD by a friend of mine who years later got arrested in a massive drugs bust called Operation Julie, which they made a film about. It was the biggest drugs bust of its time, and there were millions of tabs of acid found. The police also uncovered plans to put acid in Bristol's main water supply. They were only the ramblings of a few hippies, but as you can imagine the police were not amused! They all went to jail for a long time.

I had been given two tabs of this acid and was amazed at how small they were. I decided to take it with my friend Sophie. I swore her to secrecy and we decided to meet early that evening and take it then. Needless to say, she immediately ran off and told our friend Alex, aka Noddy, whose parents were great friends of my mother's. Noddy ran home and told her father that Sophie and I were about to kill ourselves, that we were going to take LSD and jump off the top of a tall building thinking we could fly. That's what you call Chinese whispers. Soon enough, Noddy's dad was straight on the phone to my mother saying that I was going to kill myself. The poor woman was probably relieved! So, unbeknown to me, everybody in Henley was suddenly aware of what Sophie and I would be doing, but luckily not where we would be doing it. We met by the river for this dirty deed, took our tabs and waited. And waited, and waited – but nothing happened. This was boring. Typical, I thought. I should have taken both of them; they were much too small to have any effect whatsoever. Sophie was equally bored, so we set off for the pub.

It might have been prudent to ask what to expect when I was given the drug. I had no idea that it took at least sixty minutes to take effect and that it would then last for twelve excruciating hours! It being a Friday night the pub was unbelievably crowded, and as normal I ordered a Perrier. As the drug started to take effect, people's faces began to contort and look like Edvard Munch's painting *The Scream*. It was very disconcerting the way their voices would rise to a crescendo and then fall to a whisper. I can remember Sophie at one point asking me to look at her dress as it was soaking. Why was there water running off it? After an hour of what seemed like torture I began to feel very claustrophobic and had to get out of the pub. Another friend, Anna Gilchrist, came to our rescue and suggested we go back to her house. The night was beautiful, at least it was to me – but then the traffic lights were a work of art and a wrought-iron gate was a thing of immense loveliness, so I think my judgement was a little clouded. We climbed up St Andrew's Road in Henley – quite a hill at the best of times, but that night I swear I felt like we were climbing Everest. When we finally reached the summit, I was convinced we should raise a flag, but Anna was more insistent that we just go into the house and get off the street before I got arrested.

I remember speaking to Anna's mother, which was an achievement in itself, and she offered us some food. Rice salad with chicken looked to me like a massive bowl of maggots and I thought I was going to be sick. We listened to music and I don't know what happened to the time, but eventually I was in a bed. The patterned wallpaper started to come alive, and I swear the door started breathing. I don't think I slept at all that night.

As I made my way home the next morning, I was just looking forward to getting into my own bed and sleeping the residue of the acid away. I was greeted by my mother who wanted to know where I had been and what I had been doing; as usual, I completely ignored her, went to my room and locked my door. My mother had other plans, however, and a short phone call set them in motion. I must have dozed for about an hour when my brother knocked on the door to say that there were two men here to see me. Half-drugged and half-asleep, I made my way to the kitchen to see two police officers! Well, that sure as hell woke me up. My mother, *my own mother*, had called the police on me. They wanted to know who had sold me the drug – no one had, of course, they had given it to me – but I would not give them any names and said that I had got it from a stranger in the pub. If I was ever to see this person again, I would immediately inform them. Naturally, they knew I was lying on both counts. They then began to recount horror stories of what has happened to people when they take LSD. I wanted to say that I had some inkling as my trip had been pretty scary.

I survived the interrogation and was allowed to return to my room, but I was definitely a little more contrite, and even managed to apologise to my mother in front of the police and promise never to do it again. How humiliating, and how wrong – I did take acid a few more times, and even had some good trips; but it was definitely a drug of my youth.

I thought the whole saga would be put behind us, but my mother was on the attack. Shortly before lunch, my father arrived. He was furious, and I was mighty scared. 'Get in the car,' he said, 'and don't move.' My parents talked on the doorstep for a while, and then my father – who was obviously not amused at having to drive from Windsor on a weekend that he would normally have spent with his wife and her children – looked as if he was going to lunge at me through the windscreen. My God, I was in trouble now, and I was beginning to wonder if it had all been worth it. I just wanted to go inside and get a cuddle from my mum and stop pretending that I was such a grown-up, but it was too late for that.

Without saying a word to me, my father got into the car and drove to Sonning, where we pulled into a restaurant by the river. We sat at a table and I refused to order anything. My father told me that after the night I'd just had I really should eat something, and he ordered for me. I had only eaten a few mouthfuls when my father suddenly said, 'Well, that was a really stupid thing to do, wasn't it?' I looked blank. 'Fancy taking acid in a pub!' He proceeded to tell me about his one and only acid trip. We finished our lunch, I promised I would never again do anything as stupid as taking acid *in a pub* of all places, and we agreed that the subject would never be mentioned again. He would deal with Mum when we got back. We drove home, I got out of the car and he told my mother that he had severely dealt with the situation. I was to spend the rest of the day in my room, and he felt there was no need to mention this sorry episode again.

My mother calling the police was the final straw. I knew I had to leave home as soon as I could. My boyfriend at the time was squatting in a house in Caversham, near Henley, in what was known as Millionaires' Row. The house had been bought by an elderly couple; he had died and she did not want to sell it, but equally she did not want to live there. It had been empty for years before Terry moved in. (Same name, different Terry!) It had no electricity and no running water, but it had a beautiful river-fronted garden and once you got used to the paraffin lamps and hauling buckets of water from the pump outside to a huge metal box with a Calor-gas heater underneath it to heat your bathwater, it was quite an idyllic hippy existence. I left home and didn't speak to my mother again for a very long time.

Living away from home was not all that I had expected. The launderette was one of my first eye-openers; learning to cook was another. As the house was run like a commune, everybody had their duties and we took it in turn to cook. We were all vegetarians, of course! I was well taught by the other girls in the house, and I soon became a dab hand and quite enjoyed my turn. Having thought I was such a rebel at home, and knowing that everybody believed I was going to drop out completely, I decided I would do what they least expected and enrolled at the local college to take my A levels. It seemed a shame to waste my nine O levels; I also realised that I was now on my own, and had no one to blame for my failure except myself. I bought a little moped and took myself off to college every day. I was quite a good student. I became vice-president of the students' union, and we organised marches against the government and the cuts they had ordered in student grants.

I missed my mother, but I couldn't possibly admit that. Two years passed quickly. I got my A levels, but I also became more and more disillusioned with life in a squat, and knew that I wanted to go home. I picked the phone up one day, spoke to Mum and she came that afternoon to fetch me. We have been firm friends ever since, and not a word has been said about the missing two years or my appalling treatment of her.

I spent the summer working in a pub in Henley, and then at the regatta, and as I had saved enough money I decided to spend a year travelling through America. I visited my old school friend; when her father found her in bed with her boyfriend smoking pot, we both got booted out of the house. We decided to head down to some friends in San Francisco; when we were not staying with them, we would sneak on to her father's very beautiful boat which he kept in a marina in Sausalito just outside San Francisco and sleep there. As I was on a budget and was due in LA shortly to visit the first Terry, we devised a very cunning way of eating well and not paying for it. She and I would scour the thrift stores – or charity shops as we call them in England – and we would buy old handbags and old keys. We would then go into expensive restaurants, place our handbags and 'house keys' on the table and order lunch or supper. Having eaten, we would then order coffee, which I never drank anyway. She would leave and a few minutes later I would say to the waiter, 'Could you hold the coffee for a minute as I need to get something from my car?' It never failed to work – even if they were a little suspicious, they were upmarket establishments and were hardly going to stop you with your handbag and keys left on the table. At about the time I left for LA, my friend's father had forgiven her and she was allowed to go home. Sadly, I haven't seen her since.

LA was perfect. Terry was living in a house in Latigo Canyon in Malibu and I would hang out on the beach. I got myself a little job working at a restaurant. I swear they only employed me because of my English accent. On one of my many nights off, Terry took me to dinner at Mick Fleetwood's, and over dinner the conversation turned to the subject of James Coburn's forthcoming party. James Coburn! Were they kidding? I was totally besotted with the man. At boarding school, I had based every fantasy that I had ever had on him. Terry said he wasn't sure if he was going to go, to which I replied he had to as he had to take me and that James, as I was now calling him, was my hero. Eventually, he agreed; with that settled, I now had a week to work out what on earth I was going to wear.

I can't remember what I wore; in fact, I don't remember much except how genuinely devastated I was. It was a typical LA day – bright sunshine – and a typical LA party – big house, big pool and lots of blonde women. I was itching to meet my hero and expected him to emerge from this rather magnificent house in dirty Levis and we'd live happily ever after. But no. There he was sitting on a sunlounger in a cream safari-style suit with a white panama hat and a drink with an umbrella in it. To make matters worse, he was old! Where was the Jack Daniels and that rugged look that had comforted me on many a lonely night in a Catholic boarding school? I was totally traumatised.

I continued sunbathing and doing as little restaurant work as possible. My yearning to become a surfer chick was being hampered by my complete inability to surf. I could bodysurf a little, and I was quite a dab hand with a boogie board; but when it came to standing up without my feet on the bottom of the ocean I was a disaster. One friend, Claire, was a natural surfer and a real Californian babe. She had worked for Fleetwood Mac and at some point did something for Bob Dylan who lived down the road near Zuma Beach. She knew his son well, and I think they went out at one point. She introduced me to her friends and also to her brother James. James was a lot older than me – maybe twenty-six or twenty-seven – but he seemed like a nice enough guy and had done security for a few bands and individuals when they were on tour as he was a black belt in karate. One day, James was going with about fifteen of his friends to Las Vegas to watch Sugar Ray Leonard fight Thomas 'Hit Man' Hearns. It was billed as the fight of the century, but then have you ever heard of a title fight that is not billed as the fight of the century? When the touring work was thin on the ground, James would drive an eighteen-wheeler truck delivering whatever his consignment was all over America. He had just been given a long-haul job and was going to miss the fight; for some reason he gave me his ticket. This annoyed a few people, as it was an all-boys affair and now there was a girl on the scene. I just wanted to see Las Vegas before going home, and I think James knew that.

On the way, the boys held a sweepstake and for twenty dollars we got to pick two tickets, one from each hat. One hat was for Sugar Ray, the other for Hearns. Each piece of paper had their name and a round number on it, and if your man won in the round specified on your piece of paper, you won all the money. I had Sugar Ray in the fifteenth round, and Hearns in the third. One of the guys, who slightly objected to my presence, thought the fight would go the distance and offered to swap my Sugar Ray in the fifteenth round with his Sugar Ray in the fourteenth, and to pay my stake. I was so delighted just to be there, and happy to get away without paying my $20, that I agreed. Well, Sugar Ray knocked Hearns out in the fourteenth round with twenty seconds to spare and I won all the money. I couldn't believe it – nor could anyone else!

After four months, LA started to get a little stale, and I really felt like a new adventure. I wanted to see the Grand Canyon and I had this romantic notion of driving across America, but I didn't have a travelling companion. At one of Claire's barbecues, James appeared and I thanked him for the ticket, told him how I had won the sweepstake and that I owed him dinner. Claire piped up over a beer and a burger that, if I wanted to see more of the States, I should go travelling with James. He said he would be leaving shortly on a long-haul trip and would be driving to New York. It sounded too good to be true, so after extracting a promise from him that we would stop at the Grand Canyon, I had found myself a travelling companion.

Apart from occasionally on the beach or at Claire's, I had never spent a lot of time with James. I don't think I had ever been in a truck before, and they certainly looked different from the ones I'd seen on the motorways back home. These had air conditioning, a bed in the back – which was of slight concern to me at first – and compressed-air seats. If nothing else, it was going to be a very comfortable ride. We left four days later.

I should have smelled a rat when the route changed on the first day and he told me I would be sharing the cabin with his dog. He said it was good to have a dog in the cab when you weren't there or were asleep, to stop anyone breaking in. Seemed logical enough. We had originally planned to leave California and head straight for the Grand Canyon, Arizona, then on to New Mexico, Texas, Oklahoma and straight across up to New York. As it happened, James's workload was re-routed, and instead he had to pick up a shipment of furniture from Seattle and then take it on to New York. At least that's what he told me. It meant I would miss the Grand Canyon, but it would allow me to see some of the Rockies and also Montana – which was some sort of consolation.

As I left Los Angeles, I began to wonder if this was such a good idea. James did not stop talking, and it didn't take him long to fill me in on his entire life story. He was married, which was news to me, although not disappointing news, as I had absolutely no romantic feelings for him in any way, shape or form. He kept moaning that his wife was going to leave him and that he didn't understand why. He worked hard, he said, and was always sending money when he wasn't there – which seemed to me to be all the time as he was always either away on tour or away driving his truck. I sat and I listened. We got to Fresno and our first truck stop. There are some very dodgy women who hang out in these stops which really are male bastions. They didn't have women's showers, and I certainly wasn't going to risk having a shower in the men's room. I resigned myself to not washing till we got to Seattle. James disappeared for about half an hour and returned looking a little bleary and very hungry, so we ate and hit the road, having decided to stop for the night nearer Sacramento. James said I could sleep in the truck and he would sleep in a little place he knew, which he didn't want to take me to as it was very rough.

As we were pulling out of the stop, a woman called James's name, waved and said, 'See you on your return trip!' It was the same scenario at the next few truck stops and, although I had only been with James for a short time, I began to have a very good idea why his wife was leaving him.

Despite James's inability to drive more than a few hundred miles without getting his cock out, I was settling in well to a trucker's life, and was even getting used to the fact that I hadn't washed in days. One afternoon, feeling a little jaded, I decided to lie down in the back of the cab and go to sleep. I must have only been asleep half an hour before I felt James's cold hand somewhere around my ankle. He started working his way up my leg with some dexterity – it must have been all the practice he had recently had. I came to rather abruptly, and then realised that the truck was still moving. If that was the case, who the hell was touching my leg? I pulled back the covers, then let out the most monumental scream, which made James slam on his brakes and pull over. 'There's a goddamn snake in the bed,' I shouted.

'Of course there's a snake in the bed,' said James. 'It's my snake.'

*His* snake? How can you fail to mention that you have a snake, and where the bloody hell had it been for the last few days? This snake was apparently another security measure. It had been asleep and had just slipped his mind. I'm not squeamish about any animals, and snakes are no different – but I would have preferred to know of its existence before it climbed into bed with me.

The plan was that on arrival in Seattle I would stay in a little motel near the depot that he was picking up from; this could take a couple of days and James, surprise, surprise, had somewhere else to stay. We checked into the motel and I decided to go and get myself something decent to eat. James had other things on his mind and was already on the phone. When I returned to the motel, James was still there – and so was the snake, in the bath which was half-filled with water. Running around on the floor squealing in terror as this snake eyed him from over the top of the bath was a little hamster. It was all easily explained: the snake was hungry and the pet shop was out of rats. This was too much for me. I so wished I was back in Los Angeles.

The snake was banished with its live breakfast to a container in the back of the truck, and I spent the next two days beginning to understand why Seattle has the highest suicide rate in America. It poured with rain, and there was only so much crap TV that you could watch. I had scrutinised every road that we would be taking from here to New York and had the complete itinerary noted and checked. So, as the boredom set in, I decided to take a walk down to the depot and see if there was anything I could do to get this show on the road. On arrival, I was told that James was not there as he was out on a job. Out on a job? 'How can that be?' I asked. 'We're going to New York.' Apparently not. James, unbeknown to me, had taken a two-month contract with this firm to do removal work in and around Seattle. To make matters worse, he had agreed this before leaving California. I was gobsmacked. What the hell was I going to do now?

James arrived back at the motel to find me somewhere between fits of tears and fits of anger. He tried to explain himself by saying that he really liked me and that he felt a great bond between us, mainly it seemed because we shared the same birthday. He was sure that, if I spent the next few months with him, I would feel the same. The man was mad. We could still go to New York, he said. He just needed to finish this contract. I wasn't waiting for anything and, after a row that saw me throw whatever was movable in the motel room at him, it was agreed that he would take me to the airport so that I could get the first plane out of that godforsaken city and as far away from him, his women and his snake as possible.

The first flight out was to Miami. I had always wanted to visit Florida, it was on my way home and I'd get a suntan to boot. So, eight hours later, that's where I found myself – in Miami with very little money and not knowing a single person. I found a motel, went for a walk on the beach and, feeling very sorry for myself, sobbed.

Miami was hot and full of old people. It reminded me of an

elephants' graveyard – when elephants get old, they congregate in one place and wait to die, and it seemed as if half the population was waiting to do the same. The other half seemed to be Cuban and didn't speak English. I wasn't sure if I was going to like Miami and wished that I had gone back home, but as I had gone for a year I didn't want to appear to have failed and return early. Now I didn't have enough money for the air fare and really needed to find a job, which was going to be hard as most places wanted people who were bilingual. I rang the only telephone number I had in Miami, a Colombian guy called Julio who ran a little coffee shop-cum-bar in Coconut Grove. I had been given his number by some friends in LA, and when I called I must have sounded desperate as his wife invited me to come straight over. They were a lovely couple and took me under their wing. I stayed with them for a few days, and through them I eventually found a room in a large four-bedroom house just off Collins Avenue. It was near the beach and I shared it with two other couples and an extremely glamorous, leggy blonde who was hardly ever there.

Now all I needed to do was find a job to pay the rent and hopefully save enough money either to continue my travels or go home. Julio and his wife gave me a few mornings a week in the bar; as the World Cup was about to start and theirs was the only South American bar showing the football for miles around, they were inundated. It was there that I met Danny.

Danny was a tall, good-looking Argentinean; when we met he had a broken arm. Very soon we were in love and I was going to stay in Miami for the rest of my life. I moved into Danny's house, which was a guesthouse on a very grand estate that was on the edge of a golf course. Danny and I were both pretty impoverished, so we spent most of our time making love, arguing over who would win the World Cup and sailing in his friend's yacht. On returning from one three-day sailing trip, I went to see Julio. Danny, his arm now fixed, had had to go back to work, and it was while talking to Julio that I discovered that England had gone to war with the Argentineans. I found the fact I was sleeping with the enemy quite amusing, and couldn't wait to tell Danny that we had something else to argue about apart from the football.

I spent a lazy summer on the beach hanging out with some crazy South Americans, but I had no money and no real prospects of making any. One of the girls who I hung out with worked in a go-go bar and always seemed to have lots of money. It seemed like a good idea to me – you didn't need to speak Spanish to strip. Danny was furious and absolutely forbade me to get a job taking my clothes off. Despite what he said, a few days later I found myself at Rizi's Go-Go Bar doing an audition. It was awful. There I was at ten o'clock in the morning in a bar that smelled of stale sweat, smoke and alcohol, being given some ridiculous outfit to put on with the intention of taking it off shortly afterwards. I felt clumsy and stupid – anyone who knows me would know that I must have had the smallest tits of any go-go dancer in the state – but I still got the job. It's amazing how quickly you become comfortable taking your clothes off in front of complete strangers, though. We had to dance three songs for each set. One with all your clothes on, one with half your clothes on and the other naked. It really was easy money and, after two weeks, I never gave it another thought. I can see why lots of women find it hard to give it up, but it's a grim way to make a living. Men who want to watch women take their clothes off at ten in the morning really should get jobs themselves!

I gave myself two months to save the money I needed to travel to New York and get myself home. I didn't drink alcohol and hardly ever touched drugs. I used to quite enjoy going to work, if only because it meant I could leave with a large number of dollars in my bag. Danny enjoyed the benefits of my earnings as well, and this helped soothe his enormously large male ego. The only time I ever felt uncomfortable at work was one day when he came by to see for himself what went on. It was absolutely torturous and I made him promise not to come again. So long as no one I knew ever saw me, I could pretend it wasn't really me. I would leave that person behind at the bar when I went home. I even lied to my parents about my job and pretended that I worked in a very fancy yacht club called The Mutiny. How could I tell my mother that after thousands of pounds on a good education I was achieving no more than taking my clothes off?

There was a lovely man who used to come in every lunchtime

who owned a jewellery store a few blocks up and he constantly used to ask me what I was doing working there as I seemed very out of place. Before I left, he gave me a present of a solid gold Perrier bottle top, as that was all I ever drank. I never got to say goodbye to him because an incident happened that made me decide I should never go back – and that it really was time to head home.

There was a very unpleasant man who would come into the club about twice a week. He was of Chinese origin and was allegedly a big drug dealer. He certainly always looked high, and he would sit in a booth and insist on having some of the girls sit with him. He liked blondes, so that ruled me out, and he also liked girls with big tits, so that *definitely* ruled me out. He always had a huge wad of notes that he would wave in front of the girls to encourage them to dance in front of him. The top notes were all hundreds, but underneath he had dollar bills, and which end of the pile you got your tip from would depend on whether he liked you. I never danced near him, primarily because I thought he was a creep but also because I knew exactly which denomination note I would be getting, and he could stick his dollar right up his own arse. One day, however, the owner instructed me to sit at his table. The gentleman himself was not pleased, but thought that he would have some fun by banging on about my breasts – or rather my lack of them – and kept getting his wad of notes out and pretending to place them in my cleavage. After he had done this once or twice, I began to get quite pissed off, so the next time he tried to put his money in the top of my leotard, I grabbed his wrist and twisted it. He let go of the money and it went down the inside of my leotard. He went absolutely mad, started shouting and causing a commotion and tried to pull my leotard down. Security was on him in no time, and as he was being removed from the club he kept shouting that I had stolen his money.

Rizi came over and asked me what had happened. He was completely unaware that I had a large sum of money hidden in my leotard. I said that the guy had given me a tip and then asked me if I would sleep with him. I refused, and because of that he had wanted his tip back. As I didn't want to return it, he had tried to get it back himself. The federal law is very clear that if an owner allows his customers to fondle or touch any of the girls his licence will be revoked and the place closed down, so Rizi came down heavily on my side. I was lucky, but I also knew how much money this man had spent. He would be back the next day to speak to Rizi and explain what had really happened. I left that evening knowing that I would not be coming back. I didn't say anything to any of the girls, got security to take me to my car and when I got home and shut the door I emptied all the money I had taken on to the bed. I had just over $1,200. I was certainly not going back now, and my career as a go-go dancer ended as abruptly as it had started. I had already worked for longer than I had originally intended – I'd kept promising myself just one more week, so it really was a blessing in disguise, otherwise I might now be the oldest go-go dancer in Florida!

Danny was thrilled. Together with the other money that I had saved, it looked like we were going to have a great time in New York. My visa was going to expire soon and I had to go home; but I promised Danny I would come back to see him. We planned a road trip with some friends. I contacted a company that provided a service for people who were moving and did not want to drive their car to their new home. I put us down for a ride from Florida to New York and about a week later got a call saying that they needed a Cadillac taken from Miami to upstate New York. We were off!

My abiding memory of that trip was having sex in the back of the car with Danny while our friends Ian and Sally were in the front, and neither of them had a clue. When we got to New York and we told them, as both of us thought it was hilarious, Sally looked mortified. 'What do you expect from a go-go dancer?' she said, and Ian had to play along – but I think he was secretly impressed. The next morning, we went our separate ways: Sally was going to visit relatives. Thankfully, I never saw them again.

Danny and I stayed in Christopher Street in the Village, which was home to a great gay community. It was something that I had never come into contact with before, and I absolutely loved it. The only problem was that what seemed like a lot of money in Florida was not enough to have a good time in a major city. It cost nothing to hang out on the beach, but entertaining yourself in New York was a different thing. We weren't going to be staying long, so I covered the tourist attractions and decided after a couple of weeks that I would head back to England. I was beginning to feel homesick. Danny and I swore undying love for each other: distance would never keep us apart. I left for England and did actually return after a few months when I had managed to work enough to raise the airfare, but it wasn't the same. I saw him years later in England with his wife and child and he was still as handsome as ever; there was even a little sparkle between us ...

Having returned to England, I found myself a little flat, and not living at home certainly helped keep my relationship with my mother on a more than friendly basis. We even had whole conversations! I started going out with a friend of mine who worked for The Beat, a Birmingham-based band. They were quite successful and were about to embark on a North American tour. Phil asked me if I wanted to come on tour with them and I jumped at the chance, thinking that weeks on a tour bus would be a lot more glamorous than I soon came to realise. There was a no-girlfriend rule on the tour, so Phil had to invent a job for me. I was supposed to work one of the spotlights but I was completely crap at it, so I helped out with the merchandising which Phil was in charge of. We played in New York where we stayed at the Gramercy Park Hotel. The Clash were on tour at the same time, and we would sometimes overlap: the hotels would be full of girls in short kilts, ripped tights and heavy black eyeliner.

Being on buses for most of the day just going from one city to another, and staying in identical hotels with identical decor for weeks, is soul destroying. There was one consolation, though: I was never made to travel in the roadies' bus. The smell that emanated from it was palpable. The longer the tour went on, the worse the smell. It seemed it was the norm for them not to wash and then cover themselves in aftershave; the combination of stale sweat, smelly feet and twenty different scents was nauseating. But the tour went well. The Beat had been asked to support David Bowie at Milton Keynes on his China Girl tour, and there was even talk of another tour supporting The Police, which put everyone in high spirits, and we even stopped complaining about the fact that none of the roadies showered or how boring the travelling was.

It was an exhausting tour, but I never bored of listening to the band. Ranking Roger the singer and Saxa the saxophone player certainly brought the place to life. For me, the highlight of the tour was the gig on the beach in Miami when I got to invite all my old friends. The band seemed keen to invite all of Rizi's girls to perform with them on stage! On our return home, we had a little rest before the Milton Keynes gig, where I developed a huge crush on David Bowie's guitarist and would hang around backstage in the hope that he would speak to me. He never did – he was way too cool for me. Shortly afterwards, The Beat broke up, as did Phil and I. I was unemployed and single again.

I decided that, even though my relationship with my mother was improving on a daily basis, I really couldn't live in such a small place as Henley. I decided to move to London where I ended up in a ghastly flat that smelled of cats' piss on the thirteenth floor of a high-rise block in Fellows Road, Swiss Cottage. It really was awful, but I thought it would make me get a job, work hard and move the hell out of here. I got a job within a few days, working in a restaurant called The Pheasantry on the King's Road. It was a hell of a way from Swiss Cottage, and I cycled both ways every day. Steve Thomas gave me the job, and he is still a friend today – he even came up with the title of this book, as much as I'd love to say it was me! The place was co-owned by a photographer by the name of Chad Hall. He must have been sixty, but was very distinguished-looking and I remember saying to him one day that if my husband looked like him when he got to his age I'd be very happy. He turned to me and said, 'If my wife looked like you now, *I'd* be very happy!'

It was a fun time. I decided that the King's Road was where I was going to live, so I started saving hard. The Pheasantry closed and I got a job working at the Main Squeeze, a private members' club just off Sloane Square. It was there that I met John Stephens, who I fell madly in love with, and he me. Some days I wonder why I ever left him, and I have a huge amount of affection for John to this day, especially as he allows me to be a member of the very trendy club he now co-owns – Chinawhite – even though I've never paid my membership! John and I went out for three years until about 1984 and when I left him I really regretted it; but it was too late to do anything as he had gone to America and time had moved on.

During the first year that John and I went out, I moved out of the toilet in Swiss Cottage and found a room in a house in Smith Street, just off the King's Road. I was happy there, but spent most of my time at John's house in Chelsea. I have very special memories of that time, and just to show I have no hard feelings towards him (and so that I can continue not paying my membership fee), I have to say that a more considerate lover would be hard to find than him. He certainly doesn't come from the breed of men that think lovemaking is a race and if they come first then they have won! We had many fun times together, and laughed a lot. I remember looking after a friend of mine's fabulous penthouse apartment in Park Lane when he was the bureau chief in Poland for ABC News. John would often come and stay there, and one night he came over and we were discussing my days as a go-go dancer. I decided to stand on the table and give John a demonstration of my skills, forgetting of course that these huge floor-to-ceiling windows looked out on to the Dorchester. If I could see the hotel, the hotel could sure as hell see me – at least, the security men could, as they insisted on reminding me every time we met. I'm so glad it was only a coffee table and not convenient for anything except drinks and dancing – luckily John and I retired to the bedroom for the rest of the evening.

Near to my apartment lived David Scott, who also happened to be John's best friend, and there was a lot of toing and froing between the floors. David had a business partner whose name was Johnson. They were in the oil-pipe-cleaning business. Johnson was a typical Texan oil man – very flash. He wore his jeans too short so that you could see his crocodile cowboy boots. When you went for tea, he would take milk out of the fridge and say, 'See this? It's the most expensive pint of milk in London.' He was right – Johnson would send his limousine service out for a pint of milk and have it delivered. One night, about twelve of us went to the nightclub Annabel's. We had supper in the restaurant and drank Crystal champagne all night. When, rather the worse for wear, we decided to retire, Johnson asked for the bill and promptly paid for everybody there, refusing any offers of a contribution. As we were leaving, the maître d' approached him and said, 'Excuse me, sir, but there seems to have been a mistake. Your gratuity was larger than your bill.'

Johnson, cool as anything, turned to him and replied, 'Yes. That's because the service was better than the food.'

Years later, the IRS – the American equivalent of the Inland Revenue – caught up with him and he got done for tax evasion. The story goes he put up quite a fight. Johnson's defence was that he didn't have a cent. The judge asked him what he had done with his Learjet. 'I leased it, your honour,' he replied, 'and when I couldn't make the repayments that bank repossessed it.'

'And your yacht?'

'Same thing, your honour.'

'What about your $3 million mansion?'

'Well, your honour, you know the story. You marry a beautiful woman and, when you get a divorce, you have to give them the house.'

The judge looked astonished. 'Are you trying to tell me, Mr Johnson, that you have no assets at all?'

'Yep!'

'And have you learned a lesson from all this?'

'Sure have,' Johnson is reputed to have replied. 'If it flies, floats or fucks – lease it!'

Unfortunately, Johnson's sense of humour wasn't enough to save him from a lengthy spell in a federal penitentiary or, sadly, years later from jumping out of a window and killing himself.

Around this time, I inherited some money from a trust fund that my grandfather had set up, so I went house-hunting. I knew I wanted to live in Chelsea: it felt like home, and it was near work and John. I eventually found a perfect place in Flood Street. I think the excitement of looking for somewhere to live and then doing the place up caused John and me to become a little distant. I also very foolishly thought that it wasn't necessary to go to work any more. I should have been a lot more frugal with my money. I remember going out one day to buy a fridge and coming back with a jacket. It actually cost me three times more than the fridge. I wasn't very practical. John and I soon parted company and he went to the States very soon afterwards to run Tramp in LA.

I first met my husband Tony when at the Main Squeeze. We would have lunch together at the Chelsea Arts Club. He was a lot older than me and I was quite enamoured of him. Tony owned Slick Willies, a sports shop in Kensington High Street. He was one of the first people in the country to import skateboards and had made himself a small fortune at the time.

Tony and I spent the first year of our relationship travelling and enjoying ourselves. It wasn't long before we realised that we really could not sustain this kind of lifestyle without actually doing some work, so I got a job working for John Harwood, an incredibly talented furniture designer and maker.

We were together for a good ten years before we got divorced. We led a pretty normal existence. I got up in the morning, went to work, came home, cooked supper, watched TV, sometimes went out, dragged myself out of bed the next morning, and he pretty much did the same. We might not have had the best marriage, but we did have a great wedding. It took place in Wicklow in Ireland on 8 September 1989. Montana had been born four months previously, and we decided to follow the wedding with a christening – kind of like a job lot! Tony and I arrived a few days before anyone else, and the poor priest who was about to marry us soon discovered that, even though I'm a Catholic, I'm not big on religious ceremonies. We went to see him for a bit of a pep talk about the sanctity of marriage, and he said that we needed to go to confession. Well, it had been a long time since I'd been to confession, but I duly obliged. I sat in the confession box waiting for the priest to say something. 'Belinda,' he said, 'this is when you say, "Father, forgive me, for I have sinned."' I had completely forgotten what to do, so I followed his instructions. 'Now you're supposed to tell me how long it has been since your last confession,' he prompted.

'Twelve years, father,' I answered. Quite why I decided to lie I don't know – it had actually been sixteen years – but I don't suppose an extra four years made much difference.

'This is the point where you tell me your sins,' continued the priest.

Believe it or not, I couldn't think of a single thing that I'd done wrong. I told the priest this, so he said he would help me. He ran through the list of sins and, short of murder and adultery, I had committed all of them! He gave me ten Our Fathers and ten Hail Marys – for the life of me, I couldn't remember how to say the Hail Mary, but I kept that quiet.

We took over a hotel and I know we drank them dry of tequila within the first day. Our good friends Barry and Debbie Dennis were the first to arrive but somehow managed to miss the ceremony. They made it to the reception, which is more than could be said for my dear friend Sean Bobbitt, who made it as far as Dublin Airport before he realised he had forgotten his invitation and had no idea where he was going. He stopped nearly everybody getting off the next two planes in the slim hope that they might be going to my wedding, but in the end he had to admit defeat and go home! The night before the wedding, my sister, who had come with her boyfriend Joe, decided to sleep with one of the other guests. That caused Joe a lot of heartache and he ended up staying up all night drinking with guitarist and musician extraordinaire John Martyn. John had a gig the next night in Edinburgh and invited Joe to come with him. Joe thought this was a better option than hanging around while his girlfriend slept with one of the guests, so they said their goodbyes and were off to Dublin Airport. John was a holy terror at the best of times, and could drink forever. The record company had sent a car to the airport with strict instructions that it was not to stop anywhere – whatever John said – and was to go straight to the venue. John and Joe had other ideas. The driver would not stop, so when he was at some traffic lights, they just got out of the car. After a few drinks in the pub, Joe began to feel very unwell, went out for a walk and got completely lost. He couldn't remember the name of the venue where John was playing and all he had on him was the wedding invitation, so he decided to go to the airport and catch the next plane back to Dublin and then take a taxi to the only place he knew – the church. When Tony and I arrived at the church on Sunday morning for a brief run through, I thought there was a tramp asleep on the pew. It was Joe. He smelled of booze and had had the same clothes on for three days. Luckily, someone lent him some new clothes for the reception, otherwise he might have been asked to leave! As for me, I wore a very beautiful black sequinned mini dress, given to me by my sister, Miranda. For the first thirty minutes, I wore a T-shirt over the top of it that Paula had given to me. It said: 'Any woman looking for a husband has obviously never had one.' As she herself said, she ought to know!

I first remember seeing Paula and Bob in Flood Street in Chelsea. They were taking Fifi to Brownies and she was on the back of Bob's bicycle. After that, I often saw Paula in the dry-cleaner's, and we would bump into each other in the newsagent's too. Sometimes she would say hello to me, and sometimes she would completely ignore me.

At this time, my sister Miranda was seeing someone who owned an antiques shop on Pimlico Road. He would often come to the Chelsea Arts Club for a drink, even though he wasn't a member. He also knew Bob, and Tony would sign them both into the club. Bob wanted to become a member but, rather foolishly, he fell out with the secretary – not a smart move in those circumstances, and his membership was denied. I remember Bob asking Tony if he would book him a table in the restaurant, as he wanted to have Paula's birthday dinner there. Annie Lennox and Dave Stewart were going, but we were not invited. I teased Paula that we weren't smart enough. She agreed!

She wrote me a very sweet card to thank me, and from then on whenever we saw each other we would stop and chat. On a couple of occasions when I waved to her, though, she scowled at me. Well, I thought, fuck you then, and I didn't bother any more. She cornered me one day in the newsagent's and said she missed having a chat and that I should come over and have a coffee with her one morning. I thought this was odd seeing as she had given me the cold shoulder for weeks. When I broached the subject of her rudeness, she explained that she was as blind as a bat and unless she had her glasses on – which she was constantly losing or breaking – she couldn't see a thing, so she would squint desperately to try and focus, hence the awful scowl.

It wasn't until we were both pregnant that we spent more time together and got to know each other. She had a really wicked sense of humour and we would spend hours like a couple of beached whales hooting with laughter.

A little while before Tony and I got married, we had bought a property on the King's Road. We decided to convert it into a small hotel. We also bought some property in Thailand where we used to spend Christmas. The hotel was doing well; it would have done better if more of the profits had been put back into the business. As I had guaranteed part of the business against my house, I was not best pleased. My husband and I argued a lot. My main gripe was the amount of time he spent playing snooker at the Chelsea Arts Club.

His was that I had started using cocaine.

# CHAPTER FIVE

I was arrested on 11 March 1993, charged with 'being knowingly concerned in the fraudulent evasion of the prohibition of the importation of a quantity of cocaine at Dover Docks'. I was seven months pregnant at the time. The value of the cocaine was estimated by Customs and Excise at just over £450,000.

My sister Miranda and I were making our way from Calais to Dover. We got off the ferry, went through Customs and were looking forward to getting home. It was gone nine o'clock at night and I was hungry, thirsty and tired. Passport control was not the disaster I had expected, considering I had forgotten to take my passport with me and had no other form of identification. We were waved through and then asked by a second customs officer to pull into one of the bays and park.

A female officer appeared at my window and asked the normal questions you get when checking in at an airport. Had we packed our own bags? Had anyone given us anything to carry? We were then asked to step out of the car, open the boot and stand about twenty feet away. I could see a customs officer removing my shopping and laying the items on a table. Then another four officers appeared from the ether; two started pulling the seats out, while the other two poked small metal bars between the window and the door frame. Holding a bottle of shampoo, the first officer made his way into a Portakabin and emerged some moments later with two female officers. They approached us and asked us if we would mind accompanying them. What to, I remember thinking at the time, a barn dance? We were escorted separately to different cabins, and I didn't see my sister again until gone midnight when we were bundled into the back of a police van and taken to Folkestone Police Station.

A male officer and the original female officer who had asked my sister and me the initial questions entered the room. I did say it wasn't my car and that anybody could have left drugs in there, thinking that perhaps something had been found on the floor. I was arrested at 9.13 p.m. and then strip-searched. The male officer asked me if I understood why I had been arrested. 'Not really,' I replied. There was a hospital-type bed and a lavatory, and it was known as the SS room – stuffers and swallowers. Anyone Customs believed had either swallowed drugs or inserted them into one of their orifices was kept there until they came out naturally or were forcibly removed. Nice work, if you can get it!

I asked again for my lawyer. They said they could get me the duty solicitor, but I wanted my solicitor from London. I also asked for a glass of water. After an hour and a half, no water was forthcoming, and I knew this was not going to be a very convivial time. I resigned myself to staying there for the night, lay down on the bed and, with this woman watching my every move, I went to sleep. Over the next few hours, certain people would poke their heads around the door but I never got up – I was much too tired. Shortly after midnight, a Customs and Excise officer appeared. He wore an awful cardigan and had an unlit cigar in his hand which made him look like something out of *Starsky and Hutch*. He informed me that, as my car had been used in the perpetration of a crime, it was now forfeit to the Crown. I informed him that it was a hire car and he said I would have to sort it out with the hire company. I asked when I would be going home and exactly why I was being held. He informed me that drugs had been found in my car hidden in cosmetics. Then it was definitely a misunderstanding: I didn't wear make-up, so the drugs couldn't possibly be mine. I also asked if I could call my husband, and repeated my request for my solicitor. He asked who my solicitors were. 'Offenbach and Co,' I said.

In the sixties, David Offenbach had been instrumental in setting up Release, a free service for anybody busted for drugs. Over the years, they had built up a very good reputation and were an excellent and hard-working team.

'And don't worry about your husband. There are currently six customs officers at your house. He'll have a pretty good idea of what's going on.' He left the room.

Moments later, I was bundled into the back of the police van where I was reunited with my sister and some young man I had never seen before. According to the custody records, we arrived at Folkestone Police Station at just after 1 a.m. The police officers were very polite and amenable and, after pleading with them and explaining that I didn't feel well, they let me stay in the same cell as my sister. Neither of us had been told what kind of drugs had been found, or in what quantity.

After talking for about an hour, my mind imagining all sorts of terrible scenarios, I tried to sleep. I was worried for my daughter who had never spent a day away from me, and I prayed for her to be safe. I couldn't sleep, so asked one of the police officers if I could use the phone. At 2.30 a.m., I left a message on my solicitor's emergency number. At 3.30 a.m., Customs and Excise were granted a period of further detention while they continued to pursue their enquiries. Eventually, I slept and woke around 8 a.m. It's a horrible feeling waking up in a police cell. No toothbrush, no clean clothes – but then the whole experience is supposed to demoralise you.

At 2.40 p.m., nearly eighteen hours after my arrest, I was able to speak to Christine McCormack, a representative from my legal team. Christine told my sister, who told me the amount of cocaine we were charged with smuggling. I was shocked and totally confused. I couldn't understand how that amount of drugs could have been in my car without my knowledge. Half a million pounds' worth of drugs sounded like it should have taken up a lot of space in such a little car. I later found out that the cocaine was hidden in liquid form in four shampoo bottles. Quite a complex procedure is then needed to transform it into its powder form. The cocaine was in excess of 90 per cent pure and, according to Customs, cocaine sold on the streets is only around 44 per cent pure. Customs also maintained that the street price of cocaine in 1993 was £86 per gram. I felt like telling them they should get a better supplier – I'd never paid more than £60 a gram – but the situation didn't really call for humour.

I was tired and desperately wanted to go home, but I had a good idea I wasn't going anywhere in a hurry. I hadn't eaten for nearly twenty-four hours and felt weak. I asked Christine what was going to happen next, and she said that Customs wanted to interview me. She advised me not to say anything unless I was absolutely sure I wanted to; she also wanted a doctor to see me to say that I was in a fit state of mind. Me, I just wanted to get this nightmare over with.

The interview commenced at 3.36 p.m. in a stuffy, windowless room. The tape recorder beeped to announce the start of the recording, and the two customs officers in the room introduced themselves to me. One of them seemed familiar to me, but I couldn't place him and I didn't feel it was either the time or the place to ask him if we had met before. The two officers explained the seriousness of the offence, and asked me if I had anything to say. I said that I was not guilty and that the drugs were not mine. They asked me to tell them what I had done that day and how I had come to be in France. So I began with an explanation of the day's events which, over the coming year, I repeated so many times that I could have recited my entire statement in my sleep. My version of events never changed; anybody who asked always got the same response. It was easy – I was telling the truth, whatever these two boys sitting opposite me thought.

Originally, I was going to go to France with my friend Jack Lewis, but at the last minute he pulled out. I met him the day before to finalise the travel arrangements and that's when he told me he wouldn't be able to come. He also asked me if I would take some money to a friend of his who was stuck in Calais as his wallet had been stolen. Jack gave me an envelope with £300 in it. It had his friend's name on the front – Donald – along with the telephone number of his hotel and room number.

I was really annoyed with Jack for letting me down, as I had been looking forward to the trip and had arranged with my estranged husband to look after our daughter. Tony and I had tried at a reconciliation, I suppose because I was pregnant, but it was a disaster. We had gone to our house in Thailand over Christmas, but I flew back early and he stayed another month. That was the end of our marriage. Jack had been very kind and looked after me, and I could feel that there was definitely something between us – and, anyway, what girl could resist a man as handsome as he was? It was definitely flattering having someone like him showering you with affection when your marriage was in tatters and you felt fat, ugly and pregnant! He promised to make it up to me and would take me to Paris for a weekend and he would call me on my return. He kissed me, and I couldn't be angry with him for long.

So, on Thursday, 11 March, I found myself getting up to go to France alone. I had tried calling Miranda the night before and had left her a message asking her if she wanted to come with me. It was just a shopping trip, and I would buy her lunch. She never replied, so I rang my girlfriend Natalia who I had been at school with and asked her if she wanted to come. Natalia ran a very successful nursery school in Parsons Green which my daughter attended. She said she would have loved to come but she had to take her daughter to a birthday party that afternoon. I got in the car and thought that I would stop by my sister's apartment in Kensington and see if I could wake her. I went by the bank on the King's Road to get some money, and ran into someone I knew who was going for breakfast in a little café near by. It was a chance meeting but one that, as the next few days played out, would become very significant. I rang Miranda's doorbell at 11 a.m. In fact, I persistently rang it so she had to get out of bed. She told me she'd had a late night and had a hangover. A trip to France would cure all that, I told her.

With Tom Petty and the Heartbreakers at full volume, we pulled into Dover only to discover that the hovercraft was full and that we would have to take the ferry. I was beginning to wonder if we should bother going at all. Miranda was muttering something about wanting to be back for six o'clock, which was going to be totally impossible now. The ferry journey was uneventful and we finally arrived in Calais. It seemed an age before they let the cars off the boat, and by this time I was desperate for the loo.

We made our way into Calais, and the first hotel we came to was the Holiday Inn. I pulled into the car park and Miranda and I went into the bar. She ordered a much-needed black coffee and I went for a much-needed pee! There was a map of Calais at reception which I picked up. I joined my sister, asked the barman where the Mammoth hypermarket was and he showed me the direction in which I needed to go. The map did not actually show it, as it was further out of town, but he put a cross on the road that we needed to take. I then went to the public phone – back then I did not have a mobile. I called Donald to tell him that he could come and pick up his money. He was very grateful and said the Holiday Inn was only a few minutes away. Would it be cheeky of him to ask me to drop it round, as he was in the middle of packing and was late checking out? The receptionist said that it wasn't far, but it was quite complicated to drive if you didn't know the town because of the one-way system. A taxi, she said would be better. So on her advice I headed off.

On my arrival, I asked reception to ring Donald's room, and he told me to come up. I exited the lift and headed to his room through some large glass swing doors which I held open for a gentleman coming in the opposite direction. He thanked me in English. 'No problem,' I said. Donald greeted me at the door and I went into his room. According to Customs' observations of that room, I was there for about four minutes. Personally, I think it was longer, but either way it was a short amount of time. I had never met the man before, and it wasn't a social visit. He was packing and was having trouble closing his suitcase as it was so full. I helped him with the zip and he asked me if we could give him a lift back to London. I wasn't very keen on this, as I certainly didn't want him coming for lunch with me and my sister, but, as he was a friend of Jack's and I didn't want to appear rude, I told him we were going to catch the 7.15 ferry back to England. If he was on it, I would give him a lift from Dover to London. He seemed happy with that, and asked me if I would put his suitcase in my car, as it would save him having to lug it around with him. This I declined to do. I remembered thinking at the time that it would have been stupid, purely for the security aspect.

As we were leaving the room, he picked up a shopping bag that had some bread, cheese, shampoo and toothpaste in it. He asked if I would take it with me and put it in the boot to keep cool – and anyway he had no more room in his suitcase. It was a reasonable request, and we agreed to meet on the ferry. As I was leaving the hotel, the man for whom I had held the door open on the landing was also leaving. He got into a small blue car with three other men, and I remembered thinking what a nice leather jacket he had on. I took a cab, and in less than fifteen minutes I was back at the Holiday Inn.

I went into the bar where Miranda had finished her coffee, and after paying the bill we made to leave. Suddenly, I saw the man in the nice leather jacket coming into the hotel. I turned to my sister and jokingly said, 'That man is following me.'

'Typical French,' she replied. 'They'd even follow a pregnant woman.'

We laughed, and as we went through the front door we both turned to look at him. 'At least he's got a cute arse,' I said, before we got into our car and followed the directions we had been given by the barman.

We spent a wonderful afternoon buying wine, cheese and anything else that took our fancy. We shopped for longer than expected and spent more money than I had anticipated, but what the hell. We had two trolleys stuffed with good things, and now had the unenviable task of trying to fit it all into a Fiat Uno. I opened the boot and took out the blue-and-white-striped delicatessen bag that held Donald's shopping. I placed it on the floor of the car park and started loading in the cases of beer and the bottles of wine. I then placed on top of these items the boxes containing the cheese, hams and salamis. I picked up Donald's bag and the handles broke and tore the side of the bag. It was very thin plastic. I placed his stuff on top of mine in the boot. We headed towards the ferry and only stopped to go to a tobacconist.

We arrived at the ferry at 6.45 p.m., giving us what I would have thought was plenty of time to board the ferry – but apparently not. I was informed that you have to arrive at least forty-five minutes before departure to allow time for check-in. We were told we would have to catch the next one. I explained that I was supposed to be meeting someone on the ferry but that, apparently, was my problem, not theirs. I thought that Donald would wonder where we were, but a few groceries were not the end of the world. I did feel a little guilty, though – after all, I had offered him a lift.

We checked in early for the next ferry, and I handed in my ticket to the man in the little kiosk. He then asked me for my passport. 'Passport?' I said. 'I didn't think I would need one now we were all part of the European community.'

'No,' he replied, 'You definitely require one. Do you have any other ID?'

I had nothing. I had taken cash only to avoid the temptation of going crazy with my credit cards. He was not amused, and to make matters worse my sister had no passport either. If we were international drug smugglers, we certainly weren't very professional. Miranda, however, at least had her driving licence. The French customs officer said that there was going to be trouble because I had no ID whatsoever.

'Will you let me leave the country?' I asked him.

'Yes, but there is a good chance you will be detained by British Customs when you arrive in England.'

He didn't know how right he was. I searched the glove compartment of the car and found a receipt which showed my name and address, and also the hire agreement for the car. He reiterated that I would probably be held in England until they could verify my actual identity. I had visions of poor Miranda catching the train to London to get my passport while I was held at Dover. The poor man looked completely exasperated by us, and must have thought how bloody stupid English women are.

I slept on the boat, as did Miranda. We disembarked, and the rest you know. No wonder they weren't concerned about my lack of identification at passport control: they had bigger fish to fry.

The interview lasted fifty-nine minutes, and I was returned to the cell. Miranda was not there. I hoped that my explanation would satisfy them and that I could go home. I needed to see my daughter and I wondered how I could have been so stupid as to be embroiled in this mess. I was scared, and there were more than a few frightening moments along the way.

Miranda had been placed in a separate cell to me at the request of Customs, as they did not want me to discuss my statement with her. She was taken to the interview room at 5.45 p.m. They said the same to her as they said to me – that she was charged with a serious offence and they wanted to know what her movements were that day. They also asked her to verify what I had said to her during the day, what I had done and when I had done it. Her interview lasted twenty-nine minutes. During this period, I sat on the thin foam mattress on my concrete bed and wondered what Jack's involvement in this was, or if he even knew what his friend was up to.

Then it came to me. I knew where I had seen one of the Customs and Excise officers before. He was the guy with the nice leather jacket and the cute arse, the man I had opened the door for in the hotel and who had followed me to the Holiday Inn. I couldn't believe it. I hadn't been stopped at Dover by chance; this was a well-planned operation. I became more frightened and wondered whether I should have heeded my solicitor's advice and not answered any questions until I knew the extent of what I had got myself involved in. But, before I could dwell any more on this startling piece of information that had come to light, the cell door opened and I was again taken to the interview room. The time was now 6.55 p.m.

The mood in the interview room was quite different to before. There was no hint of warmth from either officer, and I thought better of trying to engage them in conversation. However, I also knew that I wanted to get on record that I had seen one of them following me. I was sure that an opportunity to do this would arise in the interview; if not, I would have to create it myself. This time, instead of me doing all the talking, they were asking all the questions. Customs officers are like barristers: they don't ask you questions unless they already know the answer. They can catch you out easily and know if you are lying. They asked me about the vague description of Donald that I had given in my earlier interview. As the Metropolitan Police were to find out a few years later, my powers of description are awful, but I never forget a face. They questioned me about the fact that Donald had asked me to take his suitcase, and yet I had not mentioned this to my sister. 'I didn't think it was significant enough to mention,' I replied.

'But it's significant now, isn't it?' asked one of the officers.

Now was my perfect opportunity. 'Yes,' I said, 'of course it is. But then not everything seems important at the time. When I held the door open for you at the hotel and then you followed me with three other men in a blue car to the Holiday Inn, that didn't seem significant; but now that I'm sitting in a police station having been arrested for a large quantity of drugs, and you are sitting opposite me interrogating me, it becomes *very* significant.'

I thought his jaw was going to fall off it fell so far, and for a few moments there was a stunned silence. Months later, I found out that there had been two customs officers in the hotel. They thought that I had noticed the other officer, which is why they sent this one to interview me. Once they had got over the shock, they continued questioning me. What did Donald look like? Would he still have the envelope with the money in? Would his fingerprints be on the bag or the shampoo bottles? I answered all their questions. I would recognise him again if I saw him; I didn't know what he'd done with the envelope, but I presumed he'd still have it; and I hoped his fingerprints would be on the bottles – surely they could check that. It was all rather tiresome, and then they suddenly asked me a question right out of the blue. Did I know a man by the name of Brian Close? What the hell had Brian got to do with all this? Now it was my turn to look surprised.

About a year before, I had gone to a wedding in Ireland and met Brian. He was in the fashion industry and knew my husband's brother, who was also in the business. When he came to London, he would stay in our hotel on the King's Road. I had been out for drinks with him a couple of times and we had supper at the Chelsea Arts Club once. He wasn't so much a friend as an acquaintance, but as he was a client at our hotel I was always polite to him when I saw him. They asked me if I had seen Brian in the Holiday Inn in France and I said no. They asked me if I had ever met him at The Cadogan Arms pub on the King's Road. I said no – I knew the pub, as it was near our hotel, but I had never been in it.

'We've been working on this operation for well over a year,' they told me.

'Then you must know Jack,' I said.

But Jack, they insisted, was just a figment of my imagination; I really should now tell them the truth. The truth was that I was blue in the bloody face with telling the truth, and I just wanted to get out of there. One of the officers went on to say that Brian Close had organised this drugs run and that he had also met on numerous occasions with the man I had given the money to in the other hotel. He went on to say that I could go to prison if found guilty, and that I would deserve it. I decided then to be very careful what I said, and wished – not for the first time that day – that I had refused to answer any questions.

They insisted that Brian Close was in the Holiday Inn when I stopped there with my sister, that that was the reason for me going to the hotel and that I had met with him. They could believe what they liked. If they were going to insist that I was there with Brian, then they were in for a big shock because I knew different. Better still, I knew where Brian Close was, and it was nowhere near France – but I wasn't going to tell them that.

Their line of questioning returned to Jack. They insisted that he didn't exist and that it was too much of a coincidence that I knew Brian and Brian knew Donald. 'Looks like he has set you up,' said one of them, 'or you are knowingly involved.'

My barrister loved that statement in court and hammered the point home to the jury on numerous occasions – even Customs, he pointed out, had admitted that it looked like I had been set up. I hoped for a few more gems like that before the interview was terminated. 'I was not knowingly involved,' I told them quite firmly.

By now, however, the magnitude of the situation had become overwhelming and I could feel myself wanting to cry. I suddenly had the most awful thought. Miranda also knew Brian. I had introduced them one night at the Chelsea Arts Club, and we had

had drinks. I didn't know if she would even remember his name, but now Customs had Miranda alone at the Holiday Inn where they were insisting Brian was. This dreadful situation had absolutely nothing to do with her, and when I'd told her to tell the absolute truth I had meant it, but now I realised that she was going to be caught even deeper. I had left Miranda in the Holiday Inn where Customs were now insisting Brian also was – and by now even I was beginning to think he might actually have been there, they seemed so sure. I had to do something about it.

I thought I was going to faint. I told my solicitor to stop the interview, and I suddenly became quite hysterical. I was taken outside for some air and I insisted on sitting on a bench in the corridor and that someone gave me some water. I could hear Miranda banging on her cell door wanting to know what was the matter with me, as she could hear all the commotion. The customs officers asked the police to look after me and to call a doctor, and also to bring Miranda to the interview room. As she came out of her cell and down the corridor towards me, she looked very concerned. I winked at her, then flung myself towards her, putting my arms around her neck and whispering in her ear that she didn't know Brian Close. I continued crying, and was genuinely shaking, but it was OK – she had heard me.

Customs interviewed Miranda for twenty-seven minutes and gave her a packet of cigarettes. They knew her only involvement was that she happened to be a passenger in my car, but they didn't care. We found out later that the only reason she was charged was that if they let her go it would have put an element of doubt into the proceedings. They could not afford that risk. At 9.21 p.m. on Friday, 12 March at Folkestone Police Station, Mr Thompson of Her Majesty's Customs and Excise formally charged my sister and me under the Misuse of Drugs Act 1971 with importing cocaine. Miranda fainted. Mr Thompson read from a sheet of paper that I was being charged in conjunction with Daniel Burns, Laura Critchley, Brian Close and my sister. I was totally confused. Who the hell were Daniel Burns and Laura Critchley? I had never heard of these people and no one would give me an explanation as to who they were and what their connection was to the crime. He also told us that bail was being refused because of the gravity of the charge and the fear we might abscond and not appear for the court hearing.

That meant we were going to jail.

My poor little girl. What was she going to do without her mummy? And what was I going to do without her? I felt my life had come to an end.

At 12.40 a.m., I was finally given a toothbrush, and, at 8.15 the next morning, I had my first shower in two days. At 9.30 a.m., we left Folkestone Police Station for good in the back of a police van, accompanied by WPCs Smith and Fletcher. They were very decent and had looked after us well during our stay. They wished us both luck. We were taken to a large communal cell below Dover Magistrates' Court, where all prisoners waiting to be processed through the courts that day were held. The women were separate from the men, and Miranda and I found a wooden bench in a corner. There were two other women in the cell with us. We had been there about half an hour when I became very conscious that the blonde girl in the cell was staring at me. I ignored her but she kept on glancing over at me. It was making me nervous. Eventually, she walked over to me and asked me if I was Belinda Brewin. How the hell did she know who I was? I had never seen her before. Before replying, I asked her who she was. 'Laura Critchley,' she replied. Well, you could have knocked me over with a feather. She looked young and very frightened – I actually felt sorry for her – but I also knew I didn't want to talk to her. Whatever her involvement was, I didn't want to know, but she looked desperate and truly scared. I told her to calm down and breathe deeply. She sat down next to me and told me she had met me before. I was adamant that she had not and that she was very much mistaken. She then explained that she had seen me once in the Chelsea Arts Club, but that we had never spoken.

It transpired that she had been at the club visiting Brian Close with her boyfriend Danny. I deduced from this he was the same Daniel Burns with whom we had been charged. She recalled that my husband was there at the same time; he should have picked my daughter up from a friend's that day and hadn't bothered to show up, so I stormed in, gave him a piece of my mind and left. 'You were very scary,' Laura said.

'I was incredibly pissed off.'

'Well, there was a stunned silence after you left.' (In fact, all the regulars were probably just thinking, Oh, there goes Belinda – again!)

I explained to Laura that we were in a lot of trouble here and it would be best if we did not discuss what had happened. I certainly didn't want to hear her side of the story, however curious I was. 'Do you think this has anything to do with my holiday to South America with Danny?' she asked. I shuddered to think – it sounded like the poor girl was in a lot worse trouble than us. 'What's going to happen next?' she asked.

'We're probably all going to go to jail,' I replied, and she started to cry. I put my arm round her. What else could I do? I wished she had never spoken to me, but it was too late now. Maybe we should all be sticking together.

We were called up to court and, after they asked us our names and addresses, we were remanded in custody for a week. I asked my solicitor if that meant we would be freed in a week and was told that it was highly unlikely.

Both Miranda and Laura were very down. None of us had eaten or slept properly in the past two days. Laura had been arrested at the flat in London that she shared with Danny, and had been brought to Dover in the middle of the night. She too had been questioned. I felt it my duty to try and keep everybody's spirits up and tried to encourage them not to be so despondent, even though I felt totally miserable. The other girl who had been in the cell with us was led back from court in tears. She was Dutch and didn't understand why she had been arrested. It seemed to be the one thing we all had in common, and it made me smile. She had been arrested the same evening as Miranda and me, getting off a ferry with marijuana in her bag. She explained that in Holland it was perfectly legal to carry that amount and she didn't understand why she couldn't bring it on holiday with her. No wonder she got stopped – her clothes stank of the stuff and her hair, which resembled a Brillo pad, was filthy. Not only did her clothes stink, *she* stank. I am sure that the two days she had spent in the cells had not helped, but this was definitely long-term, deeply ingrained body odour.

Court broke for lunch and we were removed from the cells. This time we were taken to Dover Police Station; what a farce that turned out to be. Miranda and I were put in a cell together, and Laura and the Dutch girl were held in the one next door. Customs had finished interviewing us and, as we had been formally charged, the police were far more lenient towards us. I advised the girls to be polite at all times, as this would make our stay easier. As a result, we were allowed to spend most of our time in the exercise yard. The four of us huddled under extra blankets in a corner – it was like being on the worst camping trip ever, with a smelly dog to boot. Something had to be done and we asked the police for a washbag for the Dutch girl. They didn't have one, so Miranda and I donated the money for someone to go and buy soap and shampoo. It was not the time for subtleties. We told her she stank, she took it very well and she duly sorted out the problem. Suddenly, life's aroma – if not its general conditions – improved. (Unfortunately, she had to be reminded again two days later, and she did take slight umbrage at that. After all, she had already washed once, as she insisted on pointing out to us.)

Dover Police Station was undergoing renovation work. As a result, there was no heating in the cells, and the skylights were permanently open. It was like a walk-in freezer. The duty sergeant was concerned about how cold it was, and I asked if there was any warm clothing we could borrow. Extra blankets were brought, along with some police sweaters with 'Kent Constabulary' sewn on to the epaulettes, but we were still freezing. Steve, the custody sergeant, empathised with our problem but said that he only had one cell that had heating. We asked if we could share that one cell. Off he went and came back saying that it was a very unorthodox request but he would comply, so we spent the afternoon trying to arrange four mattresses in a cell built for one. I had the concrete bed, and the others were arranged on the floor with a six-inch path by the side of the wall. Nights were the worst: the sea air blew through the skylights and we all huddled together trying to steal a bit of warmth from the next person.

The next morning, Steve called for a doctor to examine me and take me to hospital. He thought the cold would affect my pregnancy and was concerned, although personally I felt the lack of decent food and a good night's sleep were far worse. As custody sergeant, he was in charge of our welfare and I have to say that he did everything possible to make us feel that we were staying at the Four Seasons Hotel rather than a police cell. He was a thoroughly decent bloke and, when we left, he said to me if I ever wrote a book would I give him a mention. Well, I have – and I hope that he reads it and knows just how much we appreciated his genuine humanity. By the time we left, however, I think he was probably glad to see the back of us – especially me, as my requests became more ludicrous with each passing day.

Breakfast was brought to us after the hospital had given me the all-clear. It was repulsive, inedible and totally unrecognisable as food. Just as I rang the bell to see what could be done about this, the screaming and shouting that had persisted through the night started again. As we had been settling in for the night, someone rather the worse for a Saturday night in the pub was brought in and placed in the cell opposite. He was effing and blinding and rang the bell all night, pleading for a light for his cigarette. He obviously thought the magic word was 'cunt' because every time he kicked the door or rang the bell he would shout this out. Personally, I have always found that, if you want something, 'please' is a much better way to start than 'listen, you fucking cunt'. Amazingly enough, he never got a light and, having now woken up, he thought he would start where he left off. Me being me, I couldn't help but give him a little lecture on gentlemanly conduct and was promptly told to 'fuck off, you snobby cunt'. We all burst out laughing and headed for the exercise yard. I think he was released shortly afterwards because nobody could stand the noise any longer.

We were allowed to take some of our money out of the sealed bags that our things were kept in. We gave this money to a policewoman who went to the shops for us. According to the records, we bought mineral water, all the Sunday papers, French bread, cheese and eggs. Miranda and I made scrambled eggs for the others in the police canteen, and we sat in our cell eating, reading the paper and relaxing – a little like the rest of the population of Britain but in different surroundings. Laura was becoming more despondent with each passing hour; I wondered how we would all cope when it came to going to prison. This was bad enough, but Holloway was going to be much worse. I for one did not relish the idea of going there. I hoped we would all stay together.

That evening, we asked for a takeaway and gave the money to yet another policeman who went to collect it in his panda car. It was lukewarm when it arrived back and I complained to Steve about this. He said the restaurant was a long way from the station. I asked why he hadn't put his blue flashing lights on to bring it back, and even they laughed and shook their heads in disbelief. It wasn't that I really thought it was funny, but if you don't laugh you'll cry, and I knew that if I started to cry I would never stop.

Miranda insisted on having her Chanel No 5 returned to her; this was allowed on condition that we all promised not to drink it. At least it covered the smell of the Dutch girl who, along with Laura, spent most of her time in tears. One of the female officers said she would stop at Marks and Spencer for us the next morning and pick up some shopping if we gave her the money and a list of what we wanted. As it would probably be our last decent meal, the list was endless and she kindly got the lot. I wish I could remember her name so I could thank her too.

We were all offered showers, but were warned that, like the heating, the water wasn't very hot. We all declined – it was freezing with our clothes on and no one was in a hurry to remove them and cover themselves in cold water. And then our carriage arrived to take us on the next step of our journey. After removing our Kent Constabulary jumpers and collecting our meagre belongings, we were taken out of the police station. I really wanted to keep my sweater as a souvenir and asked Steve if this was possible. Once more he shook his head in disbelief and said no. The four of us stood in the yard and the big metal gates drew back as a police transit van reversed in. Steve handcuffed the Dutch girl to one of the female officers who were going to accompany us. He then went to reach for my hand. 'What on earth do you think you are doing?' I asked him.

'I'm going to handcuff you to one of the officers,' he replied.

'You have got to be kidding.' We had come to an impasse in our relationship. Steve was adamant that I had to be cuffed, as it was procedure. Fuck procedure, I thought, there was no way I was letting anyone handcuff me. After much deliberation by the police, it was decided that I would be handcuffed to my sister. This was still unacceptable. I tried to explain that I wasn't objecting to the *person* that I was being handcuffed to, it was the act of being handcuffed that I found total reprehensible. Now they had a real problem. Steve tried to appeal to my better nature. I explained to the poor man that on this matter I didn't have a better nature – even after everything he had done for us.

Half an hour passed and I would not be moved. It seemed totally unreasonable as I had been taken to the hospital without being handcuffed; I had even been left in a ground-floor room completely unattended when the female officer asked me if it would be all right if she went to get a drink from the canteen and then went to the loo. 'Of course,' I had said.

'Please don't try to escape,' she said and smiled at me.

'Of course not,' I said, smiling back, and then sat there for fifteen minutes with freedom just the other side of the window. As far as I was concerned, it was quite clear that I was not going to try and escape – especially from a moving vehicle with three guards in it. Eventually, the situation was resolved and it was agreed that I would not be handcuffed. We finally left with Miranda handcuffed to Laura, the Dutch girl to an officer – and me handcuffed to no one.

# CHAPTER SIX

If I thought the journey from Dover to London was depressing, arriving at HMP Holloway was enough to make you feel suicidal. I spent the journey with my face pressed against the glass, wondering when I would see another field again. I tried not to think about my daughter. It was too painful. The last time I had seen her she was asleep in her bed; I had stroked her hair and kissed her forehead and I couldn't bear to imagine how long it would be before I would be able to do that again. As we drove through North London, I saw a restaurant I had once been to; the memories it held seemed so insignificant now.

No one really spoke on the journey. Each of us was wrapped up in our own self-pity, full of trepidation. I for one certainly didn't expect someone as kind as Steve the custody sergeant waiting for us with open arms at the gates of the prison. I was right.

Suddenly, there it was – the place that was going to be my home for the foreseeable future. A grimmer-looking institution would be hard to find. The barrier rose and the first set of metal gates opened menacingly to let us enter. We were unceremoniously unloaded and herded like cattle into the reception area. We were to be processed here. There was a desk where we filled in forms and two wardens searched us, took our possessions, gave us a prison number and moved us along. Stupidly, I asked if we could all stay together. 'What do you think this is,' came the obvious reply, 'a hotel?' I never asked again, but as I have said I always think rudeness is unnecessary. When someone has been polite enough to ask a civil question, I see no reason why the response should not be equally polite. It became more of an issue the longer I stayed in prison and in the end I would not tolerate it. It caused a lot of trouble.

It did not take long to see why some of the wardens had that attitude, however. Many of the inmates were foul-mouthed – indeed, some were just downright crude – and it seemed we would all suffer for it. As I was sitting waiting to see the doctor, I put my hand in my pocket and realised I had Miranda's lighter. Another of the girls saw it and immediately put her hand over it. 'Crutch it,' she whispered. Lighters are like gold dust in prison, and they were amazed I had managed to get it past the front desk. Nevertheless, even though I had never heard the expression 'crutch it' before, I had a pretty good idea what it meant and there was no way I was going to put anything up my fanny that God never intended to go there. I gave it to the girl next to me who promptly secreted it without moving from the seat – and, it seemed to me, without moving a muscle. I could tell this wasn't her first stay. Miranda and Laura's numbers were called and they disappeared.

All time in prison is spent waiting. Waiting for the day you will be released, waiting to see the result of an application you put before the governor weeks before, or just waiting for a door to be unlocked so you can go back to your cell. I was just waiting to see a doctor, and hopefully rejoin my sister and Laura. In fact, I would never speak to Laura again. I realised right there and then that I was going to have to learn patience. This was not a good place to lose your temper.

A sweet, sickly smell began to pervade the room and a number of the girls began to look around in earnest for the source of this smell. I had never smelled it before, but I sure as hell got used to it and, by the time I left prison, I could recognise the smell of someone smoking crack cocaine from miles away. A girl was huddled in the corner of the toilets with her pipe and her rock. She had obviously crutched it before going to court, and she wasn't coming out until it was all gone – and she certainly wasn't going to share it with anyone. That was my initiation into the drug culture of Holloway; very soon I began not to notice it, as it was such an everyday occurrence.

My number was called and I went in to see the doctor. 'Do you have anything the matter with you?' he asked. 'Do you have a drug problem?

'No.'

'Are you sure.'

'I don't have a drug problem,' I assured him.

'You won't get treatment or methadone if you don't say now, and we don't want you going crazy on us.'

I assured him that I was not a junkie. Anything for a quiet life. No, I was sure I didn't need anything – no sleeping pills or Valium. Could the man not see that I was pregnant and that tablets were probably not the order of the day? This doctor and I were to have more than one run-in. I was told to remove my clothing and put on a robe. Thinking that the doctor was going to examine me, I refused. If I was to be examined, I was to be examined by my consultant in a suitable environment. A female officer appeared and quite reasonably explained that it was just procedure. 'It's always procedure,' I said, 'but it doesn't make it right and no way am I going to be touched anywhere by this doctor.' No one argued. I was weighed and then taken to another part of reception where my clothes were searched, especially along the hems and cuffs. I was asked to open my robe and then get dressed. I was given some sheets and placed in a line with the other girls. I could see the crack-smoker scratching herself in the corner. It's terrible what drugs do to you. She looked wide-eyed and crazy. In fact, she really was completely mad, and whenever I saw her after that she seemed heavily sedated. Poor kid. Miranda, Laura and the Dutch girl were nowhere to be seen.

I was escorted to the ground-floor wing which housed mainly pregnant women. There were a few who weren't pregnant – mainly very young girls who were vulnerable or had been beaten by other inmates, the logic being that pregnant inmates are generally less violent than the others. I was taken to the warder's office and asked if I wanted a cell on my own or if I wanted to share. I felt a single room was what I wanted. A male officer escorted me to my room which was dark, dingy and damp. I knew I could not lie there all night with no one to talk to. I had passed some shared cells on the way and for some reason they looked a little more inviting. Suddenly, I started having trouble breathing and thought I was going to pass out. I must have made quite a lot of noise, as a couple of wardens appeared and took me outside. I recovered soon enough and told them that perhaps I would prefer to share. We went back into the office where a blackboard on the wall showed the cell allocations. There was some discussion among the staff about which was a suitable cell for me. In the end, a cell was chosen and I was escorted to a largish room with four beds in it. Mine was in the corner and I had a desk in front of the window. I had a small wardrobe to hang my things in, if I could find a hanger. The male officer reappeared with a large square pillow which he gave me, saying that he thought I was used to a bit of luxury and he hoped this might help. So far so good. Maybe not all prison officers were bastards.

There was a communal sink in the room and a metal toilet with no seat or handle. In fact, it was one complete unit and had no removable parts that could be used as missiles in case of a riot or a row in the cell. At least the loo had a door, which was more than there had been in the police cells. As I sat on my incredibly narrow bed trying to remember the last time I had slept in a single bed, I realised I didn't know where Miranda was. I went back to the office to enquire about her and was told that she had been placed on another wing and another floor. I asked if I could see her, and was told to make an 'app'. I was then dismissed. An app? I had no idea what that was, and there seemed to be no one about to ask. I went back to the cell, thought about the environment I was in and formulated a plan to help me survive this ordeal.

I decided that my years at boarding school would stand me in good stead for the pettiness of prison rules, and I was right. Also, I realised that not a soul here knew me, which meant that I could behave however I wanted and nobody would know if it was the norm or not. I didn't want any reports from the prison to be in any way detrimental to me or my case. I also didn't want to get into any fights with the varying factions that existed among the inmates, and I knew already that this was going to be my biggest problem. Even in the waiting room, certain ethnic groups had stuck together and similar social groups had formed quasi-gangs. Having weighed up the factors against me, I decided that I would be a model prisoner. I would be extremely polite to everyone, even in the face of adversity and extreme rudeness. The other thing I decided to do was not to swear, and even to pretend I found it very offensive. The truth is that I swear like a trooper – some people think I suffer from Tourette's. My language is the bane of my mother's life – she *never* swears. It was going to be hard. I decided never to discuss my case with anybody, though most of them knew either from the newspapers or from the prison grapevine what I had been charged with, and on the scale of offences mine was on the high end of serious. I also decided that, if asked, I would say I had never taken drugs and never would.

It was a case of sink or swim, and I had no intention of drowning in a shithole like this.

I spent some time in my cell and then, as the door was unlocked, I had familiarised myself with the whereabouts of the bathrooms, the recreation room and the canteen. There were also washing machines and tumble dryers, which surprised me. The big heavy doors at the end of the corridor were locked and they only seemed to join yet another group of unending corridors. The place seemed remarkably clean and my room-mates seemed tidy enough. There were bars on every window and we looked out on to a small yard that joined one wing with another. It was almost impossible to see out of the windows which seemed to be made of reinforced Perspex and were so scratched they were almost opaque. Suddenly, I heard the sound of keys in a lock and a door opening, and then what sounded like stampeding cattle. The wing was returning from wherever they had been all day.

My room-mates were a mixed bunch. Maria I liked immediately – she was a pretty East End girl with blonde hair and no pretensions. Her cockney accent cracked me up and she thought I was very proper, but we got along fine and she gave me good advice. The other two were druggies. One spent her entire time picking the scabs and spots on her face, much to the horror and disgust of me and Maria. She also never brushed her teeth which were repulsive and looked as if they had a film of filth over them. She and the Dutch girl would have got on fine. The other girl, believe it or not, had attended the same school as me. It didn't say much for their achievements – 50 per cent of one cell in Holloway was a statistic that I was sure they wouldn't be putting in their prospectus. She had been in the Paddington rail crash, had helped pull survivors out of the wreckage and had been hailed as a hero. The trauma she suffered seemed to have had a terrible effect on her life and she had ended up in jail – something to do with stealing furniture or selling stolen property, but I thought there was more to it than that, as she had got quite a long sentence considering it was her first offence and her mitigating circumstances. Her main problem seemed to be drugs – along with nearly everybody else in the prison. I would say that 90 per cent of all women in prison are there because of drug-related crimes, and I was no different.

My first night in jail was probably the worst. Night-times are grim in prison. For about an hour after lock-up the noise is incredible. People are constantly shouting, some calling out of the windows to someone on another floor or wing, others telling them to shut up. Tin cans are swung on a string to other cells in a kind of mobile drug-delivery system. It's a real hive of industry. Then along comes the sleeping tablets and the liquid cosh – a very apt name for Largactil. One swig of that and it's away with the fairies for whoever takes it. Everything quietens down and you are just left with your thoughts. I barely slept, and tossed and turned all night. The bed itself was a nightmare. Every time I moved, it creaked so much that it sounded like automatic rifle fire. You certainly wouldn't masturbate unless you wanted your entire wing to wake thinking they were under siege from an armed SWAT team. I thought I would be kicked out by my room-mates, but no one seemed to have been troubled by the noise. I was relieved and vowed to try and find the source of the squeak. But right now I had my first day in captivity to contend with. I needed to learn the rules – and fast.

There are the ordinary prison regulations, and then there are the unwritten rules which are probably the most important – unless of course you want to be beaten with a sock stuffed full of batteries or, even worse, a snooker ball. Breakfast was served at 8 a.m. and, like all meals, was compulsory. You had to be properly dressed and to have made your bed. A sweep would be made of the wing for anyone dragging their heels. After breakfast, the inmates tidied and cleaned their rooms. This was always a good time for a fight as someone would have a broom in their hand. I always preferred to do the sweeping in the cell – I felt the broom was safer in my hands even though my room-mates seemed affable enough. So far so good – exactly the same as school. That finished, we moved on to the communal areas and our allocated section. Easy. I could cope with this and I did it all with the utmost grace and not a single swear word.

I was due at my induction class and followed the majority when they went off to education. It takes a long time to go anywhere in prison. Every door has to be unlocked and certain sections have two gates – it just seemed to be an endless conveyor belt of locks and keys. Very boring. As I settled into my seat in what appeared to be a classroom-cum-gymnasium, I looked around to see if Miranda was there, but no. Some of the class were greeting each other as if they were at a school reunion. I soon realised that there are people who actually like prison, if only for a short time. There is no shortage of drugs, you get fed and there is always a bed.

How to make the most of your time in jail is an interesting topic for a class, but we obviously needed an explanation of what our time would involve, so a blackboard was dragged out. On the left-hand side of this was drawn a vertical line. This represented the start of your sentence. A line on the right signified the end of your sentence and a line that joined the two together represented the duration of your stay. It was hardly rocket science. When you got to halfway through this vertical line, it meant you had served half your sentence and could be eligible for parole. When you were lucky enough to have reached that stage, further help would be given. My God, this was slow – by the time the lesson was over we would have finished our sentences! Finally, we moved on to the educational courses that were available. At least I wouldn't be idle. I would definitely do anything to pass the time and, apparently, the library was quite well stocked. There were certain sporting activities that ran on a daily basis and you could sign up for these. This is getting a lot better, I thought, and more like school every minute. I even found out what an app was – an application for something you want or need or something which is out of the ordinary. Anything over and above what is normally allowed requires an application and sometimes these can take weeks to be acted upon.

It looked like I had learned everything there was to know about prison life, but then to my great surprise we were told that you could order things to be sent to you. How fantastic. If you ordered things from a catalogue then they couldn't be tampered with. Face creams, radios – whatever you needed. This seemed very reasonable to me. Just to make sure I had it fully clear in my mind, I checked with the teacher. 'Can I really order things from outside, pay for them on my credit card and then receive them in prison?'

'Credit card?' she asked with a hint of suspicion in her voice.

'Well, if not a credit card then one of my store cards.'

'What exactly do you mean?' she asked.

'Well, could I order some Clarins face cream from, say, Harvey Nichols, put it on my account and have it posted to me direct?'

She viewed me with some scepticism. Then she realised that I had totally misunderstood her and wasn't taking the piss. She burst out laughing. I was hugely disappointed: you didn't order from Harrods or Harvey Nichols, but from the goddamn Home Office's very own catalogue crammed full of specially selected crap things.

Well, if nothing else, it brought me instant notoriety. My fellow prisoners thought that I was taking the piss and that I had done an excellent job of keeping a straight face. Whenever I had to give my name to a member of staff, they all said, 'Oh, yes, you're the Harvey Nichols girl.' Maria would sometimes call me Harvey when she thought I was getting a bit above my station.

Lesson over, and slightly more deflated – though a lot more popular – than when I arrived, I headed for lunch. Back on my

Happy families – the Brewin clan posing on the stairs. I'm the one with the fantastic slippers.

*Above*: Newton Hall in Cambridge, the family home, and where I spent a large part of my childhood.

*Below left*: I hung out at George Harrison's home, Friar Park, during my teenage years.

*Below right*: Me, aged eighteen.

I had to put this in just to prove I had a nice arse once!

*Above*: Pictures of the items seized from my car by Customs.

*Below*: Celebrating with my sister Miranda, following the not guilty verdict.

Paula never could resist a rock star …

*Above*: With friend Bono.

*Below*: Every girl's dream: a night in with Michael and friend Johnny Depp.

Paula the mum.

*Above*: Paula with Peaches, on holiday …

*Below*: … and with Michael and the girls.

Girls' night out and … *inset*, girl's night in!

Michael was the love of Paula's life.

wing, I collected some food and sat at a table by the window. I was told it was not advisable to sit there, as that was Michelle's place – or Shell, as everyone called her. So I moved two seats along. It seemed that wasn't a good idea either. Shell sometimes sat there as well; in fact, the whole table seemed to be reserved. Mealtimes were a very cliquey affair. The Nigerians all ate together and were the least popular on the wing. The West Indians sat en masse and loathed the Nigerians who, according to them, were all thieves and liars. Mind you, I never met a Nigerian who wasn't innocent and whose father wasn't a prince; but come to think of it I never met anyone in Holloway who admitted ever doing anything wrong. It was comforting to know that you were surrounded by such law-abiding citizens and that *Rough Justice* would have enough material to make documentaries for the foreseeable future. Shell never showed for lunch, and no one had sat in that seat at breakfast either. I was intrigued as to who she was and why she was not in attendance. People didn't seem frightened of her, it's just that in prison inmates who have been there a while have a set routine and if you sit in their seat you are not showing them respect. Everyone slips into place, you find your own seat and then that becomes your permanent place. It's one of prison's unwritten rules and it's an inevitable pecking order that maintains the status quo. I personally never sat in the same seat all the time, but I certainly knew better than to take someone else's place.

The afternoon saw me attending trampolining class. While being instructed to stick to the middle of the trampoline, I was asked my prison number, which I couldn't remember. So the instructor asked me what wing I was on and, when I told him, he looked up from his clipboard and screamed at me to get down. It had never dawned on me that, at seven months pregnant, this was probably not the sport for me, and the Home Office certainly did not want to be held responsible for any injuries done to myself or my unborn child. So that was the end of that physical activity, but I was allowed to play six-a-side netball.

Back in my cell I removed the mattress from my bed, located the squeaking joints and, with some borrowed baby oil, I seemed to fix the problem at least temporarily. It was early afternoon when I heard my name being called and was informed that I had a visit. It jolted me out of this little world that I had been in for the past five days. I felt nervous, and I didn't want anyone to see me in this place. In a daze, I followed the guard through yet more locked doors and waited in line until my name was announced. I made my way to the little cubicle where I was frisked and then given a table number to sit at. My husband walked into the visiting room and the reality of the situation seemed to hit me in the stomach; I thought I was going to be sick. My grip of what was real had disappeared and in such a short space of time I had forgotten what I held most precious to me: my child, my freedom and the people I cared about.

Tony had brought me clothes and money. He told me my lawyer would be coming to see me the next day and that there was talk of a bail application. I wanted to know how Montana was. Like most kids, she was very resilient and was doing just great. I did not want her to come to the prison – well, not just yet, anyway. Not if there was a chance that I would be getting out of here. I didn't want her to see me in this environment at all. Tony had told her that I was in hospital. She was only four so she had limited understanding, but kids aren't stupid and since when did you get searched and locked up in a hospital? As much as I wanted to hold her and kiss her little face, I didn't want to do it here. Suddenly, I understood once more what was important: I had to get out of here to see my child. I had to work hard on my case, get out of this mess and get on with my life. Of course, I still needed to get by on a daily basis, but the master plan was to get out.

As Tony left, he actually put his arms around me and told me not to worry. He told me that different people wanted to visit; but I wasn't sure if I was up to it yet. We never mentioned my pregnancy. I think the idea that a child would be born in prison was too abhorrent to put into words. I only had six weeks to go.

There is an attitude that prevails in prison that it is easier to do your time on remand than as a sentenced prisoner, so if the odds are stacked against you – as they were in my case – you may as well sit tight and have the time spent on remand deducted from your sentence. I didn't want to fall into that line of thinking. Remand prisoners are innocent in the eyes of the law, so their rights cannot be curtailed to the same extent as those of a prisoner who has been found guilty. Prisoners are held on remand because they might not show up for their court date, because they might be a danger to society or simply because of the seriousness of the crime. I apparently fell into the first and last categories. However, because I was on remand I was allowed a visit every day, the amount of money I could have and spend was less restricted, and I could have food and cigarettes brought in to me, although the food was stopped shortly after my arrival because of the quantity of drugs that people were smuggling in by this means.

I put in an application to visit Miranda which was not granted on the grounds that they did not allow pregnant women on to the other wings for safety reasons. So I put in an application for her to visit me which was granted. She looked pale and had some sort of rash on her neck and face. I was truly worried for her. She marvelled at my cell and the amount of space we all had and the facilities that were available to us. Things were tougher on the other side of those locked doors. I told her the lawyer was coming in the afternoon and I thought it would be a good idea if, from then on, she and I co-ordinated our visits to be at the same time. That would ensure that we got to see each other every day without the need for these applications which could take forever to be processed. You spent a lot of time hanging around waiting to be taken back from your visit, so there was plenty of time to chat.

The first time I met Keith Dolan was in the legal visiting rooms in Holloway. I wasn't too impressed with his appearance, but I soon learned not to judge a book by its cover – you'd never find a better lawyer. He said that he did not advise making a bail application at this time. You are only allowed three attempts at bail, and you don't want to waste one using it too soon. His advice was to lie low for a bit. I explained to him my concerns for my sister and asked if she could make a separate application for bail. He explained that this was risky and could be detrimental to any application for bail that I might make in the future.

I felt a little more reassured and, with my visit over, I made it back to my wing and had just enough time to go to canteen with the other girls. 'Canteen' was different to *the* canteen where we ate. Canteen was the shop where you could buy basic supplies. Maria had asked me to get some things for her, as, having been sentenced, she was restricted in what she could spend. I had cigarettes brought into me which I used as currency to barter mainly for fruit. Sometimes I just gave them away. Supper was served at 4.30 p.m. which was ridiculous and was something about which I complained vociferously to the governor, but to no avail. We had over fifteen hours to wait for our next meal, and it was only four hours after our last meal, but the necessity of serving supper at such an hour was never explained to me. But, then, not a lot makes sense in prison. Sometimes after supper we would have 'recreation' when we could watch TV, have a bath and wander around the wing. You could only enter another cell by invitation, and God forbid you entered a cell when no one was in it. Theft was rife in prison.

Maria explained to me that the wing we were on used to be the mother-and-baby wing which was why the cells were so much larger and hence the washing machines. It had been closed down by Health and Safety because of an infestation of rats and cockroaches. The mother-and-baby wing was now housed on the top floor, well away from the vermin. If I was allowed to keep my baby, that was where I would be. I had to make an application to keep my baby with me and go before a board and answer a lot of questions. I filled out the forms and the date for my interview was set for ten days' time.

We were locked in our cells at night, and shortly after lock-up a nurse would come round with everybody's allocated medicine. If she was late, a terrible racket would ensue with people banging on their cell doors and others screaming for them to shut up. The two other girls in my cell were no better and I soon realised why my noisy bed never woke them: they were too drugged. I was constantly being badgered to ask for sleeping pills which I could then give away or sell, but I didn't. There were enough drugs without me supplying any, and I figured I was in enough trouble already. Still, at least the drugs stopped my room-mate picking at her ghastly scabs.

The next morning I decided to hang back in the cell and have a quick wash before breakfast. You couldn't bathe or shower in the mornings, which I would have preferred to do, so a wash in the sink was the next best thing. As I stood there an officer appeared in the doorway and started shouting at me. 'What the bloody hell do you think you're doing? Why aren't you at breakfast?'

I turned round to look at her. 'Have we met before?' I asked.

She looked totally bemused. 'No,' she said. 'Why?'

'Well,' I replied, 'if we haven't met before, I can't have ever been rude to you. So why are you being rude to me?' At this point, I held out my hand to shake hers and I introduced myself. It did the trick, and every time I met a new officer I would shake their hands and say, 'I'm sorry, I don't think we've met before. My name is Belinda Brewin.' It became a bit of a standing joke.

I made my way to breakfast and was greeted by the infamous Shell, who someone had pointed out to me the previous day. She had a towel wrapped around her very large pregnant stomach, a bra and that was it. What had happened to the strict dress code, I wondered. She scowled at me and muttered something under her breath. 'It's nice to meet you too,' I said cheerfully, 'and if I may say so you are looking particularly attractive this morning.' She burst out laughing.

Shell had a cell of her own and was a rule unto herself. She stayed in bed as long as she wanted and even went back to bed in the daytime which was unheard of and definitely not allowed. She would go out of the jail once a week for work experience and always came back drunk, high and with a propensity to hit anyone who got in her way. Apart from that, she was charming! I have never heard such vulgarity come out of anyone's mouth like it came out of hers. Even I was truly aghast. I would always say to her, 'Now, now, is that really necessary?' She would always tell me to go fuck myself.

There is always something to wait for in prison. If you're not waiting for a door to be unlocked, you're usually biding your time for either the phone, the pool table or a bath. The phone is the worst. I have seen some nasty fights break out because of the amount of time one person is holding up the phone, or because the person on the phone can't hear what is being said because they are being shouted at to hurry up. If everybody was quiet, things would run more smoothly and a lot more quickly, but then that would make life easier and no one in prison is looking for that. The rule with the phone was that everyone waited patiently in line. There was no queue-jumping and that was a hard-and-fast rule with no exceptions – unless your name was Jennifer. If there's a rule in jail, then there's always an exception to it. Jennifer was a large black lady with an amazing sense dress – she wore see-through blouses and multicoloured leggings – and was pregnant with her sixth or seventh kid. Every night at 6 p.m., she would walk up to the phone and, no matter who was talking, would take it from them, hang up, move them out of the way with one side swipe of her very ample bottom and make her call. She was due to give birth at any moment and she had discovered she was pregnant when she first arrived in Holloway, so it was a well-established routine she had going. Most people knew the drill and many would hang up before she even got there to avoid being bumped out of the way. No one ever questioned her authority to do this and, when I told Maria that I thought it was unfair, she laughed. 'Well,' she said, 'you go tell her then. No one else will, she's in here for murder.'

Murder? Violent crime in general is a rarity in women's prisons. In 2002, there were just over 4,500 women incarcerated in England and Wales and of those only 152 were serving a life sentence. So, if you were charged with murder, people tended to keep out of your way, unless the crime had anything to do with a child and then you kept out of everybody else's way. Personally, I felt it best to let the situation remain the same – Jennifer had never done me any harm. But I was curious to know who she phoned every night at 6 p.m.

On my second day in prison, my urge to leave was stronger than it had been on the first. Tony had ordered a newspaper from the shop opposite the jail to be delivered daily, but I knew I would never read it. I couldn't. I don't know why, but I was almost phobic about even touching it. I suppose it reminded me of what I was missing, and for the moment the outside world was too painful to think about. So I cancelled the subscription and then regretted it. Today, I would head off with some of the prison population to education. As only half of the prison population has any educational qualifications at all, and those who are illiterate don't attend classes because they haven't even got the necessary basic skills to advance themselves, I felt education should have been compulsory for everyone, at whatever level they required. Maybe it's the lack of funding, but, when you consider that over half the women in jail have a drug or alcohol problem and these are usually the ones who fall into the no-qualifications category, it would be well worth the government spending some money on educating these women out of their predicament. How, in this day and age, can we have so many people who will never know the joy of reading a birthday card from their child or even writing one themselves, let alone the pleasure of reading a book?

I decided on a computer course and filled in the necessary forms. As I finished early, I decided to write a letter to the governor about the conditions in the prison. Classes started at 10 a.m. the next day and we could all work at our own pace, which was a relief. Miranda was coming to see me after supper, as Keith was going to make an application for bail for her at the end of the week and he wanted to go over some points with both of us on the phone. Miranda was supposed to be at my wing at 5 p.m., but trying to get quickly from one place to another in jail – or even on time – is like trying to break the speed limit on the M25 at rush hour. It's just never going to happen. I was worried that we would miss Keith and that he would have left the office, but he waited and at about ten to six we eventually got to the phone. I had completely forgotten about Jennifer. Keith wanted some crucial background details on Miranda, our family and anything that would show stability and that she should not be considered a flight risk. Suddenly, I saw Jennifer approach. I stood between her and Miranda. 'You really are going to have to hang on,' I told her. 'My sister only has permission to stay on the wing for half an hour and she needs to finish this call. She's going for her bail hearing and she's talking to her lawyer – it's kind of crucial.' I half-expected her to stab me.

'Cool,' she said. 'Hope she gets it.'

I was stunned.

Miranda finished and Keith wanted to talk to me but about nothing specific and I explained that someone else wanted the phone. He said that he was going to be in the office for another hour and I promised to call back. I felt that, as Jennifer *hadn't* stabbed me, the least I could do was to let her use the phone first. So, about ten minutes after her normal appointment, she was on the line. I hung around, partly because I had to ring Keith back, but more because I was just being nosy. I was definitely surprised when this allegedly hard-nosed – and definitely big-bottomed – girlfriend of a leading Yardie got on the phone and started reciting a recipe. A recipe? How to make sticky chicken with rice and beans. I thought prison was beginning to affect my hearing, but no, she really was telling someone how to cook. Step by step. How fantastic was that? If only all the other girls knew – there would probably be hell to pay, but I sure as hell wasn't going to let on. At one point, she looked round and it must have been quite obvious that I was eavesdropping. She just shrugged her shoulders and smiled. As she quite rightly pointed out, she was in jail and someone had to cook for the rest of her kids. She said she regretted not teaching them to cook earlier, but better late than never and so the recipe she gave depended on the age and skill of whichever of her children was cooking supper that night. She always planned the week's menu in advance. It was her little secret and it amused me no end. I saw her months later on the nine o'clock news standing on the steps of the Old Bailey. She had been acquitted of the crime, although her boyfriend had got life, and sure enough she was wearing a see-through blouse, coloured leggings and had her arm raised and her fist clenched in the black-power salute. All I could think of was what on earth she would be cooking for supper that night.

The following day at education, I was informed that I could not do the computer class as I was not eligible. I didn't understand. I was in jail – how much more eligible can you get? Apparently, I had to be sentenced – after all, what is the point in spending money when there is the possibility that you may be released? Good point, but what if I *wasn't* going to be freed and I had to spend a year there with nothing to do. I'd go mad. Not only could I not attend the class, but also, as there was nobody to escort me back to the cell, I would have to wait in the corridor until classes were over. I asked every passing warden if they could take me back to my wing, but no one was going that way. By chance, the governor and two officers made their way through the locked doors and down the corridor. I took this opportunity to introduce myself and shook his hand. He looked at me as if I had lost all sense of reason, and then I asked him if he had received my letter. He asked me what it was about, and I explained to him that it was about the conditions that the pregnant women were kept in. It obviously rang a bell. Yes, he had received it and it was a very well-written letter. Never mind the bloody composition, I felt like saying, are you going to do anything about it? But, remembering to be polite, I thanked him. I then asked him if he was going to my wing as I had been in the corridor for over an hour. He was quite surprised by this and, after he dropped me back at my cell, I thanked him and shook his hand again. I said that I hoped we would speak soon.

After I had been there a few days, Maria informed me that I was going to get a beating. She had heard Shell discussing it on the way to education. I was scared, and watched my back when I had to venture from my cell; otherwise, I just sat on my bed reading. It was safer that way. After a while, Shell and three of her cronies appeared in the door of my cell. 'You can't hide in there forever,' she said. 'We will get you.'

I looked up from my book. 'What is this all about?' I asked.

'We don't like snitches.'

I had no idea what they were talking about. Maria acted as scout and, apparently, Shell had heard that I had written to the governor and complained about her antics and that she was going to be moved because of it. I *had* written to the governor, but not about her, so I decided to confront her about it. Supper was the best time to do this as there were always at least three guards, and hopefully if Shell and her crew went for me I might have some back-up. I came into supper with a copy of the letter I had written to the governor and handed it to Shell. She pushed it aside with a total lack of interest. Maria, who had once shared a cell with her, encouraged her to read it and so she picked it up and glanced at it.

I could tell by her body language that she wasn't really reading, and I wondered if she could read at all. I think I had found the heart of the problem: she used her aggressiveness to cover up her illiteracy. Shell said she couldn't be bothered to read it and that if, as Maria had told her, it concerned the whole wing perhaps I should read it to everyone. Rather than embarrass her, I did exactly that. In the letter, I highlighted the lack of fresh food that we were given, and especially the deplorable lack of fruit. I had been thinking about mentioning the amount of drugs handed out to the pregnant women, but luckily I didn't, as this would not have been popular with the troops. I also suggested that we should be allowed to shower in the morning, and that supper should be served later, as most of us were starving when we went to bed. All in all, it was what we all felt and I had voiced it. I was commended on how well written it was – considering that most of the inmates could barely read and write it wasn't that much of a compliment – but more importantly I was saved a beating. After that, I became chief letter-writer. I even helped Shell write letters home to her family, and encouraged her to go to classes to help her with her lack of reading skills. I know she went once, and she said she meant to go again, but I don't think she ever did.

Miranda's bail application was successful and, after a week incarcerated through no fault of her own, she was freed. I was delighted for her and I wondered if she would ever speak to me again. I didn't have to wait long to find out: the day after her release, she came back to prison to visit me. It was the best visit that I had there and it meant a lot to me that she came. I wondered if I would ever get out, but I really was genuinely pleased not to have the guilt of knowing she was in jail. A few days later, I received a card from her and I realised her sense of humour had not been adversely affected by her traumatic experience. It was a picture of a man in a cell wearing a prison suit with arrows on it. He was sitting at table writing, and inside the card it said, 'Dear Diary, Stayed in again today.' I laughed out loud.

The time passed with monotonous boredom and I began to feel weaker with each day. The food was disgusting, I barely ate and I hadn't had a decent night's sleep since being arrested. On my weekly medical, it was noted that I had lost quite a bit of weight and that I was anaemic. The nurse said I would have to see the doctor. The doctor wanted me to go to the hospital for a scan and an appointment was made. I was taken to the hospital with a male officer and a female officer. It was one of the worst days of my life. We went in a taxi and one of the guards had my medical notes which he handed to the doctor who was going to examine me. The last few weeks of my first pregnancy had been spent in hospital and neither my daughter nor I had been well. I was concerned that the same thing would happen again. As we sat on the third-floor waiting room, there were other people there, including a little boy who was playing with the toys on the floor. I walked in with two people in uniform who sat either side of me and no one seemed in the slightest bit embarrassed about staring at me. I can't say it didn't bother me because it did. The little boy came up to them. 'Are you police officers?' he asked.

'No,' they replied, 'we're prison guards.'

Now everybody's mouth fell open.

The doctor called my name and for a few moments I didn't acknowledge it – I was so used to being called by number. I got up to go into the consulting room; the two officers came with me and closed the door behind me. I sat at the desk with the doctor and they sat against the wall. 'Why have you been refusing to take your iron tablets?' the doctor asked me.

'I haven't been refusing,' I replied, 'I've never been offered them.'

The doctor then asked me to undress, as he wanted to examine me. I turned to the two guards and asked them to leave; they said they couldn't, as they had to remain with me at all times. I couldn't understand this – and no way in the world was I even taking off my socks, never mind anything else, with those two in the room. 'I'm terribly sorry to have wasted your time,' I told the doctor, 'but I can't continue with this appointment.' I was very polite – as tempting as it was, I refrained from telling the two officers to go fuck themselves.

'You'd better get used to it,' the male officer then said, 'because when you give birth we'll be in the room.'

Now I really was astounded. I could not believe what I was

hearing. 'There is no way in the world you will be in the same room as me when I have my baby,' I told him.

'Do you want to bet?' he replied.

That was it. I was going straight to the governor, my MP and anyone else who would listen. This was ridiculous. I was hardly about to escape – we were on the third floor of the hospital, and if I tried to jump out of the window I would more than likely die. There was only one way in and out of this room and these two officers were saying that they could not stand guard outside the door so that I could be examined. The doctor remonstrated with them and said he felt that I really needed to be looked at and to have a scan. I suppose they were only doing their job, but by then I had heard enough.

On my return, I asked to see the governor and was told to make an application. This no-swearing thing was becoming more difficult by the day. I vented my disgust in polite and docile tones over supper and was told that often women are handcuffed while in labour in case they try to escape. It has to have been a man who made that up rule. What woman in her right mind is going to try and escape in the middle of childbirth? As you are mastering your breathing technique and pushing down hard, you're hardly going to pop off the bed and sprint down three flights of stairs with two guards hot in pursuit. You don't need to be Sherlock Holmes to figure out who is going to win that game of chase. Nobody should ever be treated in this manner: it is degrading and humiliating. I was definitely not having my baby in prison. I rang Keith. 'Get me the hell out of this place,' I said.

Keith came to see me the next day and said that he was going to make an application for bail, but he was not optimistic and I was not to get my hopes up, although apparently Laura had also been granted bail. It was the day of my appointment with the board and they were going to see if I was a suitable candidate to keep my baby in prison with me. The meeting consisted of a doctor, a social worker and a few lay people, and I asked all the right questions. They looked very surprised by my crime and, as with most people in prison, were amazed by my manners.

Bail was unsuccessful, but my application to the mother-and-baby unit was successful. I had three and a half weeks to go till my baby was due. It was getting desperate. I *had* to get out of here. The doctor at the hospital wrote a letter to the governor complaining about the male officer and the way in which he had spoken to me. I was amazed that he had taken the time out of his day for me, and completely unprompted as well. Because of this, I was taken again to the hospital by two female officers who stood outside the room while the doctor examined me. It was slow, but it was progress.

On returning to Holloway, I was given a tour of the baby wing and it was quite impressive – just not large enough to accommodate every baby born to a woman in jail. I met some of the women who lived there. Two of them had been handcuffed while in labour.

My second bail application went the same way as my first and it looked like I was going to be moving upstairs to the baby unit. I decided that, if my third and final attempt at freedom failed, then I would ask Tony to bring Montana to visit me, but, until I categorically knew I wasn't getting out, I didn't want her anywhere near the place. I was very down on hearing the news that I wouldn't be going home, and some of the girls rallied round to try and cheer me up. We sat in my cell and everybody had their own bail or court story to tell. One girl – the youngest girl in the prison at the time – had more offences than her age. Her mother and father were heroin addicts and both in jail. She had been used in burglaries since she was a tiny child and would be put through small windows in order to let her parents in. She really didn't know any other way of life. Another girl had got two years for burglary which seemed very stiff as it was her first offence. Well, maybe not her first offence, but definitely the first she had been caught for, and as most people usually got three to six months it seemed unreasonable. I asked her about this and she said the problem was that she had robbed a judge's house. Now that really *is* bad luck. Maria, on the other hand, had been the manager at a bookmaker's and she had given her boyfriend and his mate the keys to the shop and told them the alarm code. It was the weekend of the Grand National, and they stole the entire takings. Then she wonders why she got caught! Now that's just stupid.

When you are in prison and you have nothing to do, you concentrate on the stupid, mundane things in life. Little things become terribly important. I needed some slippers and it drove me mad that Tony never had the time to go and buy me some. He could go into a shop any time he liked; I couldn't. In the end, to put me out of my misery, my dear friend Debbie Dennis bought them for me and then I hardly ever wore them. She, along with my sister Julia, visited a lot and never tired of my demands for whatever seemed important that day. You get attached to things that are of no consequence whatsoever. There was a girl on our wing who was eventually moved to the 'muppet' wing upstairs. The poor kid collected sanitary towels. Don't ask me why, but in prison possessions are very important.

Coming up for three weeks in jail and I was beginning to lose hope of ever getting out. I was also tiring of the politeness routine I'd set for myself. I was sick of the food, the lack of stimulating conversation and of being constantly surrounded by people either on drugs or looking for drugs. Keith was going to launch a last-ditch attempt at getting me out. This time I was going to attend my bail hearing and spent the morning packing up my belongings. I left behind my toiletries and the cigarettes that I used as currency, and instructed Maria to divide them up if I was lucky enough not to come back. I picked up my jewellery and money from the front desk and with two guards, though not handcuffed, I was taken to Folkestone Magistrates' Court where I met my barrister Jerome Lynch QC. Jerome is a very handsome man, a little smooth, but he worked his magic. I did as he said and I stood in the dock looking very pregnant – which wasn't difficult as I only had a few weeks to go – and, with my mother, my uncle Oliver, my brother Tobey and my friend Natalia looking on, the judge granted me bail. It wasn't easy, and my mother and Natalia had to put up substantial amounts of money as surety, but finally I was going home.

# CHAPTER SEVEN

I don't remember the drive home from the magistrates' court, but I do recall eating smoked salmon sandwiches that my mother had brought. It meant a lot to me that Tobey was there. After my arrest, he wouldn't speak to me and could not believe what I was supposed to have done. Once the facts began to emerge, he had a change of heart and no apologies were necessary. He had come to drive me home, back to my daughter, and that was enough.

I will never forget the moment I first saw her. I remember the smell of her hair as I kissed her little face as if it were yesterday. I must have been the happiest person alive that day.

The relief to be out of prison was overwhelming. It would take me a couple of days to adjust. Keith told me that we needed to start work pretty soon, as there was a lot of material to get through. At that stage, I had no idea quite how much there was, and that three days a week for the next ten months would be spent in his office in the West End of London poring over files and photographs.

First things first, though: I needed to have a baby.

It was ironic that the day my daughter was born I was with two policemen. Having been so adamant that I would not have my baby with uniformed officers present, I nearly did. I was at home with Montana when I started to have contractions. After a while,

I rang the midwife and she told me not to panic and that I should wait till they were about five minutes apart before going to the hospital. I rang Tony to tell him. He was on his way out for lunch with some friends of ours, Gerry and Elizabeth. Elizabeth said she would come over but I said I was fine at the moment and I would ring her when I was going to go to the Kensington and Chelsea Hospital. This was all new to me, as I had been in hospital for weeks before the birth of my first child.

As the contractions became more frequent, I thought that it would be best for Tony to come and pick me up. He said he was going to finish his lunch and would meet me at the hospital, but Elizabeth would come over.

A few minutes later, the doorbell rang and, thinking it was Elizabeth, I pressed the entry button opening the door. Next thing I knew, two police officers were in my hallway. For one awful moment, I thought I was going back to prison.

'Are you all right,' asked one of the officers.

'Yes,' I replied, 'I'm just having a baby!'

The other officer said his wife had just had a baby a few weeks ago, and he sat me on my sofa and held my hand. It was farcical but I couldn't explain the joke to them. They were concerned at how close together the contractions were and said they would give me a lift to the hospital. They seemed quite astounded that my husband was not coming to get me and was going to meet me there, but this was not the time to prevaricate and I agreed to go with them. My nightmare was going to come true: the only people with me at the hospital would be uniformed officers. They helped me down the stairs and, just as I was getting into their police car, Tony pulled up. Elizabeth had berated him about not going to pick me up and had forced everybody to leave the restaurant.

So it all ended well and I thanked them profusely. They explained that the reason for their visit was that, while searching the house of a burglar, they had discovered some paperwork that had my address on it and they wanted to know why it was there and if I had been burgled recently. They suggested I might want to come to the station and see if I could recognise any other property that belonged to me. As it happened, our warehouse had been broken into months before and that was where the stuff had originated from. The paperwork was of no consequence, but the police certainly picked their moment!

On arrival at the hospital, I insisted on eating a chocolate bar and drinking apple juice, which I later vomited all over Tony. I was now in a vast amount of pain and after being examined by the midwife I asked for an epidural. She informed me that I couldn't have any drugs as it was too late.

'Too late?' I screamed. 'What do you mean it's too late? It's never too late for drugs!'

But she wasn't listening. She said I could have gas and air and handed me the mask. Gerry, who had obviously had a few glasses of wine with Tony over lunch, thought it would be a good idea for them to try it first. So, while I lay in agony on the bed, the two of them played with the gas and air until the midwife kindly came back and retrieved it from them. Elizabeth was entertaining Montana in the glass lifts which she found more fascinating than the idea of a new baby. Every now and again, she would pop her head around the door to see if anything had happened.

I started to insist that I needed to go to the loo. The midwife insisted I didn't and that it was the baby pressing down. Now I was getting annoyed: I knew my body and I sure as hell was not letting someone tell me whether or not I needed to do a pooh. I had to go to the loo and I needed to go now, I insisted. She was right and I was wrong. I didn't need the loo and sure enough I had my baby. Little Indiana came into the world on 25 April 1993 at 4.16 p.m. I was so happy – and the only uniform in sight was on the nurses.

Paula came to see me when I got home. She said she would have visited me in jail, but I explained that I really didn't want to see anyone. She had been shopping and had bought some new dresses and couldn't wait to show them to me.

Prison became a thing of the past and was replaced with the trial. The trial was set for March the following year at the Old Bailey. Customs objected to this and had it moved to Maidstone. My solicitor then raised an objection and it would become a battle of wills and cunning that in the end we won hands down. Perhaps Customs did not want the trial in London, as their feeling might have been that juries would be more liberal and in Kent they felt the pool of jurors that they could pick from would be far more conservative. Whether this was true was not something I wanted to put to the test, and the statistics showed that Customs might have had a point. Kent had a higher conviction rate and the sentences that they handed out were much more severe. So we applied to the court and had it moved back to the Bailey. Customs had it moved back, and for the time being my solicitor let it rest. 'Let them think they have won that point,' he said. I had to trust him. He had done this many times before.

Operation Respite, as it was called, had been up and running for over a year and a huge number of man hours had gone into surveillance. Listed on the court documents were eighty-one witnesses of which thirty-eight were customs officers. That was only the surveillance team, so God knows how many were working behind the scenes. Every day, files of observations of the main suspects landed on Keith's desk and we had to go through them in minute detail. God, it was boring. There were pages of things that bore no relevance to me. Daniel Burns was seen walking down Elgin Avenue into a newsagent. He used the public phone box in that street and the number he dialled was duly recorded. He was accompanied by a brunette. Keith and I had to go through each such entry and I would have to say that the brunette was not me and where I was at that time, if I could even remember. The surveillance alone comprised over 500 pages. Sometimes a page covered a few days; sometimes it covered just one, depending on the amount of activity. There were also over 700 different witness statements and thousands of pages of exhibits. Despite this mountain of evidence that had accumulated over a long period of time, there was not one sighting of me, ever, until the day of my arrest when I went to drop off the money to Donald in his hotel. Nor was there a single photograph of me. The photographs of the main suspects and the people they met or spoke to could have filled the National Portrait Gallery ten times over. I rest my case.

I became totally consumed with the case. The more I read, the more confident I became that I would not be convicted. None of this related to me in any way. My solicitor had a different opinion: the more he read, the more convinced he became that the situation was very, very serious and, if I was found guilty, I would go to prison for an extremely long time. He had a list of things he wanted me to do, people he wanted to get statements from and people whom he wanted to stand as character witnesses for me. The main statement he wanted was from Jack. Never mind a bloody statement – I wanted an explanation. I had been too worried to be hurt, but now I felt totally humiliated and foolish. Jack, however, had disappeared. There was no trace of him anywhere. It was as if Customs were right and he had never existed.

I first met Jack on Portobello Road. I had a flower stall there on Fridays which did cracking business. Brian Close – the man I had met in Ireland and whom I was now charged with – used to sell clothing to a stallholder on the market. One day, he passed my stall and stopped to say hello. He was with Jack at the time and he introduced me. That was six months before I was arrested. I never saw Brian at the market again, but a few weeks later Jack stopped by. I didn't remember his name or how we had met and he had to remind me. After that, I saw him most weeks. Nothing much, just a hello, or if I was busy he would go and get me a drink. As the weeks went by, he stopped for longer. Jack would often get me something for lunch when I was rushed and we would sit on the pavement together and eat it. He was very charming.

I decided to go back to Portobello to see if anyone I knew had seen him around. My flower stand was usually next to a fruit and veg stall. Tony, who owned the stall, was a typical market trader, very outgoing. We often shared a joke and I would give him flowers for his wife, but I hardly knew him. I asked him if he had seen Jack around and he didn't know who I was talking about. I reminded him of the guy who used to come by and talk to me. Tony was right – lots of men stopped by the stall, why would he remember this one? I couldn't think of any reason at all, so I carried on. Then I remembered him and Jack having a long conversation about golf and the courses they had played on, so I went back and reminded him. That jogged his memory – Tony loved his golf. I asked Tony, if he saw him, to ask Jack to call me.

Weeks passed and nothing. I went back a few times and each time the answer was the same: Tony hadn't seen him. Keith said it was imperative that we speak to Jack as Customs were adamant that I had made him up. I must have looked worried and Tony seemed concerned and asked me what the problem was. I told him that Jack had got me in trouble with the police. I did not want to mention that it was Customs and Excise and that it involved drugs, as I thought this would freak him out. He said he'd definitely keep an eye out for him. The next week, when I went back the answer was the same and I started to cry. 'Don't cry, love,' he said. 'It can't be that bad.'

'It *is* that bad,' I told him. 'Jack's got me in trouble and the police are saying that he doesn't exist.'

'But that's ridiculous,' said Tony. 'I've met him.'

I asked him if he would be willing to make a statement to that effect to my solicitor. He was very hesitant but eventually agreed. I felt a bit mean because I did play a bit of a dirty trick on him. He asked me if it would ever go to court and, if it would, he did not want to go. I lied and said I wasn't sure if it would ever get that far, and, if it did, he definitely would not have to go. I knew that, once he had given a statement, we could always subpoena him if necessary.

We also got a statement from the customs officer in France who remembered that we had no passports and had told us that we would probably be detained in England. Things were starting to improve. Customs were adamant that I had met with Brian Close at the Holiday Inn in Calais and Keith thought that this might be a sticky area, as there had been surveillance and photographs of him there on previous occasions. I assured him that it wouldn't be a problem. Yes, he might have been there, but not when Miranda and I were there, or even on the same day. How could I be so sure? Because he was the man I fortuitously bumped into on the King's Road having breakfast in the little cafÈ. He told me then that he was on his way to Heathrow heading home to Ireland. I got his number and rang him. His wife said that he was not about. I asked her to get Brian to tell her what flight he was on and what time he caught it and any other proof he had that he was not in France when Customs were saying he was. Keith got everything: his flight details, his credit card details which showed that he was on the King's Road and that he had bought duty free at Heathrow and had caught a plane out of there at lunchtime and gone to Dublin. If Customs were going to persist with this ridiculous notion that I had met with Brian Close, my barrister would blow that argument out of the water. Another job well done, Mr Dolan.

Tony gave his statement and I thanked him. I also thought I owed him more of an explanation, but he said he didn't want to know the details. I even told him he would probably have to go to court, but I think he knew that and he said, if that's what he had to do, then so be it. I also went to see Tessa Walley of Portobello Car Hire to apologise for the fact that Customs had kept one of her cars for so long. I asked her if I owed her money. I had known her for years, had always hired cars from her and saw no reason why she should be out of pocket. She refused to take any money from me. Sadly, she died of cancer about the same time as Paula died, which was a terrible shame, as she was a wonderful woman. She told me that Customs had been to see her and had taken a statement. They called her as a prosecution witness, which turned out to be a big mistake. They also called my bank manager John Gallop as their witness, and that proved to be disastrous as well.

Keith rang me one morning and asked me to come to his office, as Customs had sent over the surveillance photographs. They were neatly bound in little blue books with their insignia on the front. I thought that there might have been some photographs of Jack, but to my surprise the mastermind of the ring, Mr Daniel Burns, was the man I knew as Donald. No wonder Jack was nowhere to be found. After everything that had happened, I still found myself being shocked by this.

Months passed in a monotony of paperwork. Seven months after my release, I attended Maidstone Crown Court where I, along with my other co-defendants, was arraigned and a trial date was set for 11 March 1994 – a year to the day since my arrest. It was quite a daunting experience as Miranda and I went into the court and took our seats in the dock. Laura was already there. The doors from the cells opened and three men joined us. One I recognised as the man I now knew to be Daniel Burns, but the other two I had never seen before. One was Wayne Doyle, the other Ian Tyler. There had been another 'leg' of this operation, and they were it. Ian Tyler eventually pleaded guilty to smuggling cocaine. I think he got eight years, but I never saw him again. Wayne Doyle pleaded not guilty, as did the rest of us. Laura's barrister argued that there was not a prima facie case for her to answer. The judge agreed and she was a free woman. It would have been hard for them to prove she knew anything. I was pleased for her, but I knew it could damage Miranda's chances of the same thing happening to her. If *she* didn't have a case to answer, then Miranda sure as hell didn't, but could the judge let two people go in one case on the same day?

A month passed and I remained worried about the venue for the trial, as it was still in Maidstone. Doyle's solicitors informed Customs that they were going to ask for a change of venue and were told it would be opposed. Keith had written to the listing officer at every court he could think of to see if there was an earlier available slot than that of 11 March and thought he was on to something. As Burns and Doyle were being held on remand, it was the duty of the prosecution service to get them to court as quickly as possible. We desperately needed a London court to have an earlier date. Mrs Bull, the listing officer for Wood Green Court, informed Keith that she did indeed have an earlier slot. Keith wrote to them: 'Please let me know whether that means you are indeed willing to take this case and whether arrangements can be made for the transfer of papers to you.' Her Majesty's Customs and Excise were not informed. I am sure it was just an oversight on our behalf.

Mrs Bull responded favourably and, two days later, before Judge Garland at the Royal Courts of Justice, we applied to have the case transferred to Wood Green Crown Court at a date six weeks earlier than that of Maidstone. Customs were not there to oppose it. Maybe someone forgot to tell them – yet another small oversight on our behalf. Two days later the case was transferred. The next day, my solicitor wrote to Customs and Excise informing them of the decision. They were not happy. I was delighted.

This action caused a flurry of letters and accusations. Mr Brompton, the barrister for the prosecution, objected vehemently to the courts. He stated, 'The place and date of a criminal trial are important matters. Inevitably, defendants, like prosecutors, prefer certain courts ... and neither party should be allowed to manipulate procedures.' He suggested that Keith had acted improperly in soliciting the help of a court official and that the request 'should not have been made without notice to the prosecuting solicitor'. He also suggested that 'The failure of Offenbach & Co to inform Her Majesty's Customs and Excise appears to have been deliberate.' How could he say such a thing? Where was the evidence?

I told you we won that round hands down – but probably not fair and square. But then nothing is fair in the justice system, as I was soon to find out.

As the trial grew closer, Miranda and I spent a lot of time in chambers being prepped by our barristers. Jerome Lynch, the charming man who had got me bail, had been retained as my sister's barrister, and Peter Guest was mine. By the end of the trial, I was completely in love with him – platonically, of course. He was brilliant. He was good-looking, an excellent orator and he captivated the jury. Michael Brompton for the prosecution, on the other hand, was not a scintillating speaker – and in the looks department, forget it.

Shortly before the trial started, an amazing thing happened. We were all due in court for a pre-trial review and, while we were sitting in the canteen at Wood Green, Peter appeared grinning from ear to ear. He could hardly contain himself and told us the reason for the delay in proceedings was because Daniel Burns and Wayne Doyle had escaped. I thought it was a joke, but on seeing the pandemonium that was occurring among the prosecution I knew he was telling the truth. It was totally surreal. Burns and Doyle were handcuffed to each other back to back. When they reached Commercial Road in the East End of London, they bit the bottom off one of the guards' ears, á la Mike Tyson, and beat up the other guard. They then escaped out of the back of the van and hijacked a car, pulling some poor woman from her seat. Burns was never to be seen again, and Doyle disappeared for a good few years.

This changed the whole complexion of the trial. If Burns was capable of this horrific, violent act, then he would have no qualms about using me and setting me up. I was beginning to feel much more confident – until the judge ruled that no mention could be made to the jury of their escape. I was shocked. This showed that these men were ruthless, but the judge was adamant. Customs had certainly won that round, but there are many ways to skin a cat. Patience, yet again, was the order of the day.

The trial started and the judge made it clear that he would hold anybody in contempt if mention of the escape was made to the jury, and he would order a retrial. I was talking about this to a barrister friend of mine, moaning about how unjust the justice system was. 'Well,' he said, 'there's an easy way round that.' I looked at him quizzically. 'If the information just happens to slip out while someone is under cross-examination,' he explained, 'it becomes a matter of public record and stays in the proceedings. There is nothing the judge can do about it.'

'Tell me more,' I said, becoming very animated.

Apparently, my barrister could not bring it up, or even lead me in that direction; but if by some chance the prosecution lead me in that direction then it would be their fault. Once it had been mentioned, my barrister would be allowed to ask me questions about it and draw attention to it in his closing argument. I couldn't believe it. 'Why hasn't Peter told me this?' I asked my friend.

'He's not allowed to,' he explained. 'Professional ethics.'

Now I knew, however, I laid a plan. I told nobody about it because I wasn't sure how I would implement it. It all depended how Brompton's questioning went. Fingers crossed.

The judge instructed the jury that if they found me not guilty then they must not even consider Miranda's case, as she would automatically be not guilty; but if I was found guilty that did not necessarily mean Miranda was. Then and only then must they consider the evidence against her. The jury consisted of eight females and four males. I made notes on all of them: thirty years old, red hair, chews gum; nice, homely looking, white hair, sixty.

One man concerned me and I had picked him, correctly as it happened, as the future foreman. My concern was that he was a *Telegraph* reader and they are not known for their liberal views; but the next day I realised my mistake – he read the *Guardian*. That was better.

The prosecution, in simple terms, said that Jack did not exist and that I knew what I was doing. They pointed out that my bank account was overdrawn and said I did it for the money. I had used a hire car which I had only taken for a week, but had kept it for longer without paying, which they said showed intent and dishonesty. They called Tessa from Portobello Car Hire as their first prosecution witness, and then couldn't even remember her name – which didn't go down well. They asked her if she was worried that I had taken the car for longer than the agreement time and had not paid for it. 'Absolutely not,' she replied. 'Belinda has used my cars for years. I never charge her a deposit and whenever she wants she brings it back and pays then.'

'Is this normal?'

'No, this is not normal,' Tessa replied. 'I do this because I trust her and she is honest.'

I wanted to kiss her.

They then called my bank manager, John Gallop, and went through the details of my account. They broached the fact that I was overdrawn. John mentioned that I was the beneficiary of a trust fund. This was not what Brompton wanted him to say at all. He then added that I was about to come into a large settlement from the sale of some Henry Moore pictures and that the bank was not concerned about my overdraft, even though it had existed for longer than the original time agreed. When asked what his opinion of me was in relation to money and his dealings with me, he said, 'Her honesty and integrity is beyond reproach.' I wanted to jump up and down for joy.

When we broke for lunch, I heard Peter say, 'Any more witnesses like that and we won't need to call character witnesses of our own.'

The prosecution also alleged that I had deliberately concealed the drugs in the car. These allegations were backed up by the customs officers. Photographs were produced of the drugs and my shopping to support these erroneous claims. I had a clear view of the car at all times during the search, and at no point was there a photographer present. I passed a note to Peter stating this. Under cross-examination, it was admitted that the photos had been taken afterwards and one of the customs officers had told the photographer where he wanted the items placed. Also, his notebook did not run contemporaneously. Peter quizzed him on this and he admitted leaving pages blank to be filled in later, which was totally contrary to correct procedure. One of the other customs officers, when forced to produce his notebook, had written that the items in question had been found loose in the boot or on top of my shopping, which matched perfectly what I had said in my statement. It was another point in our favour – but there was a long way to go yet.

A little way into the trial, I went to see Paula and told her what was going on. She said she wanted to come to court and be a character witness. 'You have to be kidding,' I told her. 'I'm trying to keep a low profile and you want to attend court with your big hair and your theatrical sense of dress! Do you want me to go to jail?'

We laughed, but she did write me the most fantastic letter which was read out to the court. The mere mention of her name made everybody sit up and pay attention. She said I was a wonderful person and an inspiration as a mother, and anybody who had never been on a picnic with me should have that experience once in their lives. It was very quirky and very poignant. She said that to see me with my children was to see the real me, and that the jury must see through the picture that had been painted of me by the prosecution and send me home to my family. I was deeply grateful to her for that. She didn't have to do it – I never asked her, and, in fact, it took everything I had to keep her away from the courtroom. She was a bloody crazy woman, but I loved her!

On 10 February 1994, I entered the witness box to fight for the next eight years of my life. Peter took me through my evidence. At one point, he asked me how many times I had seen Brian Close. 'Maybe ten or twelve,' I replied, and I saw Michael Brompton for the prosecution scribble frantically on a piece of paper. It made me smile. In my statement, I had said five or six times, and he had picked up on that. The end of the day could not come soon enough. I felt exhausted and mentally drained. I needed a good night's sleep, as tomorrow was Mr Brompton's chance to draw blood.

I had a pretty good idea what his first question was going to be. 'If I'm right,' I told Peter, 'I have a gut feeling that we will be OK.' When he asked it, I saw Peter look at Jerome and smile.

'Well, Miss Brewin,' he said, looking down his nose as if he had something stuck on the end of it, 'you told your barrister yesterday that you had seen Brian Close maybe ten or twelve times. Is that correct?'

I looked straight at him. 'Yes.'

He then rose. 'But in your statement, Miss Brewin, you said five or six times. Which is it, Miss Brewin? Were you lying then, or are you lying now?'

'Neither,' I replied.

He gave a theatrical little laugh to the jury. 'Come, come, Miss Brewin,' he said. 'Surely you know the difference between five or six and ten or twelve, so which is the lie? Or are they both lies?'

Without smugness – and with no hint that I had been rehearsing the line – I replied, 'Neither is a lie, sir. My barrister asked me how many times I had *seen* Brian Close and I replied ten or twelve. But in my statement I was asked how many times I had *spoken* to Brian Close and I replied truthfully five or six times. So, in answer to your question, sir, neither is a lie.'

It was like the wind being let out of a balloon, but without the farting sound. It was poetry.

The cross-examination went on and on, and it was hard, relentless work. At one point, I had to pretend to have pins and needles in my leg so that I could have a ten-minute break. I wanted to save the loo break for something really crucial. I was told it was always best to have a break when they are getting the better of you, as it slightly takes the wind out of their sails. Good advice and I heeded it well. Brompton suggested that I had made up the fact that Brian had introduced me to Jack and was just trying to embroider the truth to cover my guilt. He asked me why I never told Customs that information when I was interviewed, and I said they never asked me that question and if they had I would have told them. I pointed out that I answered every question asked of me. He also said that I had given a completely erroneous description of Donald/Daniel Burns, which I personally didn't think I had until I saw him again. In fact, I got his hair colour slightly wrong, his build incorrect and his age nowhere near on target. No attention to detail – but I had only seen him for four minutes. Brompton would not stop calling me a liar. 'I put it to you, Miss Brewin, that you are nothing more than a common liar.' His technique was working: it was irritating me no end.

He then asked me what Burns did after I left. 'I have no idea,' I said. He didn't believe me and asked again, so I refused to answer his question. The judge demanded that I answer him, and again I refused. Brompton started again. 'Unless you ask me a sensible question,' I said, 'I am not going to reply.'

He banged his fist on the table. 'Miss Brewin,' he shouted, 'will you not keep interrupting me and answer my question? What do you think Daniel Burns did after you left?'

I flew into a temper. 'I have absolutely no idea, and if you had not allowed him to escape then perhaps he would be here now to answer that question for himself!'

You could have heard a pin drop. Peter looked the most shocked of all, but I hoped he was smiling underneath. I thought the judge was going to put the little black cap on his head and give me the death penalty. Brompton and his team were just stunned. The judge called a recess and reminded me that I was under oath and I was not to speak to anyone at this time.

As the court reconvened, they brought the jury back in and a young black girl gave me the thumbs-up. I wasn't the only person to have noticed it: the prosecution must have been watching the jury like a hawk to see if there had been a change in attitude, and they sure as hell saw her. She wasn't there the next morning. Apparently, she had tried to interfere with another juror on another case and had been dismissed overnight. The judge ruled we could finish the case with eleven jurors and, as things were going well for us, we didn't rock the boat.

It wasn't all plain sailing, and don't think I wasn't scared, because I was. I just never wanted to go back to prison – that wasn't on my agenda. Courts are like gladiator arenas: it's a case of kill or be killed. We had to beat them at their own game.

Questioning continued in a very subdued manner. I think we were all waiting for Peter's turn to explain the meaning of my outburst and the manner of Burns's escape. I began to wonder if it had been such a good idea. We had lost the only young juror and one of only two black people – who were more likely to be anti-police – on the jury. I wasn't happy with that. I was glad when the weekend came: I just wanted to go home. I was having one of those moments where I doubted myself. I remember being told that I was dismissed and the judge instructing me that, as I had to give evidence again on Monday, I was not to discuss the case with anyone. Personally, I wanted to forget the whole thing.

Monday was Valentine's Day and I bought a dozen red roses on the way to court. I gave one to Jerome, some to the nice ladies in the canteen, one to the court usher and, of course, one to Peter. Peter stopped me from putting one on the judge's seat with a £50 note attached to it. I also gave one each to the three old men who came to court every day. They were obviously professional court-watchers, the legal equivalent of trainspotters. They always smiled at me and said hello. They cheered me up. I refrained from giving any to the prosecution, but couldn't resist my Monday-morning dig at the Customs' case officer. He was a West Ham fan and wore a little pin in his lapel signifying his loyalty to the club. As I made my way to the dock, I leaned over his desk. 'I see you got stuffed again on Saturday!' I smiled sweetly and carried on walking. Luckily, they never won a game while the case was on. Childish I know, but it made me happy.

Questioning resumed and Brompton continued his attack. We broke for lunch and the judge reminded me again not to speak to my legal team or anyone else. As I waited in the queue for food, a man behind me tapped on my shoulder. 'Don't worry,' he said. 'You're going to be all right. He then muttered something about knowing one of the jury.

I couldn't believe what he was saying – or that he was speaking to me at all. Had he not heard what the judge had said? Mindful of what had happened to the young juror on Friday, and worried that one of the prosecution team might be watching me, I muttered under my breath, 'Thank you.' I didn't want to appear rude and ignore him. He might say how ignorant I had been and change the opinion of me. He winked at me and I smiled. I sat on my own but could barely contain myself. I wanted to rush over and tell Miranda, Peter and Jerome what had happened. Surely it was a good thing.

Eventually, Brompton uttered the phrase I had been longing to hear: 'No more questions.' I rejoined Miranda in the dock and she gave me the thumbs-up. It was her turn next. She did very well: she kept her cool and at one point even started to cry. She had every reason to.

As the trial came to a close, Tony the market trader took to the witness stand. He was a star and, although he started a little nervously, he ended well. Then the prosecution tried to challenge the evidence of my dear friend Natalia who owned and ran the nursery school, and it was a mistake. The jury could see she was a decent, honest human being and they were not impressed.

Now there was nothing left for me to do but hope and pray.

Brompton's summing up was strong. As I listened to him describe me and my actions, he almost convinced me I was guilty. He went on and on and on. Then Peter took the floor. He livened up the proceedings and everybody seemed to wake up again. He kept it short and sweet and reiterated all the points in our favour: the fact that I had seen the customs officer in France, the fact that Burns had escaped. Basically, he explained, carrying the bags back to England was no more than a foolish error on my behalf.

When he had finished, it was the judge's turn. I was stunned by his attitude, but after I had blurted out about the escape I could hardly have expected him to be lenient with me. He wasn't fooled by my little accident. 'In my opinion,' he told the jury, 'though my opinion counts for nothing in the law, Miss Brewin is a highly intelligent, calculating woman who knew precisely what she was doing.' I couldn't believe it. Could it be grounds for appeal? He went on to say that I was feckless with money and I indulged in skulduggery. I sounded more like a pirate on the high seas. He then instructed the jury on points of law and how to separate my sister and I when it came to what to do first. He told them he required a unanimous verdict and dismissed them.

I thought I was going to go home while the jury considered their verdict, but the judge had other ideas: he revoked bail. He justified sending us back to jail by saying that the pressure to escape was more enormous now than at any other time during the trial. What a load of rubbish. So, for the second time, my sister was being punished because of something I had done. I wasn't pregnant now and conditions on the other side of that big locked door were worse; there weren't the comforts that we had had on the other wings. We were kept in the cells below the courts until they closed, then arrived back at Holloway after supper. We were not offered any food.

We came to court the next day starving. My barrister asked if we could be bailed to the court building under the supervision of his clerk so that we could get some food. The judge agreed. At least we didn't have to pace up and down the cell waiting for the jury. They had been out for all of the previous day and it was now past lunchtime. I felt nervous and sick, and we debated whether or not it was a good or a bad thing they were taking so long. I wavered between the two. Maybe they had found me guilty and were now discussing my sister. The suspense was unbearable. It looked like it was going to be another night in prison. I was right.

The next day, the judge spoke to the jury and the *Guardian*-reading foreman said they had come to a stalemate and they could not return a unanimous verdict. The judge asked whether it would help if he allowed more time. No, he was informed. Someone would not be moved. The jury was then told that a majority decision would be acceptable. Normally for a majority decision you are allowed two dissenters, but as we only had eleven jurors it had to be ten to one. We filed back to our table in the canteen; the defence sat arm's length away at theirs. I had bitten my nails to shreds. It seemed that we had only just left the court when there was an announcement over the tannoy calling us back. The jury had made its decision.

Miranda and I stood in the dock. The courtroom was packed. Every court worker that I had greeted or spoken to was there. Even the canteen girls were in attendance. I hoped they were on our side and hadn't come baying for blood. I held Miranda's hand so tightly and the foreman rose from his seat. The tension was unbearable.

'Have you come to a decision?' asked the judge.

'Yes,' replied the foreman.

'Is it a majority decision?'

'Yes, by ten to one.'

The charge was read out.

'How do you find the defendant?' asked the judge.

'Not guilty.'

A cheer went up in the courtroom. I remember hugging my sister and swinging her around in the dock. The noise was so loud that I never heard them say Miranda was not guilty, but I didn't need to. I turned to the jury, thanking them and blowing them kisses. It was incredible. Then we just stood there in the dock.

'What are you doing?' asked Peter. 'You can go.'

We looked at each other and ran from the court. The combination of relief and joy that I felt is impossible to put into words.

Outside the courtroom, people were delighted for us. The old men came up and kissed me, and one of them lifted me up in a bear hug and said that they had all been rooting for us since day one. Some of the girls in the canteen were crying and said they would miss us. When Peter finally emerged from the courtroom, after arguments about costs, I had to tell him how much I loved him. He just laughed, but I was being deadly serious!

# PART THREE

PART THREE

# CHAPTER EIGHT

The experience of that year made me realise the value of friendship. Paula and I became much closer. We had lunches together, went shopping and did things that didn't just involve the children. She was a wonderful person to be with – kind, witty and very wicked. When she left Bob, I wasn't surprised, although it certainly isn't for me to comment on somebody else's relationship. She had had a crush on Michael Hutchence ever since the early days of INXS, and had a picture of him on her fridge. We all affectionately referred to him as 'Love Dog'.

The sexual chemistry that oozed from the television set on the morning of 31 October 1994 must have made most people want to take their partners straight back to bed. Paula's interview with Michael on *The Big Breakfast* was downright lascivious and it must have taken three cameramen and a grip boy to untangle the two of them. Channel Four received a record number of complaints. Their affair started that day.

Paula had been very supportive when I left my husband and would rally round when I felt my world had fallen apart. She reminded me that I had two young children to be cheerful for. I certainly wasn't going to desert her when she needed a friend. She finally left Bob in February 1995, rented an apartment in Bayswater that we referred to as the Gin Palace and continued seeing Michael. Michael was besotted with her and she him. He found the family in Paula that he had so longed for. This, he discovered, was far better than casual sex, and life could not have been happier. Both of them were expecting some fallout over their relationship, but not on the level that followed. Michael especially was horrified at the level of hatred generated by the British press towards them.

Paula had no job. She had been fired by her husband's company Planet 24 and she needed some work. One day she made an error of judgement that she would regret until the day she died. She allowed a mother from her daughter's school to come into her life. That woman was Gerry Agar. I remember being at the apartment one day when she rang, and both Paula and Michael avoided her calls. I asked Paula what the matter was and she said that Gerry was becoming very pushy. She wasn't sure if Agar could deliver the promises of work that she had been making. As it happens, she didn't.

Paula moved from Bayswater to Mount Street and then to Clapham where she bought a house mainly on the proceeds of her autobiography. Eventually, she came to an agreement with Bob: she moved back to her original home in Redburn Street and he moved into Michael's house. By late 1995, Agar was referring to herself as Paula's PA and public-relations person. This was not strictly true but, if that's how she wanted to introduce herself, Paula did not object. She needed work. Agar bombarded people in the television industry, driving them mad with faxes and sometimes speaking to them in tones of complete adoration. She claimed in an interview with the *Sunday Telegraph* that she had just returned from holiday with the couple, though she was wrong on this. Later, though, she did go to Michael's villa in the south of France. Paula had been reluctant for Agar to join them but eventually gave in. She rang me and moaned about her presence, but she had brought it upon herself.

Agar had at some point wanted to sell pictures of Tiger and make a commission for herself, but Paula chose to offer the pictures elsewhere. She even invoiced Paula for her work, but Paula chose not to pay her.

Paula, Michael and I went for lunch on the King's Road and they had invited a television producer friend of theirs, Chris Mould. Chris had also been in France the weekend that Agar tagged along. Paula was excited because Michael and she were off to Australia in a few days. Michael couldn't wait and he talked of nothing else but the sights he was going to show her and the things that they would do. He was going to take her on the journey of his life; they would even stop in Hong Kong so he could show her where he had spent some of his childhood. He wanted to share everything with her – his past, his present and most definitely his future. I was thrilled for them.

A couple of days before they departed, Michael threw a dinner party. He asked me to invite Howard Marks, who I knew, as he really wanted to meet him. He had read his book *Mr Nice* and was fascinated by his exploits in the drug business. Howard was once on America's top-ten most-wanted list and had allegedly been responsible for 90 per cent of all marijuana smuggled into the United States. He was eventually arrested and spent a number of years in a prison in the States. My girlfriend Liz and her boyfriend Dennis also arrived. It was going to be some night! During supper, Michael insistently asked if Howard was OK for money. He said that INXS would do a benefit concert for him. We all laughed at the idea, but Michael was deadly serious. They became good friends and, as a tribute to Howard, Michael would book into hotels under the pseudonym of Mr Nice. It was a great evening, and Michael, dressed in a sarong, cooked us a wonderful meal and, while Howard rolled joints, Michael sang. The stories told round the table that night would make a fascinating book all on their own.

They left on 12 September 1996. It is alleged that in the early hours of Sunday, 15 September the alarm on Michael's Jeep went off and, while searching for the car manual to silence it, Anita Debney – Paula's nanny – found opium in a Smarties tube. It was a strange story, because even I knew that the gadget to silence the alarm was on the key ring. But hey, I wasn't there. What would I know? Agar, her timing as impeccable as ever, appeared the next day and 'in the interest of the children' she 'rampaged' through

Paula's house. Agar found some very personal Polaroid pictures that were hidden in a chest of drawers well out of the reach of anybody, and she placed them with the opium. She maintains she found heroin but threw it away. Agar threw it away? Agar claimed she rang the drugs helpline from Paula's bedroom for advice, though Paula's phone records don't confirm this.

Out of the goodness of her heart, Agar not only told Bob about the drugs, but also showed them to him. This apparently explains why her fingerprints were on the drugs, whereas Paula's and Michael's were not. Agar was so 'concerned' about the children that she spoke to all sorts of people about it. She rang Chris Mould, for example, and asked him what opium looked like. Chris, of course, asked why and she told him he would soon find out. The day the story appeared in the paper she rang him and asked his opinion on the matter. Chris was hesitant and told her that if she had anything to do with it he was appalled, especially as she had stayed in their home in France only a few weeks before. She told Chris to go back to his sad little life.

In her 'concern', she also spoke to a doctor and, realising the seriousness of the situation, she felt the best course of action was to speak to a journalist at the *Mirror*! The amazing thing is that for all her concern she only called the police ten days after knowing about the drugs. Agar claims that the reason for this delay was that she was working with Bob to allow him time to co-ordinate his custody claim for the girls and get everything in place. I am not saying that that is not possible, and I don't wish to be a cynic, but how long does it take to do a deal with a newspaper? About ten days? The journalist from the *Mirror* was very obliging. Why wouldn't he be? He was about to land himself the story of the year. He would then anonymously tip off the police. This would have to be co-ordinated properly to allow the paper a total exclusive, so Agar arranged that Debney would be at the house at an appropriate time the day before to let the police in. Nice work.

The last time Paula or Michael spoke to Agar was in 1996, and yet she had the audacity to go ahead and write a book that described what happened in my house and Paula's house the night

Michael died. Anyone who can clip newspaper cuttings together could have written that book. She maintains that I pleaded with Paula to help me in my custody battle with my ex-husband. Apparently, I thought that her celebrity status, and the fact that she wrote baby books, would count for something in court, and Paula only helped me because she felt sorry for me. The truth is I never even had a custody battle. My husband and I parted very amicably with not a lawyer or a court case in sight. Agar got that bit of erroneous information from the same place she got the rest of the information for her book: yet another incorrect newspaper article.

I was sent a copy of Agar's book and I felt like going through it with a red pen and correcting the mistakes, but I couldn't read it all. It made me feel sick. The worst bit was the insinuation that Paula indulged in lesbian sex and that she and Michael had threesomes. I can assure you that Paula guarded her love for Michael like a lioness protects her cubs – no one would have got near him – and he would not have tainted their love with cheap and sordid threesomes. Agar also describes the Polaroids that she found during the drugs bust as being of Paula in a glossy black latex suit with holes cut in certain areas. She also claims that there was a picture of her inserting a dildo into Michael's bottom. A more atrocious and vindictive story would be hard to find. I saw the original photos and to this day have a copy of the police file on them which includes copies. One is a picture, taken by him, of Paula giving Michael a blow job; the other, also taken by Michael, is of them having sex. To describe them as she did is utterly reprehensible and irresponsible. She never once thought of Paula's children as she wrote that putrid tale; she just thought of her own bank account. In my view, she is an absolute disgrace and if I ever see her in the street I might not be forgiven for what I would do.

To top it all, after Paula died, she went on national television and claimed to be her closest friend. She commented intimately on two people she had only known briefly and had not seen for five years. It was shocking. To my mind, prostitution would be a more respectable way to make a living – at least the other person *wants* to get fucked by someone they hardly know.

On the other side of the world, Paula was blissfully unaware of the disaster that was about to occur in her life. When the story of the drugs hit the papers, I spoke to her and she was devastated. 'Why can't people just leave us alone?' she sobbed. Michael did not want Paula to go back to England without support and so it was decided that Andrew Young, a Sydney-based barrister, would accompany her. The heart-wrenching decision to leave Tiger in Australia with Michael was made, and Paula left her two-month-old breastfed baby behind to see if she could sort out the mess in England. It took the Crown Prosecution Service six months to decide that no charges would be made against either of them, but the damage the wait caused was irreparable. It was the downfall of the two of them.

Paula was lost without her baby and Michael, and at times was very depressed. Michael worried that they would never have a life in England and that it would always be a constant battle with the press and Bob. The drugs bust changed Michael. He was never the same again, and he felt persecuted. He stayed in Australia for a few more weeks and there is a wonderful story of him trying to placate a crying Tiger by breastfeeding her himself. He returned to England with Tiger, feeling he had let Paula down. He could not protect her from the onslaught of the media or be there to hold her hand as the court hearings for custody loomed. He had to go on tour.

It seemed I had swapped one courtroom for another. This time I was in the Family Division of the High Court with Paula and Anthony Burton on one side of the corridor and Bob and his legal team on the other. Neither party spoke to the other. After a very gruelling day in court, and with the drugs case still unresolved, Paula, in her infinite wisdom, decided that a bottle of Baileys and some Valium would do the trick. Once in the off-licence, she also bought some Malibu because she liked the palm trees on the bottle! That night, I realised I had forgotten something at Paula's house and went back to retrieve it. She was unconscious on her bed and I couldn't revive her. I rang her doctor and also called an ambulance. Her lips were going blue and I was panicking. I eventually got her to come round a bit, and when the paramedics came they gave her an injection. A now more lucid Paula refused to go to the hospital, and Bob arrived shortly afterwards. He was reasonable and seemed genuinely upset. 'You're wasting your life,' he told her as she lay semiconscious on the sofa. 'You're very talented – maybe you should write another book. That's what I'd do if I had the same talent for fiction as you.'

It was like Lazarus rising from the dead. She stood up and pointed at him and replied with one of her cutting and witty comments, and I knew she would survive this one.

Michael, on the other hand, was totally freaked out by what had happened. He rang me in tears to make sure Paula was OK. He begged me to stay in the house with her and said that as he had a few days off soon he would come back. He felt totally powerless. He just wanted the best for his girls – which is how he really thought of all of them.

Paula put her house on the market, partly to pay the enormous legal fees that were building up, and we started packing up the house to move to Michael's round the corner. It was all too much for Paula to bear on her own. Plans were made to spend Christmas of 1997 in Australia. Bob had agreed to let all the girls go and Michael had found a house for them all. Things were looking up. Andrew Young returned from Australia to help finalise the rest of the court hearings, which I was delighted about as he and I had started seeing each other on his last trip to England.

Paula wanted to change the dates that the girls would be staying in Australia, which meant that they would miss the end of term, and Bob was not happy. He did not have custody of them by this stage, but because of the drugs bust Paula couldn't remove them from his jurisdiction without his say-so. He refused to let them go. Paula decided to challenge this in court. So on the morning of 21 November 1997 we all headed back to the High Court. Michael was upset by the news as he had arranged everything and was so looking forward to being with them. He wanted to show them how life in Australia could be better. The hearing did not go well. Paula lost and the judge ruled that she could not take the children away at all. As we made our way back, we were numb. In the taxi, Paula turned to Andrew. 'This is going to kill Michael,' she said.

We entered Michael's house in Smith Terrace and there were still boxes everywhere. We were in the process of unpacking, and Paula had great plans for the place. She was totally deflated and Pixie and Peaches could see that their mother was upset. I cooked supper for them and Paula rang Michael. Andrew spoke to him and explained the legalities of the situation and Michael said he was going to ring Bob and plead with him to change his mind. I spoke to him and he sounded lucid but upset. He asked me to look after Paula and make sure she was OK. I said I would. I never spoke to him again.

We bathed the girls and put them to bed. Eventually, they went to sleep and Andrew, Paula and I sat downstairs with Paula sobbing. I suggested we get an Indian takeaway but Paula was not hungry and, at about nine o'clock, she took two strong sleeping pills and went to bed. Andrew and I stayed for a while and moved a few boxes. It had been a long day, and I for one could have killed for a margarita. We met up with my girlfriend Liz and eventually dragged ourselves home just after midnight. I was glad to get to bed.

Just as I was nodding off, the phone rang. Who the hell was calling at two in the morning? I picked the phone up and it was John Martin, the tour manager for INXS. 'Belinda,' he said, 'I've got the most terrible news.' I remember thinking for a split second that Paula was dead. But no, he had something very different to say.

I looked at Andrew in a state of shock. 'Michael's dead,' I told him, and handed him the phone.

I had to get to Paula's house before the press did. I asked Andrew to give John the phone number there as the phones had only gone in a few days before. I jumped into the shower and dressed all in the space of a few minutes, got into Michael's car which was parked outside my house and drove like crazy. What was I going to say to Paula? After everything that had happened, after all their struggles, how could I be about to tell her that the father of her child, the love of her life, was dead. I wished Andrew had come with me, but he was going to make a few calls to Australia; in any case, someone had to stay, as I had my children in the house. When I got to Paula's I would ring Abby – she had babysat my kids all their lives and she could sit with them when Andrew came over.

I pulled up outside the house and saw that there were already two journalists there. I took a deep breath and put my key in the door. I could hear the phone ringing and I desperately wanted to get to it before Paula. There was only one phone in the house and I could hear her racing downstairs. Poor baby probably thought it was Michael ringing back to say that he had persuaded Bob to change his mind. We met halfway, me in the doorway, her on the stairs. She looked genuinely shocked to see me. 'Don't touch the phone,' I screamed at her. I picked it up and it was John Martin. He just wanted to make sure I had arrived safely and someone was with Paula.

'What's going on?' asked Paula, and I told John I'd call him back. 'What time is it? What are you doing?' I put my arms around her and pulled her into me, and she knew from my manner that something was wrong. 'What? What is it?'

'It's Michael,' I told her. 'He's dead.'

Before I could say any more she punched me – really hard – straight in the face.

Then the noise came, a long, guttural scream that resonated from somewhere inside her, a place I had never heard anyone cry from before. It was like an animal in pain. She fell to the floor. I sat beside her and she clung to me with her head in my lap and just sobbed. 'No,' she cried, 'no, not my Michael.'

I heard movement on the stairs and it was the two girls. Peaches, in her flowered pyjamas, and Pixie, with ballerinas on hers, looked bewildered and still half-asleep. Before they could rub the sleep out of their eyes, I took them back upstairs. It was three in the morning and I needed those girls back in bed. They were worried for their mum and the only thing I could think of to say was that she was sad she could not go to Australia and they ought to go back to sleep, which they did.

When I came back down, Paula was lying on the huge black sheepskin rug she had made as a present for Michael. Instead of buying a sofa she had had half the floor built up with dense foam and then covered with this sheepskin and huge red velvet cushions. The whole back of the house was glass – an architect's dream – and you could lie down and watch TV or the stars. But there would be no star-gazing tonight.

I returned John's call and he told me he had arranged for some security for the house and they would turn up soon. They arrived headed by Ronny Franklin. He used to be George Michael's security guy, and a more trusted, calm and level-headed man would be hard to find. He was our saving grace that day and completely took over the logistics of the situation. Anthony Burton, like an angel, arrived and, as Paula's lawyer, gave a statement to the journalists who were now gathering outside the house. Catherine Mayer called to say she was coming over, and I called Jo Fairley in Hastings – she was getting on the next train. I called the doctor and he sedated Paula.

Passports were needed, as Paula was to get on a plane to Sydney in a few hours. I found hers and Tiger's, gave them to security and they dealt with all the arrangements. I spoke to my ex-husband and he said he would look after our children. Then I called Bob. He was staying in Chelsea at the house of Roger Taylor, the drummer from Queen. Paula wanted to take all the girls to Australia but she was in no fit state to look after herself, never mind three children. I thought it would be a media circus and Bob agreed. I tried to explain this to Paula who, even through the shock, could see the sense in leaving them in England. It was agreed that both Andrew and I would accompany her and Tiger. Andrew was due to return to Sydney in two days anyway, and there was no way that I could let Paula get on a plane on her own. I took Pixie and Peaches over to their dad's; Fifi was already there. I asked Bob if Michael had spoken to him the previous evening. 'Yes,' he said. Michael kept telling Bob that Paula was no longer his wife and that the children should come to Australia. Bob said he was their father and that he had some say in the matter as well. He was very shaken and wanted to know if he was the last person Michael had spoken to. I said I didn't know.

I was surprised by the number of journalists outside the door; with each hour there were more of them. From Bob's I went to my house and got my passport and some clothes. I can't remember what I packed, but I arrived in Sydney without a single pair of knickers. When I got back to Paula's, she was lying with Tiger next to a speaker listening to INXS, as it seemed to be the only thing that would settle the little girl in what was a growing mass of people. Provisions, at the best of times, were always in short supply in Paula's house, and everybody was in need of some sort of refreshment. Drinks were called for, and someone suggested coffee and brandy. I went out to get milk and alcohol at about nine in the morning. The off-licence on the corner had just opened. I picked up a bottle of brandy and some champagne – I didn't touch brandy, but I needed a drink too – and then decided that it wouldn't be a great idea if I was pictured carrying champagne into the house. We certainly weren't celebrating. A cardboard box with cornflakes and milk covered the alcohol. Then, as I headed back down the King's Road, there was a newsflash on the radio and I felt myself go faint. I had to pull over.

Michael had hanged himself.

I couldn't believe what I was hearing. They must have got it wrong. I rang my house. Andrew was about to leave to head over to Paula's and I asked him about what I had just heard on the radio. It was true. He, along with everyone, hadn't realised that I didn't know. When John had said Michael was dead, I didn't wait for an explanation. What had I done? How could I have been so stupid as not to ask how he had died? I presumed, incorrectly, that it was an accidental drugs overdose. Paula *had* to know what had happened before we left the house. I didn't want her hearing it, as I had, on the radio or from a journalist.

I carried the box into the house and poured myself a drink. Jo Fairley had arrived and I told her and Anthony Burton my error. We all agreed she had to know the full details before leaving. I couldn't bring myself to tell her, as I was just taking it in myself, so Jo broke the news. She just whimpered as Jo stroked her head. I was glad she had been sedated.

I threw some clothes in a bag for Tiger and Paula. Miraculously, through John Martin on the other side of the world and Ronny Franklin in Paula's house, tickets had been booked, a car arranged and all the necessary requirements set up at Heathrow. Had it not been for those two men, the pressure of that morning would have been unbearable. I am eternally grateful to them, as I know Paula was.

Ronny called the police. We were not going to be able to get out of the street without assistance – our driver could not even get his car up to the door. In the end, it took a convoy of four police cars to get us to the end of the street. I remember Catherine and Anthony being with us on the trip to the airport, with Ronny directing operations from the front of the car. The press were all over the airport, and seats to Sydney were selling like hot cakes. Ronny stopped and spoke to a lone police car on the perimeter of the airport. I had never come into Heathrow from this entrance and had no idea where we were. Metal gates were pulled back. They were expecting us and Ronny took our passports and hotfooted it across the tarmac. Were we on a runway, I wondered. Two uniformed people returned with him and instructed us to follow them. It was a little like *Mission Impossible*, but with John and Ronny orchestrating things you just knew it couldn't fail.

I hugged Ronny and left him to go back to Paula's and make sure things were secure there. We were booked into first class. Paula was booked in as Lady Geldof – the name on her passport. Later on, there were stories in the press claiming that Paula had spent the entire flight saying it was all Bob's fault that Michael was dead, and yet she did not mind, when booking her ticket, using her ex-husband's name and title to get a first-class seat. The truth was that Paula could barely stand up, never mind book a bloody ticket. She never even *saw* her ticket. In the end, we refused the first-class seats. Andrew and I thought business class would be better so Paula could sit between the two of us and we could look after her.

And so began the torturous trip to Sydney for Michael's funeral. Paula was never the same from that day on.

The plane was full of journalists and the British Airways staff did everything they could to keep them in their seats. At one point, I went to the loo and in the mirror I caught a glimpse of my first grey hair. At least I had something else to worry about now. I thought about the events that had culminated in the death of Michael and his loss of any sense of reality and I kept coming back to the same conclusion: the strain of the drugs bust had been immense, and it had then triggered the custody battle. Day-to-day living in their household had become like a war zone. To counter this stress, both Michael and Paula had sought refuge and relief daily in the form of whatever prescription medicines they could obtain: Prozac, Valium and Royhpnol – strong doses which fucked them up. They were just another contributing factor, not the cause, but a major one in my view.

Paula slept a bit and we all took it in turns to look after Tiger as Paula's sobbing had woken her up. I was glad we would be in Thailand soon. I for one wanted to get off the plane.

When we landed, we made it to the first-class lounge and Andrew poured us all a glass of champagne. There was nothing I could do to placate Paula; she was crying uncontrollably. The Thai steward came over and told us that, if she could not stop the noise, she would have to leave the lounge. A couple of Americans who had seen the news and recognised her asked if there was anything that they could do and gave Tiger a soft toy that they had bought for their grandchild. Andrew explained to the Thai gentleman that Paula's husband had just died. He said he could not have that noise in the lounge. I was shocked at his insensitivity as he leaned over and right in Paula's face told her to be quiet. She threw her drink in his face and he retaliated.

All hell broke loose and Andrew, all six foot two of him, leaped across the sofa and grabbed the guy before he lost it completely and laid into Paula. We gathered our belongings and, with Andrew seething and already making notes on the incident for later, we headed back to the plane. Andrew stopped briefly at the door to take the man's name as he was ranting down the phone to someone. Once a lawyer always a lawyer, I suppose.

As we headed off to the gate, our path was blocked by the man from the lounge, some official from the airport and two Thai police officers. We could not board the plane and there were questions of an assault charge to be answered. Andrew explained he was a barrister and that Paula had been shouted at and upset by the gentleman who had made the complaint and that she was only trying to defend herself. Eventually, they let us go when there was confirmation of our version of events. I suppose he had to complain about us or he would have lost his job, but I hoped he would do anyway. Paula did nothing to warrant his behaviour and, contrary to the press reports on the incident, she neither hit nor kicked anybody. Of course, some of the press certainly kicked her – and when she was down, too – but compared to the onslaught that was to come it was a mere bagatelle.

Once in Sydney, we were escorted off the plane by British Airways officials and taken to a suite where we were met by the police. It was a relief to find John Martin was there, along with Davo Edwards who had worked for INXS for years and is a wonderful man. Paula was insistent that she be taken to see Michael immediately. I wasn't sure it was such a good idea, especially after such a long flight. John and Davo, however, seemed to agree with Paula and, after some discussion with the police, it was agreed that our first stop should be the mortuary. Later, I found out that they wanted Paula to go because the autopsy was due to be performed later that day and seeing him after that would have been exceptionally traumatic. Apart from taking out organs, they cut the head off the body. It was better she went now.

Paula and I left Sydney Airport the same way we had entered Heathrow – under the runways to escape the awaiting press. John Martin went out the front entrance with a blonde policewoman who had a coat over her head. It had the desired effect and the press followed, thinking it was Paula. When she removed the coat, they realised they had been duped and, presuming we were going to stay in the same hotel as the rest of the family, they decamped to the Sir Stanford awaiting a glimpse of her.

We arrived at the mortuary and I'll never forget the smell in there: it was clinical and sterile. I was frightened for my friend and she hugged me as we went through the door. A lady came out and said to give them a minute and they would bring Michael to her. Eventually, they called her name. As she made to go, she turned to me and said, 'Please will you come with me?' I didn't know what to say, but I knew I couldn't say no. I had never seen a dead body in my life and I didn't know how *I* would react, let alone how much help I would be to Paula.

We entered the room. The plain white tiles went from floor to ceiling. The neon light accentuated the starkness of the room and in the midst of all this clinical drabness lay Michael. He was on a

*Above*: Supporting a devastated Paula at Michael's funeral.

*Below*: At Tiger's christening in Sydney.

For The One I Love

Dearest Belinda —
I will NEVER EVER
be out of your debt
for looking after my
baby Im sorry I am
USeless and mad.
                    I one your friend
                    Paula
                    X

With lots of love
in every line
To the wonderful man hooligan
I'm proud to call mine!

Happy
Birthday This month!

A card that Paula gave to me, after I had taken Tiger to Australia with me and my daughters, after Michael's death.

Where it all began … on the *Big Breakfast* bed.

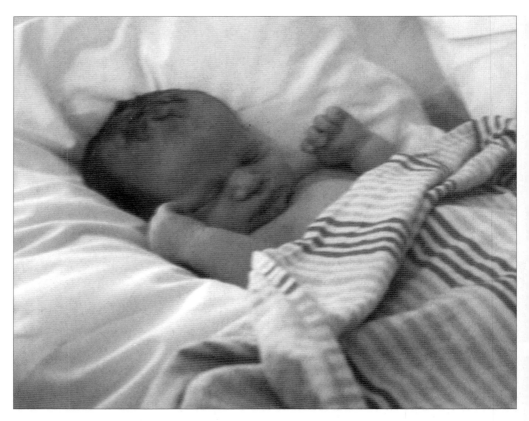

*Above*: The day Tiger was born.

*Below*: Proud parents with their beautiful daughter in Sydney.

*Above*: The Christmas we spent in St Lucia, after Michael's tragic death.

*Below*: Tiger with my daughter Indiana.

*Above*: With my daughters Indiana and Montana, and horse, Ben.

*Below*: The Rackenford Club, my local haunt.

Nervous, but determined
that justice would prevail.
On the way to the Old
Bailey as one of the Chief
Prosecution Witnesses in the
Chohan murder trial.

*Above*: The Breakfast Club girls (minus Diana Rossiter, sadly). Diana Breitmeyer, Mel Waldren, me, Andy Weedon and Corrina Knowles.

*Below*: Celebrating after the verdict, from left to right, my daughter Montana, Katie, Sonia, Flo, Lucy and Venetia.

metal trolley, naked, though covered with a plain white sheet. We were separated by a wall. It was the same height as the trolley and from a certain angle it looked as if he was lying on the top of it. Paula just sobbed and kissed his face and stroked his hair. He had a cut on his face just above his eyebrow and Paula kissed it again and again like a mother does to a baby when they've hurt themselves, to make it all better. I took Tiger from her and she climbed over the wall and on to the trolley. She lay down next to him crying, 'Please don't leave me, please don't leave me here.' It broke my heart and I started to cry too. She seemed to compose herself, then insisted that Michael needed a blanket as he was so cold. They were very kind and brought one, so Paula tucked him up as if he was one of her children going to sleep for the night. She asked for some scissors and cut locks of his hair and asked me to look after them.

I said my goodbyes to him, kissed his forehead and left Paula to spend a last few minutes with the love of her life.

We checked into the Quay West. It was the other side of town to where the press thought we were. For a few days, at least, we would have peace. Michael's father Kell phoned and came to see his granddaughter and Paula soon after we arrived. Paula had deteriorated rapidly on leaving the mortuary and the hotel doctor was called when we arrived. Against my wishes he sedated her – there was concern that she would do herself harm otherwise. Personally, I thought it suppressed emotions that ought to be allowed to come out. A message was left for Patricia, Michael's mother, which was never returned.

The next few days seemed to blend into one. Paula spent most of the time either sedated or hysterical and nothing would console her. Tiger was sick the day after we arrived, so, along with Colin Diamond and Davo, I had to take her to the hospital. I pretended the baby was mine and therefore avoided the press being alerted to our whereabouts.

The next day I was told that the Hutchence family had decided to sell the rights to Michael's funeral to a television company. The band was horrified and rang and asked if Paula had agreed to this.

I told them that no one had rung our hotel suite and asked anything about the funeral arrangements, but I knew she was horrified by the idea that it would be plastered all over the television.

Martha, Michael's manager, had arrived in from LA. She had her own feelings of guilt and spent a lot of time with Paula that day. She had told Michael the evening that he died that his meeting with Quentin Tarantino had not gone well and he had not got a part in one of his movies. That, along with the other news he had received from England, would have all contributed – along with the drugs and alcohol – to an unstable state of mind. At first, I wanted to believe it was an accident; the longer I live the more I wonder – maybe he felt he'd failed and really had had enough.

Paula and I went for a walk the day before the funeral. We strolled down by the ocean and talked about happier days when Michael was alive. She kept asking me if she thought Michael really loved her. People came up to her and hugged her; a woman in a flower shop gave her a rose. The outpouring of sympathy from the Australians was incredible. Every day at the hotel, messages from people Paula had never met poured in. Maria, a lady who owned a children's shop called Home Grown in the Ritz Carlton Hotel where Michael had died, sent Tiger some gorgeous clothes. She had sent them to the Sir Stanford Hotel addressed to Mrs Hutchence. Patricia was not happy: there was only one Mrs Hutchence, she said, and it certainly wasn't Paula. She had a belief that she kept repeating: 'Michael would never have married her.'

On returning to the Quay West, there was a rail of clothes sent over by Colette Dinningan. Michael loved her clothes and she thought Paula might want to choose something to wear to the funeral. She chose a dress that Michael liked – black with beautiful hand-stitched embroidery. It was then I realised that, along with no knickers, I had not packed any shoes apart from my flat black suede Manolos that I had worn since arriving. So, bizarrely, I spent the rest of the afternoon shopping for some.

On the morning of the funeral I had arranged for a hairdresser to come to the hotel room, and also for a masseur. I thought that this would pass the time before we had to leave, and hopefully it would keep Paula relaxed and distracted. It worked. What also helped was the fact that we had probably had our best night's sleep since arriving in Sydney. I had banned everybody from the hotel suite – especially security. It was nothing personal; it just all got too much. We ordered a jug of margarita and a jug of pina colada, went for a swim and then sat in our towels on our living-room floor, drinking our drinks and telling stories about Michael. We laughed and laughed till our sides hurt. I wondered what anybody looking in would have thought, but it didn't matter – it was great to hear her giggle for the first time since hearing the news.

The morning of the funeral had to run like clockwork as there were the television people to think of. A compromise had been reached that they would not film the first few rows, but of course that never happened. Bono rang and sent Paula his best, as did the rest of the band. I had spoken to him a few times since arriving. He was on tour in America, so his wife Ali came alone. She flew over with Andy Gill who had worked on Michael's solo album and was the then boyfriend and now husband of Paula's very good friend Catherine Mayer. They were staying in the same hotel as us. Bono told me to tell Paula that they had dedicated a song to Michael and he said he was sorry he could not be there. Paula seemed pleased – Michael and Bono had been good friends.

Unbeknown to Paula and me there had been arguments flaring up all over Sydney involving who would sit where and next to whom. Who was more important? Which side of the church had the better view? On the day of the funeral, Paula yet again got the blame for disrupting the arrangements. We got into our car as instructed and went straight to the cathedral where we were escorted to the front row on the right-hand side of the church by an usher. Apparently, we had taken the best seats in the place. Personally, I wondered who deserved them more than Michael's daughter and the mother of that child, but then I was never asked. We were accompanied by Andy Gill and Nick Cave. Nick was going to sing, and he categorically refused to let the television company broadcast him live on air. Patricia was upset by this but Nick would not be moved on the subject.

Patricia and Tina arrived and sat on the left-hand side of the church. Paula had not seen them since her arrival in Sydney and got up and walked over to where they were sitting. She bent over to kiss Patricia and to ask how she was coping, but Patricia jostled her and told her to go and sit down and that she had killed her son. I think everybody who witnessed it was shocked, and from then on the battle lines were drawn. There was certainly no pretence any more. No wonder Michael moaned on many occasions that he wished his mother would realise he had his own family now and that they were everything to him.

The INXS boys and Michael's brother Rhett carried the coffin out of the church into bright sunshine and, as the hearse pulled up, there was a bolt of lightning, a clap of thunder and it started to pour with rain. There were huge crowds outside the cathedral and the cavalcade of limousines stretched for as far as I could see. It was nice to see a friendly face in Kell and his lovely wife Susie. She squeezed Tiger's hand and smiled. Paula, Andy and I got into the limousine and were then joined by Nick Cave and his girlfriend. The rain held up the drive to the crematorium by five minutes. The crowds sang 'Never Tear Us Apart' and we drove through the streets of Sydney flanked by police outriders. It was rather surreal and I felt like an extra in a film of John Kennedy's funeral.

The crematorium proved too much for Paula, who could not come to terms with the treatment she had received from Patricia in the cathedral. I took her and Tiger back to the hotel. It was one of the saddest journeys of my life and Paula was utterly inconsolable.

For me, the trip to Sydney was to accompany my friend and to pay my respects to Michael. It was not about who had the best seat in the house, dissecting the cause of his death or apportioning blame. Michael would have been ashamed at the treatment meted out to Paula because, however crazy things were, theirs was true love. The funeral was a tragic affair made worse by the behaviour of some members of the family. Colin Diamond, Michael's most trusted friend and executor of his will, had the right idea: he didn't stay for the funeral, and flew out of Sydney that morning. It was alleged by Patricia that Paula was demanding to take Michael's ashes with her. In fact, she was happy to accept whatever they decided on. She was far too grief-stricken to bother with bickering.

Maybe it was a good time to go home; there was no reason to stay in Sydney. The arguments over Michael's money were about to start. It wasn't going to be pretty and the greatest love affair that had ever happened to either Paula or Michael was now at an end.

# CHAPTER NINE

The return to England brought a wealth of new problems for Paula. This was life without Michael and there was no going back. Reality hit home hard and she found it almost impossible to deal with from day one. The misery of returning to an empty house was utterly depressing: the letterbox had been prised off the door and the mail stolen, I suppose in an attempt to find a non-existent suicide note. The rubbish – which mainly consisted of dead flowers and Tiger's dirty nappies – had been rifled through. But now there were other pressing issues in Paula's life for her to deal with.

Hughie Green was Paula's father's arch-enemy. Jess Yates, like Hughie, had been a television star; but, unlike Hughie, his career had ended bitterly with the revelation of his affair with a young girl – details of which had been leaked to the press by none other than his old friend Hughie. Paula loved her father very much, but sometimes worried that she had inherited the depression he had battled for so much of his life.

While Michael was still alive, he and Paula had gone to Bali on holiday. While they were there, Hughie Green died. Suddenly, allegations started flying around that Paula was Hughie's illegitimate child. She was horrified. The *News of the World* printed a huge story on the subject. Paula rang her mother, who had not spoken to her since she left Bob, and asked her if there was any truth in the story. Her mother categorically denied any involvement at all with Green. Paula was relieved: Tom Jones would have been cool, but Hughie Green was a definite no-no! On the information from her mother, Paula went ahead with a DNA test. It would prove that the *News of the World* had lied and she would sue. It never worked out like that. They hadn't lied; her mother had. Paula was devastated. She was Hughie Green's daughter.

I subsequently spoke to Linda Plentl, Green's daughter and Paula's half-sister. She was angry at the way these revelations had been aired – from the pulpit in the church at her father's funeral. And yet she found the idea of having a sister after all these years kind of exciting. She is a marvellous woman with a beautiful family who were always kind and supportive of Paula. It was a shame that Paula felt so insular and unwilling to make an emotional step towards them; I think they would have been good friends.

The situation was made worse by the fact that Paula had been involved in another legal battle. Her father had died and his lover was claiming his estate; Paula disputed this. Why should this woman have possessions that she knew her father intended for her? On finding out she was not, in fact, Jess Yates's daughter, the courts ruled against her claim. In the space of a few months, she had lost everything – her past and her future.

The postman arrived on a daily basis with sacks full of letters. Paula took great comfort from these and was always amazed that complete strangers had taken time out of their lives to write to her. Some mornings I would arrive to find her sitting in a sea of envelopes spread across her floor. Some were simply addressed to 'Paula Yates, Television Presenter, London', and others just 'Paula Yates, Chelsea'. They all got there. We spent days replying to every letter with an address on it. She kept and filed each one, and I still have them. I know she would want me to mention all those people who wrote, because it meant so much to her at that time. She never really understood how she had touched people's lives and how genuinely people cared.

Soon after Michael's funeral, I got a call from Colin Diamond to say that Michael's house in Chelsea would have to be sold. Paula was going to have to move. Maybe that was not such a bad thing

– a fresh start was a good idea – but it was all coming a little thick and fast and she wasn't coping well under the pressure. Colin asked me to see if I could find a suitable house to rent and Michael's estate would pay for it for a year until she recovered enough to go back to work or start writing. Paula coped with the news by getting drunk. The house was in some way her last link to Michael and it was going to be difficult to let go of it.

Bono's wife Ali called and asked how Paula was. She said that they were concerned with Christmas coming up that she should not be on her own. I agreed. I was supposed to be going to Thailand with my children and cancelled it – Paula had not wanted to go as we had discussed meeting there with Michael on their return from Australia. Ali said that they would pay for a holiday somewhere else for all of us and she put me in touch with her travel agent. There was a cancellation over the Christmas period in a rather splendid house in Saint Lucia, which they booked. We would have to do nothing. There were maids, a chef, a private pool and we even had our own driver. It was perfect and I was eternally grateful for their kindness.

My family had owned banana and sugar plantations in Saint Lucia before independence, and they still owned property and some land on the island. Our plantation manager, Harry, still lived there. He had worked for my family for years and was now an old man in his seventies. I promised my mother I would look him up and invite him for dinner. Once we were settled in, I called him and told him where we were. 'Oh,' he said, 'you mean your grandfather's house?' I didn't know what he was talking about – he was an old man, maybe he was going senile. He arrived, and sure enough it transpired that it *was* my grandfather's house. He had sold the mountain to an Italian developer on the condition that they built him a house on the top. It was stunning and had the most beautiful views. Christmas was rather a low-key event, but it certainly beat staring at boxes of Michael's possessions in Chelsea.

One day, I arrived at Paula's house to find Martin Bashir sitting having tea with her, holding her hand. I was never a great fan of his – he is far too slimy for my liking. Martin was famous then because of his Princess Diana interview; his massive stitch-up of Michael Jackson was yet to come. I'm not a Jackson fan in any way, shape or form, but you can see how he may have allowed Jackson's mob to believe they had full control over the film and yet only gave them the right to choose what footage was used, lulling them into a false sense of security and trust before doing the most derogatory voiceover to go with it. The Jackson team just did not foresee, foolishly I may add, what kind of commentary he was going to add.

Paula had not given an interview since returning from Michael's funeral and the papers were offering ludicrous sums of money for an exclusive. There was much discussion over which newspaper to go with. Each would match their opposition's figure, so it was just a matter of picking the one that Paula felt would portray her in the correct light. She had been much maligned in the press and I never fully understood why at that time. Later, she may have deserved some of it, but their reaction immediately after Michael's death was beyond me. I remember at the time a fantastic picture of the Radio 1 DJ Zoé Ball appearing in the paper. She was on her way home after a night out and she was pictured holding half a bottle of Jack Daniels and a cigarette. Apparently, she was cool, but I couldn't help thinking that if it had been Paula the headline would have been DRUNK, SLUT AND AN UNFIT MOTHER.

Negotiations with the newspapers were drawing to a close and Michael had been dead for nearly three weeks. I was dubious about the interview as I thought it would look tacky for Paula to do it so soon after his death, even though she had no choice. Martin Townsend, then the editor of *OK!*, came up with an excellent solution. *OK!* would have an exclusive interview with her approximately three months later. For this Paula accepted a lower figure and promised not to say a word to any other publication before the interview ran. Martin also agreed to give Paula full approval of what was written. It was a risk he took, but he trusted her to say enough and she appreciated his integrity.

After the deal with *OK!* had been signed, Martin Bashir's protestations of friendship and his visits soon stopped. After Michael's death Paula felt used and very hurt by certain people and the Bahsir incident did not help Paula regain her self-confidence. For a while she refused to leave the house or answer her phone.

This was no good at all and I remember having many conversations with Catherine Mayer on how we could pull our friend out of the doldrums she seemed to be stuck in. Catherine thought that maybe Paris fashion week would be the place to put the sparkle back in her eye. Paula and I headed off on the Eurostar to stay at one of my favourite hotels in Paris, Le Crillion, positioned nicely on the Place de la Concorde and in walking distance from the Buddha Bar. The hotel staff were really kind to us and upgraded our room to a suite. Tiger was permanently attached to Paula's hip and I jokingly said that the child would never walk and, as a teenager, would insist on being carried to school. We had a fabulous few days, ate caviar, drank champagne and Paula insisted on pinching the bottom of the traffic cop that seemed to be permanently by the traffic lights outside the hotel. He never seemed to be directing traffic; I think he just waited there for Paula.

We went to a couple of shows, the highlight, of course, being the performance by Collette Dinnigan, who had been a great pal of Michael's. Whilst walking along the Champs-Elysee one morning we passed a newspaper kiosk and Tiger, who was in her buggy said, 'Look it's mummy,' and sure enough there was a picture of Paula on the front of OK! magazine. The man on the stand told Tiger her mummy was very beautiful and, thinking no more of it, we carried on with our stroll.

We were leaving for England the next day and had been invited out for dinner that evening by some friends and so arranged to meet at the Buddha bar. Paula was not really in the mood and she and Tiger only stayed for a starter. I excelled myself that evening by getting very pissed, changing outfits with a girlfriend of mine in the middle of the dance floor and then stumbling back to the hotel to sleep.

I had just gotten to sleep when I was rudely awoken by a strange man in uniform shaking my arm. What the hell was this guy doing in my bedroom? He had an excellent bedside manner though and asked me why when I had a lovely suite did I want to sleep in the corridor? What was he talking about?

Then it all came flooding back to me.

I had got out of the lift and, feeling a little unsteady on my high heels, I decided to sit down on the sofa in the corridor and take them off. Well, it was late and I had had a few margaritas and it was obviously comfortable so I lay down. I was mortified to recall it all, but the man kindly helped me up, opened the room door for me and bade me goodnight. Very chivalrous of him I thought.

Paula laughed over her croissant the next morning and surprisingly enough my headache was not as bad as I had expected – probably because when I was woken I then drank about two litres of water before getting into bed. Paris had certainly lifted Paula's spirits and there hadn't been any incidents. Not so far, but then we hadn't left the hotel.

We checked out, got to the train station and went to board the train.

'Passports, please,' said the nice uniformed man. I showed him mine and when he asked Paula for hers she said she didn't have hers. She didn't think she needed it, after all they hadn't asked for one when she had left England. Where had I heard that before? I was having that incredible feeling of déjà vu. I too had once been in France without a passport and had then ended up in jail; I hoped that wasn't going to happen here.

The officer seemed to recognise Paula, but said it was the child that was the problem. How did he know it was her baby? She might be trying to steal a child out of France that wasn't hers. A more senior officer was called and someone from immigration appeared; there was no way we could leave the country with a child without proper documentation proving the child was hers. Then I remembered the news kiosk and the copy of *OK!* magazine. I asked the immigration officer if I could prove that Tiger was Paula's daughter, could we leave without a passport. He said we could but he also said that when we arrived in England we could have problems. It really was like a recurring nightmare! I knew when we got to England, Paula would have no trouble telling the British police who she was so we were almost home free. All I had to do was hot foot it over to the Champs-Elysee and hope that the nice man hadn't sold his last copy of the magazine.

He hadn't and an hour later with a copy of *OK!* as a passport, Paula, Tiger and myself were on a train heading home. I always said we should have sent a picture of Paula at passport control with the magazine in her hand to the owner of the publication, Richard Desmond. His friend Mohammed Al Fayed, owner of Harrods, had for years been trying to get a British passport. If only he'd realised all he needed was his picture in *OK!* magazine, his problems would have been solved.

A trip to the Priory under the guise of grief counselling was soon on the cards. The holiday had helped, but Paula needed some professional guidance. Drinking and Valium were certainly not going to make life better for her and, though I understood why she was going down that path, there were also four very good reasons for her to get on with life: her children. It became a constant battle for Jo, Catherine and me. Paula could be a bloody nightmare at times.

For some reason, Paula was not forced by her doctor at the Priory to take the twelve-step programme – a well-tested method to help on the road to sobriety and recovery. Apparently, she did not need it; she was not an alcoholic. Maybe not – but she sure as hell liked to get drunk to forget, and I felt that surely that alone needed treatment. Instead, she sat in her room, watched daytime television and just hid from the world. That, to my mind, was not the answer. I would bring Tiger, whom I was looking after, to visit her every day, and on some occasions I swear she was drunk.

I objected to the fact that she was paying vast sums of money – and when that ran out – to Rupert Everett doling out more cash. One day, I arrived earlier than normal to find Paula's room empty. Thank God for that, I thought. Maybe she had gone with the rest of the residents to group therapy. Suddenly, I saw a figure at the open window and Paula climbed in wearing nothing but a nightdress and with a plastic bag held between her teeth. She was very surprised to see me. Having confiscated the bottle of vodka the bag contained, I was extremely cross – but, looking back, I suppose it was quite funny. She pleaded with me to let her have it and I refused. Foolishly, though, I agreed not to tell the doctors about her little misdemeanour as long as she promised there would be no repeat performance. She lied and said it would never happen again; I only half-believed her.

Miss Yates's antics hardly helped the recovery of the other residents of the Priory, but particularly the poor boy in the room next to her. On one of my first visits to her, I became aware of a tapping sound that quickened in rhythm and then stopped. I didn't take much notice of it until I heard it again about an hour later. 'What's that noise?' I asked Paula.

'It's the boy next door,' she replied a bit blankly. 'He's having a wank. He's a sex addict.'

I thought she was joking, but once you knew what it was there was no mistaking the sound. It was very disconcerting, and Paula and I would try desperately not to laugh as he was about to come. On one occasion, Paula tripped up the stairs and ripped her nightdress to reveal her ample bosom just as the young wanker had left his room. It would have been difficult for him to miss this sight, and I think his recovery was put back a good three months. He asked to be moved not only to a different room but to a completely separate floor.

A while later, Paula rang me in great excitement. Caroline Aherne of *The Royle Family* fame was also a resident, in the hope of curbing her drinking. Maybe she could influence Paula to admit that she had at least a small problem. Things seemed to be going well until one visit when it transpired that an empty half-bottle of vodka had been found in the wastepaper basket in Caroline's room and she was going to be chucked out for breaching the rules. Caroline swore she knew nothing about it and the other residents suspected that it had something to do with Paula. I knew it had to be her.

I soon discovered that on a daily basis Paula would sneak down to the local newsagent's and buy herself a bottle. Not any more. The poor boy behind the desk had no idea she was a resident of the Priory and promised never to sell her alcohol again. She was made to apologise to Caroline and her doctor agreed that she was in a worse state than he had realised. It's not surprising he never noticed, as he hardly ever saw her. He said there was little that could be done unless she wanted help. I suggested having her committed, and it was under this threat and with the Social Services looming menacingly in the background that Paula eventually saw fit to check in to a much stricter lockdown regime. She would call me from there cursing me and saying that I had put her in jail and that she would never speak to me again. In fact, she rang me almost daily to tell me this.

Apart from the Social Services, one of the reasons she agreed to this six-week lockdown regime was that it was the summer holidays. Her elder girls would be with their father and Tiger could accompany me to Australia with my girls for a month. It slightly changed the itinerary of our holiday, as there are certain things you can't do with a small child but it wasn't a big deal. The only problem I could foresee was how long it would take Tiger to get over not being breastfed every night. The poor kid cried herself to sleep the first few days and, even though she did sleep in the bed with me, there was nothing I could do to console her. After that, it was plain sailing and we had a fantastic time.

We visited Kell and Susie, Michael's Dad and his wife; we went to the Aquarium and the Zoo and hung out on the beach. Life was good, and Paula, I hoped, was on the way to recovery. Colin Diamond decided to send us to Lindeman Island, partly to get us away from the paparazzi, as it was becoming increasingly difficult to do anything in Sydney without it being front-page news. After all, Tiger was Michael's daughter and she had not been back to Sydney since her father's death. Everyone seemed to want a photo of her.

We booked into the resort under false names and, as you could only get to the place by boat, nobody bothered us. Club Med fielded phone calls from the press and denied we were even staying there. It was two weeks of peace and I couldn't remember the last time we had all had the pleasure of that. The activities for the children were phenomenal. The girls just had the best time ever. They learned circus skills and had dance lessons, dressed up and did plays and that was just at night. I was sad to leave, particularly as all of us had made some good friends there. Especially my friends Max and Ali. Sadly, Max was to die a few years later, but Ali and I are still in touch and remain friends.

On our return to Sydney, having not seen the television or read a paper in days, I was unaware of the antics of my friend Miss Yates. Far from knuckling down to getting better, she had got herself thrown out of the clinic (or 'jail', as she referred to it), which was quite an achievement in itself – if not one to be proud of. Michael's father heard the news first and the reason for her expulsion. Rather than discuss it with me, Kell decided to try and remove Tiger from the care of her mother and I, by making accusations of abuse and neglect to the Sydney Police. It is easy to see why he made this move and he only did it out of love, care and concern for his grandchild. On the other hand, I was charged with looking after her and had done so for many months prior to this and I surely wasn't going to let any harm come to her. I also loved that child.

One thing I did know: I could not leave her in Australia. Tiger had to return home with me. I received a phone call informing me that the police were on their way to the hotel to serve me with some papers forbidding me from travelling outside of Australia with Tiger. I spoke to a lawyer I had met through Andrew Young, by the name of Lisa Panucci, she was unsure of how successful Kell's claim would be but it would definitely delay us and there would be a court hearing. Over the years, she had become a great friend to both me and Paula, and she was retained in her legal capacity to fight on Tiger's behalf in the acrimony that ensued over Michael's will. And a bloody good job she did as well.

What concerned Michael's father so much was that Paula had allegedly been asked to leave the centre for breaking their no-sex rule. She was adamant she had merely flirted, but her idea of flirting could be pretty close to sex, as anyone who watched her on the *Big Breakfast* can testify.

It was possible that the problem was not even having sex itself so much as the person with whom she might have had sex with. A no-good, not even ex-junkie who she insisted on inviting to live in her home after being 'discharged'. Kell was not happy with the arrangement and, when I heard, I too was furious. What a waste of six bloody weeks. She and I were about to have strong words and any minute now I wouldn't be able to leave Australia. Well, not with Tiger, anyway. It better have been a good shag, I thought, because it wasn't worth it as far as I was concerned.

I received a phone call from Colin Diamond telling me to get out of the hotel I was in and fast, as he too had heard the police were on their way to serve me with papers forbidding me to take Tiger out of the country. We had to leave before they could serve them on me. I instructed the girls to gather their things.

'Don't fold them,' I yelled, 'just get them in the bags and quick!'

I rang the front desk. We had stayed at the Quay West during Michael's funeral and they were fantastic then and were no different now. A car was brought into the underground car park and the children and I lay low on the seats as we raced across town. We arrived at another hotel car park, into the service lift and straight up to a suite. It was like something out of the movies. Tiger had a coat over her head at all times. We could not leave the hotel room and our flight wasn't for a week. But there was no way I could keep three kids cooped up for days in a hotel room.

I spoke to Colin and suggested we go to Thailand for the last week of the holiday. It was on our way home and British Airways said we could leave the following day. So that was settled. I hid with the girls in the hotel until the next day. I never got to say goodbye to anyone and I was not allowed to call either. That really upset me, as so many people had been so kind and they must have thought me very rude to leave without a goodbye, never mind a thank you. What saddened me most was the amount of time I had spent with Kell; he could have called me and talked to me. Paula had not wanted Tiger to visit Michael's family when I was there, but Tiger was in my care and I personally did not understand why and ignored what she had said. Now I wondered why I'd bothered. At the time I was very hurt by Kell's actions. I could not even ring him and ask him why. I was forbidden from using the phone.

The next day, we left the hotel in a blacked-out people carrier and made the journey to Sydney Airport. We arrived safely. Tiger was in her buggy and I instructed my two girls not to leave my side. There would be no looking around the duty-free area today. My heart was in my stomach as I checked in, but the lady smiled and handed me four boarding passes. I tried not to look guilty but

I couldn't help it. At passport control and immigration, I broke into a sweat.

When the officer checking our documents asked me if we had enjoyed our stay, I could barely speak to reply, 'Yes, it was wonderful.'

Finally, we made it to the lounge reception and the steward showed the girls and me into the first-class lounge. We sat on the sofa near a television and I went to get drinks and sandwiches for Monty and Indy. All the while taking Tiger with me. This kid was not leaving my sight. Twenty minutes passed and I felt my heart rate return to normal. Tiger was strapped in her buggy making short work of a packet of crisps when the automatic doors from the reception area opened. There were two men scanning the room. I raised the magazine I was reading to hide my face and held my breath. I could hear footsteps and then they stopped. With my head bent as if I was reading, I saw two shiny black shoes come into my line of vision and the owner of the shoes spoke: 'Miss Brewin?'

I looked up and there were two police officers. We'd been rumbled.

I had told Monty, who was old enough to understand, what was happening before we left the Quay West. Indiana just thought it was another Australian adventure and Tiger didn't need to know, nor would she have understood. Monty now looked frightened and I knew I was. The police explained that they had papers which did not allow me to take Tiger out of the jurisdiction. They asked me to come with them, which I refused to do. They explained that if I did not let them take the child they could arrest me, though neither of them sounded like they really wanted to. As I had not been named as the person neglecting or abusing the child, then I was free to continue with my journey with my own children and they would care for Tiger from this point. It just wasn't an option, so the girls and I picked up our bags and, not for the first time in my life, nor the last, I was being escorted away by two policemen.

To give the police officers their due, they seemed very uncomfortable with what they had been asked to do but Kell had been to court and he had the correct paperwork. Monty was crying, 'Please don't let them take Tiger.'

How was I going to explain this to Paula when I got home? That I hadn't been able to look after her child and that I had visited someone whom she had specifically told me not to. I, in my infinite wisdom, had felt that Kell, as Michael's father, deserved to see his grandchild. Paula had said that all they wanted was to take Tiger away from her and it seemed she might be right. I had totally misjudged the situation and with dire consequences.

The police explained that I would have to go to court and refute the claims that had been made. As far as they were concerned, the child looked fit and well and they felt the court would feel the same. I was totally despondent. The police rang Kell and informed him that we had been apprehended at the airport and that I had refused to continue my journey without Tiger. By this point, Montana's tears and the mere presence of the police had frightened both Indy and Tiger and the two of them were howling. Kell must have heard the noise and asked the police what all the fuss was about. The police explained that all three girls were very distressed and scared. Kell was not an uncaring man and I was glad I had not misjudged him completely and he told the police he didn't want to cause anyone this amount of upset.

The officer said, 'If you drop the allegations we can let them go, they have just enough time to get their flight, what do you want us to do?'

Kell said, 'Let them go.'

I kissed the officers and they seemed genuinely pleased, and the girls and I ran for our plane. As the plane taxied down the runway for take-off, I felt I had never been so happy to leave anywhere in my life. It was a sad way to end our Australian holiday but we were all together and that was what mattered most.

After Paula was discharged, I was approached by a large television network about a holiday programme and asked if Paula would like to present an episode. In principle, it sounded ideal. I had seen one the week before where they sent a celebrity to a fantastic holiday resort in the Caribbean. How difficult was it to lie on a beach and extol the virtues of sun, sea and sand? We had a few meetings. Paula wanted to go to India but it was decided that Sri Lanka was the place. The fee was only a few thousand, plus a holiday with a small speaking part, but it seemed an easy way of getting back to work.

The itinerary grew daily, but we were assured it would not be a gruelling trip. Paula and I worked out that the three places she was going to cover were no more than an hour and a half plane ride away from each other. We were looking forward to it. There was just one snag: the World Cup was on and we didn't want to miss it. A clause was added to the contract to say that we had to stay in a hotel that had satellite television on the days when England were playing. It seemed like a reasonable request to me.

Before we left our stopover in Dubai, I knew we were going to have a problem. One of the team was already banging on about the budget. If we ordered a drink, 'Are you aware you're on a budget?' If we ordered a sandwich, it was the same. We hadn't even arrived and I wanted to shove his bloody budget up his arse. We arrived in Colombo early in the evening. Tiger was a little fractious and we still had a connecting flight before we arrived at our destination. There was just one problem: there *was* no connecting flight, and there never had been. We were travelling by bus. Paula and I just looked at each other – eight hours on a shitty old bus!

It looked like an old American school bus and the seats were metal and narrow. I was glad I'd stolen a pillow from the hotel in Dubai. Paula was horrified at the time, but now she was jealous and wished she had one. In the end, I gave it to her so that Tiger could rest on it. The suspension on the bus was non-existent and the roads were terrible, so the two of us ended up with more bruises on our bums than a girl should have, unless she's had great sex. It was not a good start to a trip, and things did not improve.

Paula and I made our feelings known to the crew, but by then it was too late. All the 'days off' were to be spent travelling by bus to the next destination, not – as we had been led to believe – lying around on a beach. She did the work to camera and was very good, but she was not a happy bunny. We spent hours and hours and hours on this godforsaken bus. For one trip we refused and they got us a car, but not without mentioning the budget. In fact, it wasn't much better, and what made it worse was that the driver only had one Brian Adams tape which was stuck in the machine so we listened to it repeatedly for a solid six hours. In the end, to relieve the boredom, we rewrote the lyrics to all his songs and some, I have to say, were an improvement – especially the bits where Paula barked during the chorus.

It was a gruelling workload and the travelling was way too much in such appalling conditions, particularly for a baby. Paula, exasperated and tired after another long day, told Budget Man exactly what she thought of him and how totally unprofessional they were. This did not go down well, and from then on we avoided each other.

The next day would be fun: England were playing and we were staying in a hill resort. I was going to spend the evening in front of the television with a margarita. Heaven. But there was no television in my chalet. I checked Paula's: same result. This was not possible. The front desk said that there were only two televisions and that these rooms were taken. I was sorry, but an England World Cup match was too important to miss. This was unacceptable: it was in the contract and Budget Man would have to sort it out. Not wishing to seem like a prima donna, I insisted that the people with the TVs were either moved or that they allowed me to use their room for the duration of the match. They moved. Budget Man was appalled – but not so appalled that he shied away from asking if the crew could all come to my room and watch the match. I agreed. I then proceeded to drink an entire jug of margarita, shout at the referee and fall over. That was it, the final nail in the coffin of bad behaviour, and I was glad we were going home soon.

It was a relief to arrive back in Dubai where we had an eight-hour stopover. Tiger was tired and hungry and the thought of getting arrested because Paula insisted on breastfeeding was making me nervous. The budget would have to allow us a room in the airport hotel. It was granted, though not with the best of grace. There was a knock at the door. It was Budget Man who had come to inform us that he and the crew would be eating in the dining room and he would prefer that we did not join them. I couldn't believe what I was hearing, and Paula was terribly wounded by his attitude, so I rang the front desk and asked for a rather more extensive menu than room service generally allowed. A bottle of vintage champagne and some beluga caviar certainly went some way to alleviate the insult. The problem was, the portions of caviar might have been expensive but they weren't big enough; as we were still hungry we thought it would be churlish not to order some more. It was delicious.

That was lunch sorted. Now we had a few hours to peruse the menu and choose supper. It arrived in the form of more champagne – vintage, of course – and lobster. We ordered a movie and Tiger snored the whole way through it. On leaving the hotel, I could see Budget Man gesticulating and incandescent with rage at the front desk. When he saw me, he almost lunged at me. 'That,' I told him before he had a chance to say anything, 'will be the last time you ever tell me where I can and cannot eat.' He just stood there open-mouthed. Apparently, our bill was nearly £700. It would have been so much easier – and a hell of a lot cheaper – if he had just been nice.

Paula and I loved the Rib Room at the Carlton Towers. It was our favourite place to eat. Michael, the maître d', would keep a table for us and, after what was always a delicious lunch, we would stroll down Sloane Street and window-shop. I could never resist the shoes in Prada or the clothes in Gucci. As for Paula, there was nothing in Dolce & Gabbana that she didn't want.

Many good times were had at the Carlton Towers, and many interesting lunches. Paula and I had a wonderful lunch there with Sarah Ferguson, the Duchess of York. I personally was not too keen on the meeting, but then I of all people should know better than to believe everything you read in the press. She was absolutely charming and very funny. I am so glad she turned her life around. She invited Paula and the girls to come and visit her and her daughters at Christmas. I wish she had gone. I was in Australia at the time, and I arranged a driver for her, but she got to the drive of the house and lost her bottle. She made the driver turn around and take her home. I don't know if Sarah ever knew this; maybe she thought Paula didn't bother to make the effort. I wish I had been there as I would have told her she had nothing to be frightened of. It's a shame. I think the Duchess could have been a positive influence.

There were a few other regulars, one of whom was Terry Venables and another Bernie Ecclestone, head of Formula 1. One day, Bernie was there with two handsome Italian-looking men and he invited us for a drink after lunch. Paula, who was just a hopeless flirt, blossomed in their company. The conversation got round to an incident that had occurred on the pit wall at some recent Grand Prix. Paula, knowing nothing about sport, didn't realise that the pit wall was not an actual wall. Bernie said that he hadn't actually seen the incident. 'I'm not surprised,' Paula said. 'It's because you're so short. Anyway, how high was the wall?'

There was a stunned silence and Bernie started to laugh – much to my relief.

'Don't worry, Bernie,' she added, 'I'm a midget too, but if you were to stand on all your money you'd be the tallest person in the room. Me, I'd still be the same height.'

He roared with laughter. An intelligent, articulate man who had great sense of humour, it was a pleasure to have met him.

My favourite, though, was Terry, and we had many a pleasant time spent in his company. He is a charming man to be around, has a great sense of humour and mischief and is a man who loves his football. What more could a girl ask for? I tried to get Paula to take an interest in football but her knowledge of the sport only extended to her friend Ian Wright's marvellous physique. I insisted she widen her horizons and, as she spent an inordinate amount of time sleeping in my bed, she had no choice but on occasion to watch *Match of the Day*. Before Michael died, and when I was single, my Saturday nights were meticulously planned. I would go the entire day without listening to the radio or watching television, enabling me to watch *Match of the Day* without knowing the results. It made it much more exciting. It was always the same routine. I would order a pizza, eat a tub of H‰agan Dazs ice cream and have a wank. An ideal evening really. After Michael died and Paula started coming over, I had to stop the wanking part, which was a real shame. We might have been friends, but we weren't that close!

Paula's interest in football increased, but only in terms of which players she wanted to meet, and that had more to do with their good looks and thighs rather than any footballing skills they might have possessed. One evening, I found myself watching football on my own with my pizza and my ice cream when the phone rang. It was Paula and she was watching the football at her house. I was impressed. She sounded confused. 'Are you OK?' I asked her.

'Well,' she said, 'you know that bloke that you're always talking to at the Carlton Towers?'

'Do you mean Terry?'

'Yes.'

'What about him?'

'Well, he's on the television.' She sounded utterly surprised. 'Is he famous?'

I couldn't believe it. Was he famous? Was *she* stupid? I hung up on her in disgust!

The next time Paula and I saw Terry, I told him what she had said. 'Don't worry,' he replied, 'I don't know who she is either. Is *she* famous?' At least Terry was joking.

Not all footballers brought us the same amount of joy as Terry. One day, Paula and I went to the recording of one of Chris Evans's shows. Chris was thrilled to see Paula and afterwards we went for a drink at the pub. Vinnie Jones had been on the show and was there with some friends. Paula and I were going to make one of our rare evening outings to the Carlton Towers and the lads said they were all going to go to a little wine bar near there called Motcombs. Would we like to come? It seemed like a good plan so off we all headed.

Vinnie bought champagne. I was driving and so only had a glass. Things started getting a little loud and Vinnie's language was deteriorating rapidly. One of the lads had brought a girl from the audience with him, and she asked Vinnie if he was a famous footballer. 'No,' he jokingly replied. 'Me, I'm fucking Hollywood.' At this point an elderly gentleman who was dining with his wife asked Vinnie to keep his voice down and the language cleaner. A few seconds later, all hell broke loose. Vinnie went to hit the guy. He ducked and Vinnie ended up hitting the man's wife. It wasn't hard and it was more of a deflection, but that was not the point. I told Vinnie to apologise immediately and it might be a good idea if he offered to buy them a bottle of champagne or pay for their meal. He wasn't listening and grabbed me with both hands by my sweater and lifted me off the floor and against the wall. He told me rather menacingly to keep out of his business. His friend, a one-time fellow footballer, told Vinnie to put me down. He did, and then promptly headbutted his mate.

Blood started pouring from the large gash above his forehead and I thought this was an opportune moment for Paula and me to leave. I grabbed her by the hand and made my way to the door. The girl from the audience was on the phone telling somebody that she was in a wine bar in Knightsbridge, and Paula Yates was there with Vinnie Jones and a fight had broken out. Presuming she was speaking to the press, I grabbed the phone out of her hand and threw it out on to the street – the poor girl might only have been talking to her mother. We got in the car and I decided to drive by the bar to see if things had calmed down. On the pavement stood Vinnie's friend, blood still pouring from his head. His shirt was stained scarlet, and I stopped and told him to get in and I would take him to the hospital. He did not want to go – I later learned that Vinnie was on probation for doing something similar and he didn't want to get his friend into trouble. Nevertheless, he needed treatment. I decided that Paula's house was the best bet. My children were at home and hers were at Bob's. He took off his shirt and pressed it against the wound to try and stem the flow of blood. We got to Paula's and I took him into the bathroom. He lay on the floor and I straddled him. Poor boy – he'd never met either of us before and here he was stripped to the waist with some woman breathing down heavily on him and another one slightly pissed in the background. I washed the cut and told him I thought it needed stitches. He suggested that maybe Vaseline would stop it. Paula was sent to search for some, and a few minutes later she appeared in the doorway. 'I don't have any,' she announced with a completely straight face. 'Will KY Jelly do instead?'

The two of us couldn't stop laughing; Paula didn't see the joke at all.

The next day, of course, the press printed a story that bore no resemblance to what actually happened. According to them, Paula had behaved badly and someone had called her a drunken slut, or words to that effect. Vinnie had defended her honour and was a complete gentleman. Normally he is, but, as the expression goes, 'When the drinks are in, the wits are out.' We've all done it – it's just that not all of us headbutt our friends.

After one of our many lunches at the Carlton Towers, Paula and I strolled down Sloane Street in search of a birthday present for a friend of ours. It was a beautiful sunny day and I was wearing a sleeveless summer dress. A £50 Gucci condom-holder later, we made our way back to the car and went to pick the girls up from school. We got home and I parked outside my house and let everyone in. Indy and Tiger wanted ice creams so I made my way to the shop which was just around the corner. As is always the case, I went in for one thing and came out with twenty. I was carrying two bags of shopping when my boyfriend pulled up and parked by the house. He took the bags off me and, as we made our way through the gate, two men jumped us from behind. One put his arms around my boyfriend, pinning his arms to his side, and put a knife against his throat. He bundled him into the garden.

I was almost at the front door when I heard the commotion behind me. I looked round to see a man lunging at me. I knew he was coming for my watch. It was a gold Cartier. In a split second, I placed my hand over my watch, folded my arms, crouched down with my head against the door and waited. Then it came: a foot in my back and a fist in the side of my head. I could feel something warm trickling down my face. It was blood. I was banging my head against the front door.

My daughter Montana opened the door. She had her school shoes in her hand – for once in her life she had taken them off as she should have done – and she started hitting the guy on the head with them as he continued to hit me and try to snatch my watch off my wrist. There was no way I was going to give it to him – at this stage, I didn't realise he had a knife.

I screamed at Monty to shut the door and call the police. I was worried that he might push his way into the house, and the children were in there. She did as she was told and, as the door shut, I felt one of the gold links on the bracelet give way and break. As soon as he had it, he was off. I was so angry that I ran after him, shouting to my boyfriend to get in the car and chase them. I saw them jump into a parked car and I heard one of them shout, 'Hurry up, she's coming.' The car started and they drove off in the direction of Kensington High Street. I was in hot pursuit and, as I turned the corner, I saw them stuck in traffic. I caught up with them and – don't ask me how – I put my fist through the car window and took the keys out of the ignition. I then started to run back home. The men got out of the car and looked totally lost. I thought they were going to come after me but they were in shock. As I ran back home, I realised how much pain I was in and I collapsed.

My boyfriend saw the men standing rather bemused in the street with an immobilised car. He pulled up and one of them had the cheek to say he didn't want any more trouble. Trouble? He should have thought about that before pulling a knife and kicking the shit out of me. He wanted the car keys and told my boyfriend he would swap the watch for his keys. My boyfriend agreed, even though he didn't have them – I did! The mugger threw the watch through the open car window and my boyfriend drove off. They obviously didn't know the area because they could have escaped into Holland Park – they were only about ten feet from the entrance. The sound of police sirens were heard in the distance and they started to run.

Meanwhile, back at the house, Montana was on the phone to the emergency services. The woman on the phone had asked her what had happened and she said her mother was being attacked by two men. They asked her if I was hurt and she said yes. They told her not to open the door but to go to the window and tell them what was going on. By the time she got to the window, I was halfway down the street. Monty then started crying and told the operator that I had been kidnapped. 'They've taken my mum,' she cried, 'they've taken my mum!'

The police arrived en masse and told me off for being so foolish as to chase after the muggers; but they also said they were secretly impressed. So was I, actually – I was just so angry that they would try to steal something that was mine right on my doorstep. Anyway, they came off worst: not only had they not got my watch, but also I had stolen their car and they were about to be arrested. That's what I call a bad day.

I took my watch into Cartier and the estimate to repair the bracelet was just over £800, which was more than their car was worth, so maybe it was me who was going to have the worst day after all. The manager appeared and he asked if I was the girl from the newspaper article – he could tell by the cuts and bruises on my face and arms. 'Yes,' I replied.

'In that case,' he told me, 'it will be a pleasure for Cartier to fix it for you free of charge.'

It was a very frightening experience, and I wouldn't recommend trying my method of crime-fighting to anyone. It affected me for a very long time and I remember my neighbour coming up to me the next day as I was getting something out of the boot of my car. He put his hand on my shoulder and he gave me such a fright that I burst into tears. He only wanted to see if I was OK.

Somewhere in all the madness, Paula went house-hunting. The rented house was fine but she longed for somewhere she could call home, put some roots down and have some stability for the children. She was adamant that she wanted a mews house. God knows why, they are usually quite pokey, but I think it was the dolls' house childishness of them that appealed to her.

She rang me saying she thought she had found the perfect house and would I come and look at it with her. It was just off Notting Hill, a stone's throw from where she was already living and very close to me. We arrived at the property, where entry was achieved through secure gates and there was a large courtyard in the mews. My initial reaction was that Paula was right, this was perfect. It was private, secluded and safe. The children could play outside with no danger of Tiger straying on to the road. They would be away from the prying eyes of the paparazzi.

There seemed to be only four other properties in the mews and none of them was on top of one another. We looked around the house, which had a little turret and was very quirky. I knew Paula was in love with the place. The smallness of the rooms disturbed me but she was sure.

As we stood viewing the outside of the building, one of the neighbours appeared. He came over to us and what was to follow totally shocked me. He said that he had heard that Paula was interested in buying the property and he wanted her to know that she was not welcome in the mews, that nobody there wanted her. I stood there, stunned, as did Paula. Tears started to roll down her cheeks but still he did not stop. He continued to abuse her, saying it was a respectable place to live and that the likes of her were not welcome, that no one wanted the press intruding on their privacy and he suggested that this should be the last time she visited the place, because he for one would make her stay in that house unbearable.

I couldn't believe it and Paula was shocked at the vitriolic way he laid into her. Funnily enough, she never bought the place but I was glad to read some time later that her would-have-been neighbour Jonathan King had been arrested for abusing young boys and had now swapped his beautiful mews house for a cell provided by Her Majesty. No wonder he didn't want any press interest in his respectable life.

The expression 'let he who is without sin cast the first stone' comes to mind and luckily most people do not go around abusing children. If I were him, I would never have crawled out from under that stone. I was thrilled the day he got convicted. It wasn't just Her Majesty's pleasure Jonathan King was being held at, it was mine as well.

Paula's trips to the Priory and her battle with depression and binge drinking continued. She was given large doses of medicines that I felt didn't really help and would be disastrous if mixed with alcohol. We once spent a weekend at my mother's house in Henley and we took a friend's boat on to the river. It really upset her because we had done the same the previous summer with Michael and had had a glorious day: he had serenaded the people walking their dogs on the bank with his rather marvellous opera singing. We walked back to my mother's house and I could see Paula had that 'I need a drink' look about her. It was OK, though: my mother was teetotal and there was no alcohol in the house.

When we got back, Paula decided to have a sleep, so I left her there and went to get some food to cook. When I returned, I thought she seemed a little woozy. Maybe alcohol, maybe Valium. She insisted, as she always did, that she was fine. We had been to the market in the morning and the girls had bought hair slides and ribbons and were now doing each other's hair in the garden. I cooked us all lunch and, as it was nearly time to leave, we collected our belongings. As Paula made her way to the car, I could hear a clinking sound of glass coming from her straw beach bag. Not only that, there was a small trickle of liquid dripping out of the bottom of it. On closer inspection – and much to Paula's horror – I discovered a bottle of champagne. She also had a whole collection of silver picture frames. 'What are you doing with my mother's silver?' I asked her.

She tried to insist that they were not my mother's and that she had bought them that morning at the market. 'Really?' I asked. 'In that case, why do they contain pictures of me and my brother and sisters?

Paula was very contrite and we put them back. My mother laughed about it and it became a family joke: Paula's coming, hide the family silver!

One of the things that I found the hardest thing to deal with was her obsessive-compulsive behaviour. After Michael's death, it manifested itself in a big way. I was on a plane with her once and the movie *As Good As It Gets* was showing. Jack Nicholson portrays a character with obsessive-compulsive disorder, and Paula could not watch it. I thought it was funny; she thought it was about her life. It brought home to me the seriousness of her condition. She had a key to my house so that, if, in the middle of the night, she felt sad or lonely, she could jump into a taxi and climb into bed with me without waking the rest of the house. I am not the tidiest person in the world and, if I woke up and saw that all my shoes had been straightened under my dresser, I knew that Paula was in the bed. She could not sleep if everything wasn't just so. Some days she would clean my house for hours.

Apparently, this obsessiveness was made worse by her anti-depressants. Another side-effect was weight gain. Personally, I can't help thinking that, if you start out depressed and then get fat, it's going to depress you even more. The other bizarre thing I learned was that if you take Prozac for any length of time it is possible that you can't have an orgasm. So, if you were depressed before, and now you're fat and can't come, you're going to be downright manic!

One night, Paula stayed over and she did her normal thing of wandering around and reading magazines. She had always suffered from insomnia, but now it was quite acute. The only cure seemed to be stronger and stronger doses of sleeping pills. On the way back from the bathroom, she spotted my fish tank. She got back into bed but the thought of those fish in that green water was upsetting her equilibrium so much that she knew she would be unable to sleep until it was clean. So, at four o'clock in the morning, she got up and cleaned it out. The next day, I woke up and saw a piece of material at the bottom of the tank. I fished it out to find it was a pair of my knickers. As I didn't have any J-cloths, she had used my underwear instead!

There is one thing that I feel compelled to write about and I know Paula would not forgive me if I didn't mention it. It concerns the allegations that Paula trapped Michael into their relationship by getting pregnant. This is completely untrue and caused Paula an enormous amount of pain. It also caused Michael a great deal of anguish. The truth is that Paula was having fertility treatment and the two of them would make regular trips together to the clinic. A newspaper printed a story saying that Michael had never wanted the baby. He was furious. 'I've spent the last year wanking into a plastic cup,' he fumed. 'Trust me, no one wanted that baby more than I did.' He didn't want Tiger to grow up believing something like that, so before leaving on tour he gave a sworn affidavit to Anthony Burton refuting the article and leaving instructions to sue. He died shortly afterwards and Paula took on the battle for him. He was adamant that the press would not get away with such scurrilous lies, and Paula felt the same. She sued and she won, but it did not stop another publication repeating the initial story. The threat of legal proceedings seemed to make no difference. Paula sold newspapers.

Andy Coulson, who was then at the *Sun*, told me that, if he had a story about Princess Diana or Paula on the front page, the paper was guaranteed to sell. I remember a fabulous meeting with Paula and Diana on the Fulham Road in a lovely jeweller's there called Butler & Wilson. Michael was buying Paula a vintage bag and they had not had the best week of press coverage, having made the front pages nearly every day. Diana came up to Paula and asked her how she was. 'I know this is awful,' she said, 'but every time I see you on the front page of the papers I think to myself, Thank God for that, I've got the day off!'

# PART FOUR

# CHAPTER TEN

Time is a great healer, and Paula seemed to improve. Maybe that is why I found it so hard to deal with the emptiness I felt after her death and, though I don't think about her all the time now, she is never far away. Little things remind me of her. I cannot see a cherry-blossom tree without thinking of her, and of course whenever I go to the Carlton Towers I always raise a glass to her and wish her well. I went there recently with Fifi. Terry Venables was there and we all had a drink, told stories about happier days and laughed at some of the things Paula had said and done.

The practicalities that I had to deal with after her death distracted me temporarily. There were two houses to be cleared and sold for a start. I was not looking forward to that job. It would have been impossible to hire a professional team to clear them as there were too many personal things that had to be sorted. I arrived at the St Luke's Mews house and just stood for a few minutes in the living room. It was cold and I switched the heating on. I saw something move in the kitchen and it made me jump. I quietly opened the front door again so that if it was an intruder I could run straight out on to the street, or at least if I screamed someone would be able to hear me. I edged my way to the kitchen and the intruder jumped off the table and ran right past me. I leaped back, my heart in my mouth, and then I started to laugh. It was only a cat. It had climbed in through the open ventilation window in the kitchen. It was feral and had probably been abandoned, so I was glad it had found a home. It was nice to think that the house was not completely empty.

It took a couple of days for the heating to kick in and for the place to warm up. I started in Paula's bedroom and sorted out her clothes and letters. I boxed up items that the children were going to have now, and separated other things that should be kept for when they were older. It was strange rooting through Paula's possessions, and even though she had appointed me to do the task I still felt I was intruding. For a very long time, I was unable to read the notebook she wrote in while she was staying at the Priory. It just seemed too personal, and the anguish in it was heartbreaking. I was going to be here forever if I insisted on reminiscing over each item and reading every scrap of paper that Paula had written on. I was going to have to be more ruthless.

The next day I woke up itching; it was driving me insane. I pulled back the duvet and my legs were covered in bites. I must have had about thirty of them. What the hell were they? Where had they come from? My boyfriend said they looked like fleabites. How was this possible? I didn't own any pets. Then I realised it must have been the cat – and to think I had even bothered to feed it in the hope I might tame it. I went back to Paula's and within seconds of being in the house the fleas were on my clothes. I shut the door and called the council who came and fumigated the place. Apparently, the cat had spread them throughout the house and fleas can lie dormant for months. I had turned the heating on and they came to life.

As no one could enter the house for a few days, I decided to head to Hastings with Bob and see what we could sort out with Paula's other house. I organised a van and a driver who I knew could be trusted and we started moving things. Bob organised the removal of some furniture and placed it in storage. Soon both properties were cleared of cherished personal items. The estate agents had advised me not to strip the houses completely bare, as it was easier to sell a place that looked lived in and homely. I took their advice, and both houses went on the market.

The very next day, I got a phone call from a tabloid journalist, with whom I had had a run-in before. She asked me about Paula's will and the sale of her house. I asked her not to write anything that would upset the children, and if she needed to fill column inches then I would give her a few quotes to keep her happy. She said that if she needed anything at all she would call. I thanked her for that. The following day, I got another phone call, this time from the estate agent who was selling the St Luke's Mews property. He sounded very distressed. It appeared that a couple had booked a viewing with the intention of buying the house. This was just an elaborate faÁade to gain entry to the property. Once inside, the journalist had distracted the agent downstairs and her 'husband' had run upstairs with a camera hidden under his jacket and taken a photo of the bed that Paula had died on. He also took other photographs. I was horrified and immediately called Anthony Burton, who in turn called the newspaper's legal department.

The pictures were never printed, but they did publish an appalling article lecturing me on the morality of selling Paula's house with all of Michael's possessions in it, along with the children's things. This was not so: the house was sold empty. Not one solitary possession was sold with it. She made some mention of a doll's house being callously left behind. Tiger had two doll's houses, and she had them with her. This one was broken and it was left there to be cleared when the house was sold so that the room looked lived in. I was furious. I sued them and I won damages which they settled out of court. They also had to print an apology to me in the paper. I rang the newspaper but the journalist refused to take my call. I thought she might like to apologise to me in person, but she didn't have the balls. It might come as no surprise to learn that Agar also wrote in her book that I sold Paula's house with all of Paula and Michael's possessions included. The difference was I wouldn't accept an apology from her.

Life moves on, and you can't be bitter and angry forever. I had my own children to care for, and Tiger was at a huge transition period. She had a whole new life opening up in front of her, and it was the duty of all those people who loved her and her parents to make sure that the right thing was done by her. It was very hard for me not to be involved in Tiger's life on a daily basis as I had been, but she had her own family now, and I knew I must allow her that. My girls loved Tiger as if she was their sister, though, and were glad that she still stayed with us once a week. I supported Bob throughout the court procedures in his attempt to keep Tiger with her sisters and with him. It was the only correct thing to do. I spoke to Kell, Michael's father, and at first, quite understandably, he did not agree. He soon saw sense and I was glad he added his weight to Tiger's cause.

Around this time I had a very bizarre phone call from Hughie Green's son, Christopher, asking me if I would support his claim for custody of Tiger. Had he completely lost his mind? Why on earth would he think I would even contemplate such a suggestion? He had only met the child a very few times and, once, when she was very young, at his sister's house when Paula and the two Green children had sat for a photo shoot for a newspaper. What made him think that Tiger going to a place she did not know (he lived in Canada) with a person she did not know could possibly be the right thing to do? He was furious. He also went on to write a book and, surprise, surprise, was very derogatory about me. Mind you, if the worst thing he could say was that I had filthy hair, he'd have to do better if he was trying to offend me. I wondered how his sister Linda had turned out to be such beautiful person; it didn't seem to be a family trait.

The court ruled, and sense prevailed. Tiger was not to be shipped off to Australia to live with Michael's half-sister Tina, whom she hardly knew; she was to stay with Bob and her sisters. I was delighted, and I looked forward to Wednesdays when I would pick her up from school and she would stay the night. She and Indy played Barbie for hours, and sometimes I would imagine that Paula was going to come through the door and suggest we get a Chinese.

I knew this situation could not continue forever, though. I really wanted to move. I needed to be able to breathe and I felt claustrophobic in London; with the events of the previous few years, I felt we all needed a break and a fresh start. I had put the house-hunting on hold when Paula died, but now I wanted to move lock, stock and barrel. My boyfriend and I were looking to buy somewhere in the West Country. Property prices were reasonable and you got a lot more for your money. One afternoon in Devon, I saw it: the house that we were going to buy. It was perfect, an old farmhouse with seven bedrooms and fifty acres. The owners seemed nice enough, but that didn't matter – I was only buying their house. It would have been impossible to imagine then the problems and heartache that would come to pass over time. Some were of my own making; others, it seemed, I would inherit from the vendors.

The original part of the house dated from the fifteenth century. It had beautifully proportioned rooms with exposed beams and lovely fireplaces throughout. It was off the beaten track and approached down a wooded lane with grass growing in the middle. I don't know why that amused me so much; maybe it was the contrast with years of city life. In the spring, the wood was a blanket of bluebells and it was a joy just going home. At the bottom of the lane, you went over a little bridge and across the stream which ran through our land. The lane at the side of the house divided our land from my neighbours' farm. They had shared access across this to allow entry to their buildings. I introduced myself to the neighbours, Lyn (the husband) and Chrissie (the wife) Williams, who made us very welcome. Thanks to them, we soon became acquainted with the neighbourhood and the local drinking establishments such as the Rackenford Social Club. Run by a wonderful Cornishman called Pixie, and a great favourite with all my house guests, it cost £5 a year membership and, though it would make a working men's club up north look like the Ritz, a nicer bunch of people would be hard to find. It has the best-stocked bar in Devon and the margaritas, made to my own recipe, are as good as any you would find in Mexico.

As I pulled up outside the house in Holland Park, I felt a slight wave of sadness. It was a scary step moving from a city that had been my home for the previous twenty years. We were moving in three days and there was still a lot to be done. My boyfriend's son, Shane, and an old friend, Max, had come from Canada to help us move and to stay with us for a few months. There was a lot of decorating to be done when we got there. As we unloaded more boxes and bubble wrap from the car, a newsflash come over the radio. An aeroplane had crashed into the World Trade Center. It was 11 September 2001. Everyone remembers where they were when they heard the news. Me, I was standing on Addison Crescent, W14.

We sat transfixed in front of the television. Sky News beamed live pictures across the world and, when the second plane hit, we knew then the first could not have been a freak accident. We were speechless. The next day I couldn't pack fast enough and was so thrilled to be getting my children away from London. Three days later, we were in our new house. Surrounded by boxes, we sat on the floor, ate fish and chips and drank champagne. I was going to be so happy here. I would live here until I died and the children could bury me down by the stream. I had my life all planned out.

The arrangement with my boyfriend was that I paid the deposit on the house and he would then pay the mortgage. It seemed fair and, as we had spent a good few years together, now seemed like the right time for more commitment and trust. It was going to be strange not having money of my own, but look what I was getting in return: a beautiful house with wonderful grounds. Giving up Prada shoes was hardly going to be a sacrifice, and wellies were much more suited to my environment now in any case. For a brief moment in time, I was blissfully happy. It did not stay like that for long.

The first few months were spent ripping up floors and painting over twenty-year-old Laura Ashley wallpaper. Montana was thriving at Blundells school and Indiana was under the watchful eye of Nick Folland, the headmaster of St Aubyns. All I needed was a horse and my life would be complete. As my boyfriend spent rather a lot of time working either in London or America, I felt it unfair to ask for one, especially when there was so much work to be done on the house. But on one of his trips away I received a phone call from a lady in the village. She informed me that there was a very nice thoroughbred available. Was I interested in it? There was no harm in looking and it was a good excuse to put the paintbrushes away. On arrival, I learned that the owner of the horse had fallen off it and injured her shoulder. She had gone into the local town to get treatment, and it transpired that the person treating her did rather more than just rub her shoulder. When her husband of eighteen years learned of the affair, he took the horse into town, tied it to the railings on the pavement outside the place where she was being treated and said, 'If you want to fuck my wife, you can muck out her bloody horse as well.' The horse was taken to a friend but she could not keep it; if I could take it that day, I could have it for nothing. It was checked over by the vet, and was in my field the next day. Now my life was really complete.

I was surprised how little I missed London; whenever I went, I was desperate to get home. It was dirty, smelly and far too crowded. I couldn't stand the traffic and I always got the obligatory parking tickets. I did miss Nicky Clarke's – even in the country a girl needs a decent hairdresser – but the problem was soon solved when I discovered Mel and her husband Anton at Toni and Guy in Exeter. Finally, a good blow-dry was only a drive away. I didn't mind wearing wellies all day if my hair looked good.

Then one day my boyfriend decided to leave me. It really was as straightforward as that. He didn't like the country, he didn't like the mud and more to the point I don't think he liked me any more. I was devastated. We had bought a house together, a house that I could now not afford on my own. I had moved my entire life and family and we were supposed to live happily ever after. What the hell had gone wrong? I spent a lot of time feeling very sorry for myself, and very scared. He had even given me money for Tampax; where the hell was I supposed to find the money for the mortgage?

Shortly after my boyfriend's departure, I received a telephone call from Ken Regan. He left a message on my mobile which I ignored. In fact, he left quite a few and I ignored them all. I had enough problems at the moment.

I first met Regan in the late nineties at the fifth-floor bar at Harvey Nichols. I was there with a girlfriend and he was with a man I knew. Regan was about five foot ten and about seventeen stone. He was fat, sweaty and definitely not shaggable. In fact, I thought he was gay. He dyed his hair – off-putting enough in a man at the best of times, but to make things worse his was a peculiar shade of orange. We had a few drinks that evening and I didn't see him again for a while.

Regan, it seems, was smitten with me from the first moment he met me, and perhaps I should have seen his behaviour then as a warning sign for the future. In all the years I knew him, I never saw him with a woman. In fact, the only thing you could be sure to see him with was a briefcase full of cash, and he loved to show it to anyone willing to look at it. I found out later that he told people I was his girlfriend, which I never was and thankfully never have been.

Regan would send me gifts. One was a £4,000 solid-gold Cartier watch. I told him I could not accept it from him, but he said I had to have it to replace the one I had lost. At the time it was a very nice gesture and I accepted it. He later tried to give me diamonds, which I refused, and he invited me to a Grand Prix. He had pit passes and had hired a helicopter which he claimed had cost him over £5,000. I didn't go. He was forever inviting me to his house in the country, or out for lunch. I never went. Surely he would soon get the hint. He inundated my children with presents and would say to me, 'I've won the children over, now I've just got to work on the mother.' He used to tell me that my ex-husband was a fool to let me go; he would never have been so stupid. I could have whatever I wanted, he told me, he knew how to keep a lady. His attentions were getting to be rather irritating; when I found out that he was referring to me as his girlfriend, I found it worrying. I was not scared of him, but he was creepy. He made my flesh crawl. There was no way in a million years you could have him climbing all over you; that would be totally repulsive.

Some years ago, he rang me and asked if he could take me for lunch. I said no – it was my daughter's birthday and I was taking her to the Virgin Megastore so that she could buy a Nintendo games console. I met Paula and her girls for lunch and we all had pizza. Monty and I then walked down the King's Road to get her present. When I got there, Regan was waiting outside. He had already bought the gift for her. I felt like he was stalking us and I remember telling Paula that I had not told him which branch we were going to – he had obviously guessed that the King's Road branch was nearest my house – and I certainly didn't tell him what time I would be going. I had no idea how long he had waited there.

Shortly after this, I was shopping in Sainsbury's on the Cromwell Road when a friend of mine rang and asked me if I had seen the front cover of the *Evening Standard*. I bought a copy, but it still did not make sense. Some men had been arrested in London and one of them had fled the scene and run over a policewoman while making his escape. He was stopped a few miles later after a high-speed police chase. It was Regan. I never followed his arrest or his trial and even today I am unsure exactly what he was arrested for. I do know now from the police that it was in connection with the importation of a Class A drug which I believe was heroin. There were numerous other charges laid against him, one of which was passport fraud. He only served four years in jail. Having committed the crime, he did not have the bottle to serve the time: he turned supergrass in order to get a reduced sentence.

I didn't hear from him again until Paula died, when he sent me a card to say he was sorry to have heard the news. I never replied. Then, out of the blue, in about August 2002, over four years since I had last seen or spoken to him, he started calling again and leaving messages. He said he had a friend who was starting a magazine and I might be able to help her. Still I ignored the calls, so he left me a rather irate message saying how rude I was not to have returned them and that he had given my number to his friend and she would contact me directly.

We met in the Carlton Towers but there was not really a lot I could do to help her. My main problem was trying to keep myself afloat financially. I certainly did not want to invest in a business. Regan was nothing if not persistent, and eventually I spoke to him. I explained my situation and said my level of rudeness was only surpassed by the level of stress I felt I was under. He seemed genuinely concerned and said he had a proposition to put to me concerning some land that he owned. It might help me, he said. It had to be worth a shot. My bank balance was eighty pence overdrawn, and I was praying that I could sell the house before it was taken away from me. Things, surely, could only get better.

How many times can a girl be wrong in her life? It's difficult to keep count with me.

I spent an inordinate amount of time in tears. Some days I wondered if I had enough petrol in the car to get my children to school; at other times I wondered how we would eat. I desperately needed a job and I desperately had to sell the house that I so loved. Lyn and Chris used to invite me over for cocktails, and three martinis later the world seemed a little better. The worry about how I was going to get my children to school, though, was soon surpassed by the fact that I might not be able to keep them there. I had no money to pay the fees. I rode my horse a lot and thought about what I could have done to make my boyfriend stay. Stupidly, I had thought we were in love, but obviously I was wrong.

I could not ignore the inevitable. In late August, the house was valued in readiness to be sold. Showing estate agents around a house you don't want to sell is heartbreaking. To make it worse, we had ripped out one of the bathrooms and now I couldn't afford to put it back, never mind replace it. With half the furniture gone, we also looked like we were camping. Nothing boded well and it was reflected in the price. The other thing that would apparently put potential buyers off was the state of the lane in the winter. Spring, it seemed, was the ideal time to sell my house. That was a lot of mortgage payments away, so I rang the bank.

Having remortgaged the property, I replaced the bathroom and took the ceiling down in the dining room before it fell down of its own accord. I painted every room in the house and hung curtains. Now all I needed was furniture – some sofas and a couple of beds were essential. Regan suggested I use his furniture that was in storage. He had lost his house when he went to jail but had managed to keep his furniture. He gave me the number of the removal company and said that I could ring them up and get them to deliver the container directly to the house. I was a little wary at first, but I was hardly in a position to be fussy. On calling to make an appointment to have the furniture delivered, I learned there was a large outstanding bill. I told Regan and he sounded furious. 'The company should have been paid it,' he fumed. 'I'll speak to Mike.'

I had no idea who Mike was, but as he sounded like an employee I was thankful that I wasn't in his shoes as I was sure he was in for a few fierce words.

For months, Regan had wanted to show me his 'empire' and eventually I went to the offices of CIBA Freight Ltd near Heathrow to meet him. He showed me their facilities and introduced me to the staff. Then I met Mike – Mike Parr – who worked there and he talked me through the logistics of how everything operated: they would collect goods from Customs, store them in the huge drive-in fridges and cold rooms, load them on to trucks and then deliver them. Everything seemed perfectly above board; how could I have known that Regan was spinning me a tissue of lies? Maybe he had lied to Mike as well and told him that I might be a potential buyer of the business, hence the deference granted me that day.

The furniture was eventually delivered on 23 October 2002. It certainly helped, but most of it was modern and totally unsuitable for an old house. I put a lot of it in the barn. Adam and Ryan, the young sons of Webbie, a friend of mine, came to help me and Regan unload the stuff, and I made them all bacon sandwiches. It was the only meal Regan ever had in my house, and he had waited a long time to get his feet under my table. He spent most of the time moaning about how old the house was and that he could never live somewhere like this, which was a good job because he was never going to get the chance. He liked new houses; they were 'cleaner'. Regan told me that he could help me 'improve' my house and that I should start on the drive. He suggested that I take up my circular gravel drive and replace it with paving stones. He could do this for me and he would bring me photographs to show me the kind of work that could be done. A herring-bone pattern, perhaps? I just nodded but said nothing. When he then went on to say that I should remove the surrounding hedgerow and a couple of the trees to replace them with a brick wall and 'nice electric gates', I had to say something. Had he completely lost his mind? Electric gates? This was a farmhouse, not a footballer's pad in Essex. Definitely not. I liked it just the way it was. I had to walk away before either I told him to shut up or I laughed.

It was time to feed the horses. While the others were still

carrying furniture, Regan followed me to the gate with a bucket of oats. He did not want to go any further because of the mud. What is it with boys and mud? I thought. As if it wasn't bad enough that I had to listen to him moan about the state of the house, now I was going to have to listen to him moan about my land. From the top of my land to the stream at the bottom, there is a 350-foot elevation which, though steep, means it is ideal shooting land and it drains well, except for the piece of land by the gate which forms a plateau. When it rains, that area can get very waterlogged. To make it worse, the cattle and the horses would churn up the area and some days if you weren't careful you could lose a wellie.

Moan, moan, moan; I wasn't even listening. Regan said I should build a drainage ditch there. That was the first and last time it was ever mentioned. I never agreed, I certainly never asked him to dig on my land and he never said he was going to.

Webbie, chief know-it-all and maker-of-anything in the valley, came to collect his sons and to check my hydraulic ram that pumped the water from the spring to the reservoir and then onwards to the house. I had been without water for days and we had been using the well in the dining room. It was an interesting experience pulling buckets of water up to flush the loos, but the novelty was wearing a little thin. Regan, wishing to appear knowledgeable on the subject, started to tell Webbie how to fix the pipe that had rusted and sheared. He suggested that the new pipe be made out of stainless steel to prevent it rusting. He would have one made and asked Webbie to let him have the dimensions. Webbie thought it should be cast iron to withstand the pressure and the constant movement. Me? I didn't care. I had listened to enough shit for one day. I just wanted a couple of sofas, some water and some peace and quiet.

After that day, Regan would ring me often. Half the time he had nothing to say and was just enquiring how I was; at other times he rang to tell me the progress on 'the land situation'. He told me that he owned land and a house near Hatton Cross tube station and he wanted help in getting it developed. He was getting the papers and the deeds together and suggested that he take me to view the land as I would have a better idea of the scale of the project. 'It's better than sex,' he told me. 'When you see it, you'll want to play with yourself.'

Well, one thing was sure – I'd rather do that than play with him. From anyone else, I would have found the comment amusing, but from him it just made me cringe.

Regan started finding any excuse to come to my house, and quite a few times he turned up unannounced. I really hated that. One day, the phone had been ringing all morning – literally every ten minutes. I knew it would be Regan, so I didn't bother to answer it. Two hours later, as I was sitting in the kitchen with some friends, there was a bang on the window. It was him. He shouted that he had been trying to call me and I had not answered. I went absolutely ballistic. I had a huge stand-up row with him and told him to 'get the fuck out of my house'. He apologised and said he would not do it again. He lied, but luckily I had witnesses who could verify the fact that Regan came to my house uninvited and most definitely unwanted on a number of occasions.

Whenever he turned up unannounced and I was by myself, I would pretend that I was just leaving the house and could not stop. I would listen to whatever it was he wanted to ask me, then I would get into my car, go up the road, round the village and come back home by a different route. Just because there was a possibility that I might be working for him, it didn't mean we had to be buddies. I could never understand why he would drive an hour and a half to be turned away at the door. Half the time I didn't even make him a cup of tea!

On one of these occasions, he brought a form and said he wanted help filling it in – he really did use any excuse. The form he had was an application for employment with Railtrack. He needed a job for his parole conditions and he asked me to help him answer the questions. He then told me that he had gathered all the papers relating to his land and he wanted me to come and see it. He had already shown me a video of it which made very uninteresting viewing – ten acres of wasteland a stone's throw from the airport. Even so, anyone could see the potential. I asked him why he did not just go to work at CIBA instead of messing around with the railways. He explained that his parole conditions forbade him from owning a company, so he couldn't be seen to be involved with CIBA. It seemed fair enough to me, and I didn't really care to ask any more.

He then said that he would like to bring me into the company to help get new clients and organise the place better. Regan insisted that, when he had been at CIBA full time, the place ran like clockwork and no one was allowed to run up credit; in the four years that he had been away, it had gone to the dogs. He said he wanted to get the place back in shape, and that he wanted me to shake up the office. Regan said he would make me the managing director and pay me £52,000 per annum for which I had to work two days a week. Then he changed his mind. He hated the idea of me suffering in any way and so he would pay me £72,000 per annum for the same number of days.

I needed a job and I needed it now. This would certainly go a long way to alleviating what was becoming a very desperate situation. It would enable me to keep my house and my children at school. Time was running out and I wasn't sure how much longer I could stretch the patience of the bank. He also told me that he thought the land would be worth up to £40 million if the planning authorities approved it for development. For this he would pay me 1 per cent of the deal. Once I was in my position at work, he wanted me to employ him officially. He had an HGV licence and he suggested he could be employed to drive one of the trucks. This would satisfy his parole requirements and he would be on site to run his company 'as it should be run'. It seemed a reasonable request. I remember saying to friends that I had got a new job and it was too good to be true. Well, at least I got one thing right: it really was too good to be true.

I took the file on the land at Hatton Cross to a friend of mine who specialised in commercial law. He said that he was not the person to speak to and that what I wanted was a planning expert. He put me in touch with someone he knew. I spoke to Jane Gleeson at RPS Planning on a couple of occasions and we arranged to meet so that she could explain to me in greater detail her views on the possibility of getting the use changed from agricultural land to development. Christmas was coming up and we arranged to meet in the New Year. I was being taken away over Christmas and was really looking forward to the break. My children were with their father, and Christmas in a house with no children is no fun. Regan seemed to think that, if his parole did not forbid him from travelling, then he would come on holiday with me. He absolutely could not have done and I told him so. He seemed to be quite offended and around this time I received a letter from him. It was the first of many.

Regan wrote that I was like a drug. The more he saw or spoke to me, he said, the more he wanted to see me, though he knew it was both useless and one-sided. He told me that he wouldn't see me if there was pressure and added that he'd felt that way for years. I thought I had thrown all of his letters away but months later I found two in the bottom of my desk. I was relieved that they proved that the man was obsessed and his feelings were not reciprocated. In one of the letters he said he hoped that I found what I was looking for and that he wanted to find a way of getting what he wanted. Little did I know just how far he would go.

I hoped that, by the time I came back from holiday, things would have calmed down. Unfortunately, I was not in a position where I could refuse the job – it was a lot of money for basically nothing. I knew nothing about bonded warehouses, haulage or airline freight, but I would have to learn. I justified it to myself by saying that many people work for bosses they can't stand, and at least it was only two days a week and I was earning good money.

January did not see the start of my employment. Regan kept telling me to be patient and that things were not ready to proceed yet. I didn't understand – either I had the job or I didn't. The office was there so why couldn't I go and get on with it? I was getting worried. I didn't want to put the house on the market if I didn't have to, but I wasn't in a position to be strung along or just live in hope. I decided to wait and see what transpired from my meeting with Jane Gleeson before I re-evaluated the situation.

Regan kept up the phone calls and I wondered if I was being taken for a fool. It had been nearly three months now since talk of the job had started. He rang me to say that he wished to attend the meeting with Jane. Their offices were in the City of London and we met there.

The meeting with Jane Gleeson did not go well. She had said that it would probably be ten to twenty years before the council would allow a change of usage on the land. Regan did not believe her; he thought that with the building of the new Terminal 5 at Heathrow there would be a huge demand for more development sites. He believed that it would be five years and, as he said, £40 million was worth waiting for.

After the meeting, he said we were going to go to 'the office' and talk to the accountant. Regan wanted him to explain to me the turnover of the company and see where the shortfalls were occurring and how we could go about rectifying the situation. He told me to follow him in my car, which I did, but when we passed the motorway junction for CIBA I tried calling him to find out where we were going. His phone was engaged. I was getting a bad feeling. Why was he playing games?

We continued down the M4 and came off at the Windsor turn-off. I know the area well as my father had lived there for years. I tried calling Regan but the phone was still constantly engaged. When I eventually got through, he said he thought it would be nicer to meet in a hotel. A hotel? I certainly wasn't going to have a meeting with him or anybody else in a hotel room. What if it was a scam so he could try to sleep with me? A lot of weird thoughts went through my head. But I had come this far so I had to see it out. I was relieved that I had taken my own car and not gone on the train, otherwise I really would be stuck with Regan.

When we got to the Runnymede Hotel, Regan called the office. He told me that the accountant couldn't make it but Mike Parr was on his way.

Mike Parr arrived. He was much shorter and fatter than I had remembered. He reminded me of a pit bull terrier and was not my kind of person at all.

Regan asked if they could have a few quiet words so I left the lounge area and sat at the bar. They were sitting around a table a few yards away from me. When I rejoined them, Regan was saying to Parr, 'Maybe it's time that he realised it's me.' He suggested that Parr went back and spoke to 'Neil' and told him 'the offer' was from him.

Regan explained to me that he was going to buy Neil out of the company and that Parr was brokering the deal for him, but up until that point Neil did not know the offer was coming from Regan. I was confused. Who was Neil?

Neil was the English name of Amarjit Chohan. Apparently, everybody called him that, as it was easier than saying Amarjit. I presumed he was an investor in the company, and by the way Parr and Regan were talking I didn't get the impression that they liked each other. Maybe Neil would not have sold his interest in the company to Regan if he had originally known it was him. Parr said he was desperate to sell and that he would go back and speak to him. Before he left, Regan asked Parr if he would stay on at the company and he agreed, saying he wanted the same salary he was on now and 10 per cent of the profits. Regan accepted this and they shook hands.

After Parr left, we walked to my car and Regan told me that Parr was a fool and that he would have given him 10 per cent of the whole company. 'That's the problem with people,' he said. 'They never grab what they can.'

As I drove down the motorway back to Devon, I wondered what had been achieved. I still didn't have a job to go to, and a promise of one was not going to pay the bills. Regan rang me and said he was going to have a meeting with Neil. 'Be patient,' he said, 'we're nearly there.'

A week later, on Thursday, 30 January, I received an email from Regan to Neil Chohan that I had been copied in on. It stated that Regan was 'pleased to get out of the closet today and discuss my interest in taking over CIBA'. It also said that Regan had 'no problem with you [Neil] remaining on'. He was adamant that he 'would want Belinda Brewin to be Managing Director and take over credit control'. It was something, but I had almost had enough of empty promises. I would give it until the end of February. Regan arrived at my house four days later. He had rung in the morning saying it was important that he spoke to me. I had no water again, and that was all we seemed to speak about. When he left, I wondered why he had yet again bothered to drive so far for nothing. I certainly did not feel any more secure about my position, though he did say that I would be starting work next week and that he would backdate my pay. I still wasn't convinced. In fact, until I had the cheque in my hand, I wouldn't believe a word he said. He could see I was fed up; I didn't bother hiding it now.

Another week passed and Regan called to say that everything had been finalised and he needed me to sign a contract of employment. He arrived at my house with three copies. On one page, it set out the terms of my employment and the amount I would be paid. It had been knocked up, amateurishly, on a computer. It wasn't even on headed paper. I signed all three copies. The accountant and he were the other signatories; when everyone had signed, he would give me my copy. He then told me he needed me to be in London for the following two days. He would arrange for me to stay near the office at the Runnymede Hotel. I still wasn't holding my breath, but at least there was progress.

I arrived at the Runnymede Hotel on the morning of 12 February and tried to check in. There was a problem with the booking so I rang CIBA. Regan said the room had already been paid for and he passed me to Mike Parr who said that he had booked the room personally and there should not be a problem. I handed him to the person on reception. It was soon sorted. In my room, I changed into a black Dolce & Gabbana suit with a bright-yellow silk lining. It was a good look for an important meeting. I had spoken to my ex-boyfriend that morning and he suggested that, as I was coming to London, we could have dinner together. I agreed.

The meeting at CIBA was at two o'clock. I arrived on time and I was introduced to Neil Chohan by Regan. He was a tall man with a big frame and he was wearing blue tracksuit bottoms. So much for my suit, I thought. He had dark hair, a moustache and a nice friendly face. From whatever little you can glean of a person on first meeting them, he seemed like a nice enough man. Regan, Neil and I went into the boardroom. Neil handed three sheets of paper to both Regan and me. It was an analysis of turnover, balance and debts of the company. The turnover exceeded £3.5 million and what was owed was a little over £1 million. Regan asked Neil if he was happy with the sum of £3 million for his interest in the company. Neil said he was and Regan enquired how he would like it paid. Did he want part of it paid in cash?

Regan then explained that his backers wanted to move quickly and this deal needed to be done and sorted in the next few days. Neil agreed to the timescale. It was also agreed that I would be the managing director and that papers would be signed that day confirming this.

Neil said he wanted to stay on at the company. I thought this was strange. Why, if you had just earned £3 million, would you then want to work as the warehouse manager, which was what he was suggesting doing? If it was me, I would be at home riding my horse. He explained saying he would 'get bored doing nothing' and that he 'wasn't a greedy man' but he had to 'keep active'.

Regan, on the other hand, *was* a greedy man. He had very different plans for Neil.

We all shook hands and, with the meeting finished, we went back to the main office. The shipments were controlled from there, and above it was the accountant's office. Neil introduced me to all the staff, including Mike Parr, as the new managing director. The accountant, Lionel De Silva, had the necessary forms to be signed. I signed Company House Form 228a which appointed me a director, and he welcomed me to the company. Neil was also to sign the document and, additionally, Form 228b relinquishing his directorship.

Regan and Neil had other business to discuss and there was no need for me to stay. I left the two of them there and I never saw Neil Chohan again. In fact, hardly anyone saw him again.

My ex-boyfriend and I met at the Carlton Towers. I don't know why, but it was nice to see him again. I should have just slapped him for what he had done to me and turned on my heels, but I didn't. Instead, after eating, we ended up getting a room in the hotel where we drank an extremely expensive bottle of champagne and part of a bottle of Hennessy XO brandy.

The next day I was very hungover. I had this awful feeling that Regan would have been ringing the Runnymede Hotel since some ungodly hour wanting to have breakfast with me. He had probably just turned up there to find that I was nowhere to be seen. I got dressed in what was now a very creased suit and I made my way back to the other hotel. I prayed Regan was not there and that I would not have to go to CIBA until later. I needed a shower, some clean clothes and a sleep.

Once at the Runnymede, I rang Regan. He said he was busy and that I should call him in a while and we would meet at CIBA. Later, he rang and changed the plan. He told me to go into the office and get a cheque from the accountant. I didn't feel comfortable with this arrangement. Even though I was the managing director, I felt it was a little vulgar on my first day in the job to be demanding money. I rang him back and told him so. He seemed preoccupied and said he would try to meet me there and he would speak to Lionel.

I ordered a club sandwich, had a shower and tried to sleep. I was beginning to feel better. I spoke to my ex and we arranged to meet later that afternoon. He was picking up his brand new Audi RS6 – a beast of a car – and I said I wanted to go with him. I spoke to Regan again and he said he would not be able to make it and I should just go to the office and pick up the cheque. When I arrived at CIBA, the accountant was not there – Thursdays were his day off. Surely Regan knew that – what was he playing at now? I rang him back and he told me not to worry. He would be there tomorrow and it would all be sorted out. 'Have a bit of faith,' he said. I was almost out of faith, but what was another twenty-four hours in this epic test of my patience.

I spent the afternoon at the Audi showroom in Mayfair waiting for the car to arrive. When it was finally delivered, it looked fantastic and sounded even better. We went across the road and had champagne in the Ritz to celebrate. We then went back to our room at the Carlton Towers. The next morning was Friday – Valentine's Day – and we decided to spend the weekend together. My ex was going to come to Devon, although the harmony was not to last long – as soon as we arrived there, we had a row and he drove straight home.

Before heading south, though, I had to go to the office. I arrived at CIBA refreshed and well rested. I went upstairs to find Lionel and Regan waiting for me. Regan wished me happy Valentine's Day; I thought he was going to try and kiss me so I walked past him and shook Lionel's hand. We arranged that I would not be in work until the following Wednesday. I signed some forms for the bank giving me the authority to sign company cheques. In case any bills needed paying when I was not there, I signed ten blank cheques and gave them to the accountant. I also, under instruction from Regan, wrote out a cheque for my wages for January. He had kept his promise and backdated my pay.

It was as if a huge weight had been lifted from my shoulders. I would go to the bank, pay in my cheque and then go home to my children. Life was going to be so much better.

# CHAPTER ELEVEN

I recognised the handwriting on the envelope: it was Regan's. It had to be a Valentine's card, and I hoped it was in better taste than the underwear he had sent me a few months previously and which I had returned to the shop. Personally, I think it is weird to buy underwear for someone you are not intimate with, and the idea of Regan looking at lingerie on the Internet, imagining me wearing it, is downright perverted. It wasn't just a pair of knickers – there were boxes of the stuff. Hundreds of pounds wasted. And apart from the fact that he had bought it, which would prevent me from ever wearing it, most of it was purple and green – really not my colours.

The Valentine's card didn't fare much better. The sad thing was he rang me to ask if I had received it, and then told me it had taken two hours to choose. It would have been funny if he hadn't been serious. Apparently, he couldn't find a card with the right sentiments in it till this one. It read:

> Valentine when I'm with you
> You always make me smile
> But when we're far apart
> You know I miss you all the while.
> If only you could be with me

Each hour of every day
I know my life would be complete
In every single way.

He then wrote in the card, 'I hope you give me the chance to show you. I love you.' Not in a million years, mate. Once, when he had come to my house unannounced, he tried to put his arms around me and I could feel him getting an erection. I thought I was going to throw up.  I wondered how I would cope with having to work with him, but two days a week I could manage and he would be out in the truck on deliveries for most of that time. I wasn't in a position to be fussy. I also knew I had only got the job so that he could guarantee seeing me twice a week. It wouldn't be forever and I had been through worse things in my life, or so I naively thought at the time. Regan rang me over the weekend and said that the following week he wanted me to work three days instead of two. I had already aired my concerns about not being able to work in the school holidays. My children, in theory, spent half the holidays with their father and it would be fine to work then, but I wanted to spend my half at home. Regan agreed that I could do four days some weeks and take time off in the holidays. The children were flexi-boarders so that would fit in well during term-time. As the Easter holidays were approaching, I thought I may as well do as much work as I could early on. Regan wouldn't even be there. He was going to be in Birmingham – at least that's what he told me.

When Regan realised that it was my children's half-term, he seemed very concerned about what arrangements had been made to care for them while I was in London. I told him that they were staying with friends and then going to stay with their father, and he seemed happy with that. Now I realise that he just wanted to be sure that they would not be staying in the house.

That weekend, Neil Chohan, his wife Nancy, her mother and their two young children disappeared.

I drove to London on Tuesday night. I felt a little unwell but put it down to tiredness and the drive. I arrived for my first day at work early. I wasn't sure what I was supposed to be doing and had to find myself something to do apart from check my emails. I also didn't want to ask anyone what to do – I was supposed to be in charge here. There was a huge amount of invoices outstanding, some by months, so that seemed a good place to start. I got a list of bad debtors and started making calls. It seemed that some of them were unaware that they owed money; others said they had paid Neil in cash. I asked them to send me a copy of their receipt and I would amend our records. By lunchtime I was feeling hot and dizzy. I tried to ignore it; I couldn't go sick on my first day. I was glad when the day was over.

I went for a drink with my ex-boyfriend who was horrified that I was working for Regan. They had never met but he had heard about him, and what he had heard he didn't like. We had another row and I left in a huff. I called my friend Hoot and his girlfriend Debs, and they said I could stay with them. Halfway there, it began to rain. I realised I'd left my coat behind, but I could always get it the next day. Now I needed to go to sleep. I felt ill.

I woke on Thursday morning feeling even worse. I had flu. I got out of bed without waking anyone and headed off to get my car which I had left on a meter the night before. I was late and the bloody car was clamped. This was not going to be my day. To make matters worse, I didn't have my phone with me – I had left it on Hoot and Deb's sofa bed. I went to a phone box and called Regan to explain what had happened and that I would be late getting to the office. I didn't mention the fact that I felt unwell as I didn't want to sound like I was whinging. It didn't matter – he was still in Birmingham and, as everyone else had been doing their jobs long before I arrived yesterday, they certainly weren't going to be looking to me for guidance. I rang Hoot and Debs but they were still asleep. The clampers were going to be ages, so I woke my ex who was staying in a neighbouring hotel, lay down on the bed and waited for my car to be mobilised. The longer I waited, the worse I felt. I wasn't fit to go to work and I certainly didn't want to be stuck in London unable to drive home. As soon as my car was unclamped, I was going to Devon. I left London just before midday.

Meanwhile, down in Devon, things were afoot. My neighbour Chrissie woke as normal for a day's work. That's odd, she thought.

There were unfamiliar cars going up the lane. The lane only goes to my house, her house and Keith Luxton's farm, but even he uses a different route. The road is not a shortcut to anywhere and the only reason you would use that lane is to visit one of us or if you were lost. Whenever I went away, Chrissie would feed my cats for me and check on the house. When a digger appeared on my land, she could just see the top of it over the hedge from her living-room window; she thought that most peculiar and rang my mobile. She left a message telling me that there were some men digging up my field and to ring her back. She knew it was my first few days at work and she assumed I didn't reply because I was busy. She presumed that I knew all about it and that it was all right.

My phone was still stuck in Hoot and Deb's sofa bed. When I finally got through to Hoot, he said I hadn't left my phone there, which I thought was strange. In fact, they found it a few weeks later. The journey home seemed to go on forever and I was so relieved when I finally crossed my stream, knowing the comfort of my own bed was just round the corner. As I pulled into the drive, I couldn't believe it. There was Regan's car. It was parked in front of the French windows to my study. For one awful moment, I thought Regan had spoken to Mike Parr, whom I had informed that I would not be coming in to the office as I was sick, and I thought that he had taken this opportunity to come and play nurse. Then I saw another car. What the hell was going on here?

I got out of the car and, in the small grassy track that divides my two fields, I could see a man whom I vaguely recognised. He was no more than thirty feet from where I stood. I couldn't remember his name – I had met him years before with Regan. I asked him what the bloody hell was going on. He said that they were building a drainage ditch for me and that Regan wanted to surprise me. Surprise me? I was absolutely livid. I said I had forgotten his name and he told me it was Bill. 'Well, Bill,' I said. 'Tell Regan I am very surprised and really not amused.'

Then I saw the other man. He looked like the Missing Link. He was sitting in a swing-shovel digger looking rather proudly over his work – a bloody great big hole in my field. I was so angry I could barely speak. It wasn't so much that I didn't want or even need a drainage ditch; it was that no one had bothered to ask me, and to make matters worse it was Regan doing it. How dare he think that he could do what he liked on my property? What would he do next? I would go away on holiday and come back to a paved drive, no trees and electric gates. My only relief was that Regan himself was not there.

Then I noticed the track. It is only a few yards long and I tip grass cuttings at the end of it and have the occasional bonfire when I'm burning leaves, but now it looked as if there had been a forest fire. The small dry stone walls that lined each side were burned black and completely exposed. All the hedgerow was charred and the fire must have been of such ferocity that it had burned a fence post so badly it would have to be replaced. The trees were scorched and the trunks badly damaged by the fire. What the hell had they been burning here? Now I was apoplectic with rage. My language reached new heights, and, when Bill told me that Regan had burned a sofa of his, I simply couldn't believe it. He had brought a sofa all the way from Salisbury to Devon to burn it on my land. Why the hell didn't he just take it to the municipal dump like everybody else?

Before I could say anything else, a huge truck drove up the lane. The driver got out and said there were two other trucks on their way. Where should he dump the stone he was delivering? I thought I was having a bad dream. Now they were going to turn my field into a car park. I couldn't take any more. I went into the house. I came out a little while later to find huge mounds of stone in the track and inside the field. Bill was in the ditch directing the Missing Link where to dig. How big does a drainage ditch have to be? This was massive – at least six feet deep, fourteen feet long and four feet wide.

I asked Bill when Regan was arriving. I had a few choice words for him. He said it wouldn't be today, as it was getting dark. He then started complaining that they had spent all day waiting for the stone to be delivered and it was late, but they would be finished tomorrow. Bill went on to say that Regan had thought I would be thrilled with what they were doing and that he had spent a lot of money – apparently, there was nearly a thousand pounds' worth of stone there alone. But it was just the principle of it. It was my land, not his. I quite liked the mud, and I certainly preferred it to the abomination that I was eventually left with.

Eventually, I heard the cars leave. I spent the rest of the evening curled up under a duvet in front of the television with a roaring fire and a Lemsip. I spoke to Chrissie and told her how cross I was. She said she thought it was odd that I had never mentioned I was having any work done, but as I had not replied to her message she presumed I just forgot to tell her. She had witnessed Regan come uninvited to my house on a couple of occasions and I had shown her some of the letters that he had sent me. We both just laughed at the nerve of the man.

The next day saw all three of them arrive: the digger-driver, Bill and Regan. I felt worse than I had done the day before and, as I opened the front door and walked across the drive, Regan came to meet me. He said that if I was ill I should stay inside by the fire. He said that Bill had told him how angry I was and that he couldn't believe I could be so ungrateful. He was trying to do something nice for me. 'It's the principle of the thing,' I told him. 'You don't just go around digging up someone else's property. If you want to surprise them, send some bloody flowers.'

'You'll be pleased with it when it's done,' he said, before adding that he wouldn't be doing anything like this again, especially with my attitude. He acted as if I had slighted his good nature.

I spent the rest of the day shivering under a duvet. The only times I saw Regan were when he knocked on the door and asked if he could make tea. I could see the gate to the field from my house, but the ditch and the men were hidden from view behind the beech hedgerow. They left late in the afternoon, having covered the entire plateau, not just the ditch area, with sixty tonnes of stone. I absolutely hated it.

There wasn't a soul in a ten-mile radius who didn't hear me complain about my field. Once I had recovered, I did nothing but moan. One evening, over a margarita at the Rackenford, I was talking to my friend Trevor Downing about the car park I now had in my field. Trevor, who is a retired gamekeeper, came to have a look at it and said he thought it was 'a proper job'. Maybe I was being a bit of a madam after all. I spoke to Webbie and asked him if he could remove the stone. After much discussion, it was decided to leave it, let the cattle work it into the ground and then in the spring put topsoil on it and reseed. That at least might make it look better. I hated lying in bed and looking out of the window on to a pile of stones. That was not what I had moved to the country for.

I soon settled into a routine at work. I would drive to London on a Tuesday evening, stay overnight and be at work by eight the next morning. I was usually the first in the office and that suited me fine. It also meant that I could leave around four o'clock which was a godsend on Thursdays when I headed home because it meant I could avoid the rush-hour traffic. Regan spent most of his time out delivering or trying to collect money that was owed to the company. Some mornings he would sit the other side of my desk and have a cup of tea. Usually, before he sat down, he would pat his belly and say 'Fourteen stone ten' or 'Fourteen stone eight', depending on what weight he was that morning. He had lost three stone since I had first met him, but I never understood why he insisted on this ridiculous ritual. Did he think when he mentioned the magic figure, whatever that was, I would be unable to control my urges and would hurl myself across the desk at him? His weight bore no relevance to my distaste for him sexually – that was inherent in my being.

I never once went for a drink with Regan after work, or had any real contact with him. I think he found this rather frustrating. He wanted to rent a house in Windsor for me so that I had somewhere to stay when I was at work. He also wanted to stay there himself so that he did not have to drive from Salisbury every day. He just wanted to be able to control my life and I had to avoid that happening at all costs. I sidestepped these conversations and said I was quite happy staying where I was.

I did my job and, slowly but surely, and with the help of Lionel and one of the employees called Mr Singh, I began to understand what I was supposed to be doing and how the computer data related to the pieces of paper that filled the boxes lining the office wall. While trying to collect the monies owed to CIBA, it was often necessary to look back at this information to see if the bill had been calculated correctly and exactly what had been shipped. It was hard to collate all the necessary information, especially as there were two years' worth of boxes missing. Where had they gone? I searched high and low but with no luck. I asked Regan where they would be and he told me that Neil had obviously not wanted them to be found because of his various nefarious dealings. I had no reason to doubt Regan, and it was the start of a sea of misinformation that he spread throughout the company and among the employees. He led us all on a merry dance.

Around this period, a handwritten letter arrived from Neil. Regan sat at the table in the middle of the office and showed it to me, Lionel, Mike Parr and Mr Singh. I had never seen Neil's handwriting before, but Lionel confirmed that it was his. It stated that he had been stupid and greedy and that he had become involved with some nasty characters who were now after him. He was sorry to have left the company in the state that it was in, but he had no choice in the matter and hoped that things would improve under the guidance of Regan and me. The letter was posted from France.

Regan would go to France fortnightly to do a cigarette run. He would stock up on whatever he could and sell it on at a profit. He always maintained to me that he bought the stuff on the ferry and never got off the boat as it would violate his parole conditions. I only have his word on that. But with hindsight I am sure it would not be difficult to find some kindly person to post a letter for you.

It was not the first or the last letter that Neil wrote to certain employees. In one such letter, Neil wrote to Mike Parr stating that he still had 'major problems' and was being chased for £3 million – the same figure that Regan was going to buy his interest in CIBA for. He also stated that he would 'soon have travel documents for the whole family, and then we will travel to my country. I will stay here for a few weeks and then we will leave for home, where we will be totally safe.' He also stated that he was too afraid to talk to anyone at the moment, which explained the total lack of communication. 'I really regret my actions that have put me in this mess and don't know how to get out of it,' he wrote. 'I won't

go back to prison again, not for anything. I hated it so much.'
That sentence was exactly what Regan had said to me on
numerous occasions.

Neil stated that he had problems with investigations involving
PAYE and US Customs. Regan implied he was implicated in some
drug ring. Neil also wrote that 'Nancy [his wife] is driving me
crazy, always trying to call her family, it's too dangerous at
present.' The letter was drawn up, yet again, amateurishly on a
computer and then signed at the bottom by Neil Chohan. It would
seem that there is no doubt that it is his signature, but the
positioning of it in relation to the script is indicative of a blank
sheet of paper being signed before printing.

I can't remember the exact date that the police first started making
enquiries about Neil, but it was around March 2003. Certain
people at the office had been contacted and asked about his
whereabouts, and it seems that all roads led to me. I was sitting at
my desk when a call was put through from PC Honey (I jest not!).
She asked me what I knew about Neil. I explained that there was
a large amount of money unaccounted for, which was true, and
that certain monies that should have gone through the business
account had been put through his personal account. It seemed
quite logical to me that he had taken his entire family to India and
they were sitting on a beach somewhere.

There was a pause. 'I've heard a slightly different version of
events,' she said. Well, there were so many flying around that I
wasn't surprised. 'I've heard,' she continued, 'that you gave him £3
million in cash and a private jet to leave the country. Now do you
see our difficulty?'

Actually, I didn't, and I couldn't help but laugh. Where had I
suddenly got £3 million and a private jet from? 'If I had £3
million,' I explained, 'I certainly wouldn't have given it to Neil and
bought an interest in a haulage company. I would have paid off my
mortgage, gone on holiday and ridden my horse for the rest of my
happy little life. Next question, please.' When I put the phone
down I thought it was totally ludicrous and laughable.

There was concern in the office for Neil – not so much for his personal safety as for all the bad things he must have done to make him run away. There was talk of how much trouble he would be in if the police caught him. A few weeks later, I was called to the boardroom and was greeted by two police officers, one of whom was Detective Inspector Charlie King. As the months went by, I grew to respect him immensely; but on that day I didn't know him from Adam and, as he later observed, my attitude 'stank'. He asked me questions about my meeting with Neil on 12 February, and about the money I had allegedly paid to him. 'I've already given your colleague answers to these questions,' I rather arrogantly told him.

Charlie looked bemused. 'My colleague?' he asked. 'Who was that?'

'PC Honey,' I explained.

She wasn't his colleague. She was from the Missing Persons Bureau. Detective Inspector Charlie King was from the Murder Squad.

I told him I thought Neil was in India. 'You're wasting your time,' I stupidly told him. 'Surely the police have better things to do.'

As he left, he told me that they would be back. He was right about that. In fact, he was right about everything.

Over the next few weeks, the police appeared at the office quite frequently. They mostly came to speak to Regan and Mike Parr. Occasionally, they spoke to other employees but after each visit, Parr and Regan would disappear to the boardroom. I was never privy to their discussions. Regan hated the police. He said that they were making a nuisance of themselves and making it difficult for him to run his business. Police officers arrived and looked at the printers in the office and took away ink samples and print paper. They also took away some shipping documents. I still thought that they were wasting their time. My only contact with them was to make the tea. That was how I first met Detective Inspector Andy Rowell and Detective Sergeant Tony Bishop.

At the same time as the police were making their enquiries, Barclays Bank was concerned about the level of CIBA's overdraft.

They wanted to terminate the arrangement that they had with Neil, which would have rendered the company unable to trade. If the airlines could not be paid, they would withdraw their services and we would all be out of work. Immediate action was necessary. Regan, Parr, Lionel and I went to the High Court to see if we could legally continue to trade until Neil showed up. Lionel produced the Company House papers I had signed and verified that Neil had wished me to be the managing director, and the courts granted us a stay of execution. This would keep the bank happy and everyone would remain employed.

Regan asked if I would swear an affidavit stating that Parr was present at the meeting I had with Neil on 12 February, which he was not. They said that I was also to say that, when Regan had offered Neil £3 million, he had turned to Parr and said, 'Don't worry, I won't forget your half.' Neil had never said this. How could he have done when Parr was not there? I categorically refused.

Parr scurried off to see a lawyer, most likely finding my salary an outrage. He continually said that the company could not afford to pay me, but as far as I was concerned that was not his decision. Regan said that Parr would 'do as he's told, unless he wants a slap'.

Parr spent a fair amount of time out of the office at his solicitors, and made applications to the court with regard to the company. Lionel seemed upset by this, and Regan was downright furious.

The Easter holidays were soon upon us. The girls spent some time with their father and I continued to work. The atmosphere in the office was becoming strained. The police made more frequent visits, and Regan became more irritated by them. I just kept my head own, did my work, took my cheque and went home. Regan expressed his concern for Neil to me, saying he hoped that he had not come to any harm. I insisted that someone in the office must know where Neil was, and they should tell the police. Their concern was for the two children. They weren't interested in whether or not Neil had paid his taxes – they were the Murder Squad, not the Inland Revenue. I thought it was a terrible waste of police time. However, I didn't have the information the police had. Why would I? I'm no detective.

The police were first alerted to Neil's disappearance by Onka, the brother of his wife Nancy, who lived in New Zealand. He did not believe that his sister would have gone to India without telling him. He called the police but did not get the response he wanted – maybe they had gone on holiday, they suggested. Onka insisted they were missing and got in touch with Neil and Nancy's local MP. With a bit of pressure, the police investigation got under way.

According to Regan, the police had searched the family home and found flight numbers and information pertaining to their departure to India. No one at CIBA had any reason then to doubt what Regan said. For a start, he spoke to the police more than anyone else, so he was bound to have a better idea of how the investigation was going. But information soon came to light that indicated this might be more than just a routine missing-persons inquiry. It was not until a few weeks later that any of us, including Regan, was aware of what they knew.

My children returned from their father's and I was happy to be leaving work for a couple of weeks. With any luck, things would have sorted themselves out on my return. I was at home when the phone rang. It was Detective Inspector Andy Rowell. He wanted to show me some documents. I informed him that I would not be in London for a couple of weeks. Could it wait till then? He said not. He would come to Devon to see me. He would let me know when he could arrange this.

Regan said that, if it was him, he wouldn't let them anywhere near where he lived. Andy rang a few days later and said he wanted to come on Thursday, 17 April at 10 a.m. The day after that was Good Friday, which was followed by the Easter bank holiday weekend, and he wanted to do it before then. I, of course, agreed.

Around the same period of time, another truck full of stone was delivered. Once more, I wasn't home, but Webbie's son, who was doing some work in the garden, signed for it and had it dumped along the track on the same spot that Bill had lit the bonfire. On my return, I immediately rang Regan to ask why there was a need for more stone. He said he had no idea why it had been delivered. He knew the guy at the quarry and perhaps it was a bit left over from another load. Regan said not to worry and that we could use it to do the lane by the stables. I said that was OK, but was adamant that there was to be no more stone put on the field.

The truth was that Regan *had* ordered the stone. He knew precisely what he wanted it for, and it certainly wasn't for the lane by the stables.

When I informed Regan that the police were definitely coming to my house, he said I should refuse to allow them on to my property. He suggested I meet them somewhere else and that they would only make my life difficult. Personally, I saw no problem with them coming to my home – it was a damn sight more convenient than going to a police station. But on the morning in question, Andy rang to tell me that he would not be coming to see me. He told me that they had new information that might mean he wouldn't have to come at all. If the situation changed, he would ring me after the weekend, but in the meantime he hoped I would have a happy Easter. I wished him the same.

Regan also rang me. I told him that the police were no longer coming to the house, but he seemed to know this already. Apparently, the police knew where Neil was and they were going to arrest him that afternoon for wasting police time and other related tax offences. I managed to gather later that Regan had rung the police and said that Neil had contacted him and asked him to get him a passport and bring him £20,000. Neil was in Wales. So, instead of coming to me, the police hotfooted it to Wales.

On the day that the police should have arrived, a digger was delivered to my home. Webbie and his son Ryan were on their way to my house to cut down a beech tree in the back garden. As they were coming down the lane they met a lady who was lost. She had a swing-shovel digger on a trailer. Webbie knew her – she was from JB Plant Hire – and she was trying to find out where I lived. He showed her where to go and she unloaded the digger on to my drive. I had no prior knowledge of its delivery, nor did I know that Regan and his motley crew were about to arrive, but that was nothing new. As stone had been delivered earlier that week, I assumed the digger was to be used to level the lane.

Saturday brought an influx of visitors. Webbie came to finish off logging up the beech, and Steve Cotter, who worked for Chris and Lyn, was parked in the lane by my stables and was working in their garden. When Regan arrived with Bill and the Missing Link, we all commented on what a mess they were going to make this time. My field had become a standing joke.

Regan arrived in a white transit van. It was locally hired – the phone number on the side gave that away. He parked it in my drive and Bill and the Missing Link parked next to him. In the back of the van were three or four short sections of brown piping. They had slits cut along the circumference, apparently for drainage. In hindsight there was no reason for the van – they could have fitted on the back seat of a car – but it never occurred to me that they needed the space not for what they were delivering, but for what they were taking away. Regan explained that they had not put enough piping in the ditch and before they looked at the lane they would rectify their earlier mistake. I was exasperated by the entire ordeal and just let them get on with it. Webbie, Steve, Lyn and I all commented on how useless they were and there were lots of comments about city boys trying to tell the locals how to do their job. The lads all agreed that they could have done a better job of building the ditch. For a start, they had used far too much stone and had laid it far too thick. It must have been a foot deep, and it made opening the gate very difficult.

Regan, Bill and the Missing Link took their cars on to the field and parked them at an angle about fifty feet from the hedge. It would block the view of anyone who might be on the other side of the valley. The chances of anyone seeing them were almost nil as there were no houses there. The digger was taken into the field and Regan realised it was short on fuel. That was probably due to the fact that I had allowed Chris and Lyn to borrow it the day before as they were in the process of laying their patio and they too needed to run some wavy coil pipe for drainage through their garden and into the field. Regan left to get more diesel which he managed to scrounge from a farm nearby. On his return, I made them tea.

Regan then reversed the van right up to the open gate and parked it with the rear doors open so that any view I might have had of the field from the house was blocked. In fact, with the van in position and the hedge being where it was, they had covered all the angles and almost formed a circle around the ditch.

I was in the kitchen making the girls some food when Regan knocked on the window. I went out into the courtyard and he asked me if I had any overalls they could use. I went into the workshop and took down three blue all-in-one overalls that I had bought months before. We had got them to do the decorating in, and they had never been used outside. My daughter Monty made them more tea, and I went over to the field to see if they needed anything in town. As I approached, Regan came out of the field, took me by the arm and walked me down the lane to the stables. I didn't think about it until later, but he obviously did not want me to see what they were doing. He started telling me what they were going to do in the lane and how the stone would improve my access and prevent a mud bath in the winter. Stone in the lane I could handle. I was happy with that.

When I returned from the supermarket, the ditch had been completely dug out. Bill was again standing in it, this time in my borrowed blue overalls. The brown piping was lying on the field and they were about to lay it. I left them to it. The ditch was filled and the stone, which had been scraped to one side, was laid back across the top. The van was no longer open or blocking the gate. Regan asked for a wheelbarrow and he loaded up some of the newly delivered stone into it and tipped it across the top of the now slightly mucky gravel. It would soon look as good as new.

When they had finished I offered them tea but Regan refused. He said he had things to do and needed to get on. I thought it odd that he had passed up an opportunity to spend time with me, but I wasn't bothered. He looked very intense as he climbed into the van and drove off. The others followed swiftly.

They never did the lane, but then they never had any intention of doing it. They had got what they came for.

# CHAPTER TWELVE

I recognised his voice straight away. It seemed the only people who ever rang me these days were the police. It was Andy Rowell. He needed to come and see me after all. The children were starting school in two days, I had friends staying and to make matters worse the day he wanted to come was my younger daughter's birthday. It really wasn't convenient. I said I would be in London on the following Monday and that we could meet then. He said he needed to have a 'frank discussion' with me. I agreed and said I thought the whole situation was very odd indeed. How was it that for weeks no one knew where Neil was, and then all of a sudden he calls Regan? It just didn't make sense. I didn't want to meet in the office, and I certainly didn't want to go to a police station. Being a creature of habit, I suggested the Carlton Towers. Maybe he would buy me lunch. Chance would be a fine thing, but we agreed to meet at around midday.

On Monday, 28 April 2003, I drove to London and was at my desk at eight o'clock. I informed Regan that the police wanted to see me, but not in the office. He didn't seem concerned, although he did say that it would probably be best if I did not mention the fact that he had been on my land. He believed that the police 'have it in for me' and they were 'looking for any excuse' to upset him.

If the police asked, I was to say that he had been in Devon working on my hydraulic ram.

I greeted Andy and the other detective, Graham Thurlow, and suggested we go into the restaurant as it was quieter. I got the feeling that Graham didn't like me much; I don't think I was wrong, either. Andy said I needed to tell him the truth which, as far as I was concerned, I had. I had not given Neil £3 million, I had no idea where he was and I truly believed he and his family were in India.

'If we were to check your bank account,' Andy asked, 'would we find any large sums of money missing?'

'If you check my bank account,' I replied, 'you'll be lucky to find any money at all, let alone find any missing.'

They asked me why Bill had been on my property and I said he had been there with Regan and another man building a drainage ditch. The two detectives glanced at each other. 'What do you mean?' asked Andy. I told them what had happened when I had returned home unexpectedly two months previously. I also informed them that the three men in question had come back last weekend and dug the ditch up again to put in more piping, and that Regan had not wanted me to tell them he had been on my property.

Graham suggested that I was not telling the truth. I asked him if he was implying I was lying. 'No,' he said, 'I just think you're not telling us the whole truth.'

I started to cry. 'You can apologise for that,' I told him. He didn't, and I'm still waiting for the flowers. I suppose he had a job to do, though, and in the grand scheme of things me being upset was totally inconsequential.

They asked me if Regan had said anything about Neil's whereabouts and I related what he had said about him being in Wales and the fact that he was about to be arrested. I also thought it strange that letters came from France – a place Regan went so often – and then all of a sudden Neil was somewhere else; but I couldn't shed any more light on any of it other than to say that it didn't seem right.

Andy and Graham were going to go back to their office to

discuss the drainage ditch. 'There's a chance we might have to go and look at it,' they told me.

'You're welcome to,' I agreed.

Andy would call me later and let me know; he also gave me his mobile number. I half-wished I hadn't told them about it, as they were probably obliged to investigate it now and I hated the idea of wasting any more of their time.

I had to go back to CIBA as, before I had left, Mike Parr and Regan said they wanted to have a meeting with me on my return. Andy suggested that I tell Regan they had been very unpleasant towards me. He was half-right – Graham had not been particularly friendly. I was to tell Regan that they were going to go to my house, rip it apart and make my life hell, unless of course someone could verify where Neil was. I wasn't sure if Andy meant what he said – maybe he was just warning me and that was what they really were going to do. I had nothing to hide, but I could see their patience was running low. These men were no idiots, and they had the law on their side.

When I returned to the office, Regan and Parr were waiting for me. Regan wanted to know what the police had said, so I informed them how horrible they were to me and that they were threatening to go to my house and rip it from top to bottom. I said that someone must know where Neil was, and that this had gone beyond a joke. Regan told me I should just refuse the police entry. What was the point in that? If they wanted to gain entry there was nothing I could do to stop them – they could always get a warrant.

My mobile rang: it was Andy Rowell. I didn't take the call. I couldn't – I was sitting at a table opposite Regan. Parr said that the company was in dire straits and they could no longer afford to employ me or even pay me my last month's salary. Regan told him that was not his decision to make and that, as I had worked, I should be paid. At least we agreed on something. I suggested that I could increase the number of days I worked for the same money. Parr didn't want me in the office at all, and certainly not on my salary.

If the company was not solvent enough to pay me, there seemed no point in demanding the money. I suggested taking a drop in pay to get us through this period and redeeming it later when things improved. This seemed an amicable way to deal with the situation. My phone rang again, and once more it was Andy. I switched it off. Regan insisted that I be paid for the previous month; then he privately told me not to worry – he would speak to Parr who was getting 'far too big for his boots'.

By now it was seven o'clock. I left the two of them in the office and said I would see them in the morning. A few hundred yards from the office, I pulled into a lay-by. I switched on my phone and rang Andy Rowell. I apologised for not taking his calls earlier and explained that I had been with Regan and it had been impossible to talk. I told him that neither Parr nor Regan had come up with any additional information on Neil, and I wasn't sure how much longer I would even be employed. Andy then informed me he was about twenty minutes from my house. They were in Devon. They certainly didn't waste any time.

If the police were going to my property, I definitely wanted to be there; in any case, it was a good excuse not to have to go into the office, especially after the very frosty meeting I had just had there. I told Andy I would be calling CIBA to tell them I wouldn't be in because my presence was required by the police in Devon. I called the office. Parr answered the phone so I told him what was happening, and then I spoke to Regan.

'What are they going to do there?' he asked.

'I've no idea,' I replied.

Five Murder Squad detectives rolled into my drive just as it was getting dark. I was a couple of hours away, somewhere on the M3. They surveyed the site. Andy rang me to say they would be coming back at nine o'clock the next morning. I was still feeling guilty for what I thought would be a pointless exercise and a total waste of public money, all down to me mentioning a stupid drainage ditch. The police, though, had other information that led them to believe it might not be as futile as I thought.

The next morning, at precisely nine o'clock, two cars pulled into my drive. Andy and Graham I knew. Graham managed to grunt a cursory hello, which earned him a cup of tea, but only just. Andy introduced me to Detective Sergeant Tony Bishop,

Detective Sergeant Russell Ferris and Detective Constable Simon Laslett. I voluntarily signed the search-warrant papers giving my permission for the police to do whatever they had to do. They had got a court-approved one in case I refused entry. I wasn't supposed to have seen it, but I did. It allowed the police to enter my property on suspicion that I had kidnapped someone. I found that disturbing. I showed them the location of the ditch under the huge amount of stone and roughly outlined the area and size of it. There were a lot of huddled discussions and Andy said that they would be going to Exeter to co-ordinate things and to get a police helicopter. They needed an aerial view of the land. They would be back later.

The helicopter circled low and several times over the area. I could see a camera and a couple of officers through the open doors on its side. This would get the locals talking – not a lot happens in the Exe Valley, and rarely anything that involves a police helicopter. The speculation that evening in the surrounding drinking establishments would run at the pace of an out-of-control forest fire. Half an hour after the chopper arrived, it disappeared down the valley and out of sight.

I wasn't sure what to do with myself. I checked my horses and one of them had ripped his blanket on some barbed wire. I decided to take it to the saddlery and get it sewn up, more to pass the time than anything else. The children were not expecting me back from London until the following day, Wednesday, so they were safe at school and none the wiser. I was happy with that – there was no point upsetting them when this would soon be over. I put the horse blanket on the front seat of my car and turned right out of my drive and up the lane. It is very rare that I take this route – normally I would go left, but a trip to the saddlery is not an everyday occurrence. As I made my way up the lane, I reached a crossroads and saw a car coming towards me.

It was Regan. He was driving and Bill was in the passenger seat. They pulled up alongside me. I was extremely surprised to see them.

'How are you?' Regan asked.

'Very stressed. The police are all over my property.'

'Well, I've come to give you moral support. Where are you going?'

I pointed to a nearby house and said, lying, that I had to return a horse blanket I had borrowed.

'I need to have a chat with you,' said Regan.

Then it was Bill's turn to speak. 'Why don't you get in the car? We can go into town for a coffee.'

There was no way in the world I was going anywhere with those two. 'I'll just drop the blanket off,' I said. 'I'll be right back. It'll only take me two minutes.'

I drove down the road and, as soon as I was out of sight, I rang Andy Rowell. 'Regan and Bill are in the lane near my house,' I told him. 'They want me to go for a coffee with them.'

'Right,' said Andy. 'I'm going to send two police officers back to the house. Go and see what they want. But, Belinda …'

'What?'

'Don't get in the car with them.'

There was no worry of that. I got out of the car, placed the blanket in the boot so it was out of sight and went back to where they should have been waiting for me. They had gone.

I was quite shaken by the experience. There was no way that they had come to see me; they had come to see what the police were doing. Regan had also approached my house from a different direction to one he had ever used before when he visited. It is a longer route, but it gives a better vantage point to view what was going on at my property. I waited on the side of the road for about ten minutes and then went home. Tony and Russell had arrived and were parked in my drive, out of sight of the entrance. Regan had not come down the lane. They suggested I go back and wait and see if he showed up. An hour later, it was obvious Regan would not be coming back.

Andy Rowell returned and informed me that they were going to start digging the next day. Yet another digger would shortly be delivered to the house. Andy and Graham sat at my kitchen table and asked me if I was sure I had not asked Regan to come to the house. Of course I was sure. I hadn't even spoken to him since my call to the office the previous evening. If Regan had been so concerned about me, he would have waited, but I was the least of his worries. Personally, I think I surprised him: the chances of bumping into me on that section of road were very slim. Both detectives seemed bemused as to why Regan would come to the house, especially as he knew they would be there. I wondered if they thought I was making it up. I bet Graham did. I think he thought that everything that came out of my mouth was a lie. Luckily, while they sat drinking their tea, the phone rang.

It was Regan. I mouthed to Andy that it was him. 'Why didn't you wait for me?' I asked.

'It looked like you had enough problems without me adding to them,' he answered.

'Where are you?'

'On the way back to London.'

Andy was writing a question on a sheet paper for me to ask him. 'Why was Bill with you?'

Regan didn't answer my question. He said he had to go, but that he would call me later. I was relieved. Regan's call proved I hadn't fabricated the entire incident. I dialled 1471 to retrieve the number he had called from, and I read it out to Andy who wrote it down. I had a terrible sinking feeling that this was not going to get better, but tomorrow was another day which would hopefully shed greater light on this whole mystery. I felt totally bewildered and very alone. I wished I had someone to talk to. I was glad the police were with me, as I found them vaguely comforting.

I hardly slept that night. It was partly due to the fact that my mind was imagining all sorts of crazy scenarios – none of which turned out to be as bad as the truth – but mainly because the two officers who were parked right under my bedroom window insisted on turning their car engine on every hour. At around 3 a.m., I got out of bed and went downstairs. I knocked on the car window and asked them if they wanted to come inside. Both Tony and Russell refused: they had to 'protect the site'. It was pitch black and freezing cold. I said I would light a fire in the study and they could open the French windows. It would be the same as sitting in the car but a hell of a lot warmer and a damn sight quieter. They still refused, so I asked them if they could refrain from switching on their engine so frequently, as I felt like I was sleeping on the hard shoulder of the M25.

When they were eventually relieved of sentry duty by Graham and Simon, the Tiverton Hotel must have seemed like five-star luxury. I wondered if they were there to make sure I didn't go anywhere, or to see if Regan would come back. Why would he? He'd already been back once.

Pleasantries between the police and I continued, apart from with Graham. At one stage, he was commenting on the size of the house and the number of bedrooms, and it seemed as if we were actually having a pleasant conversation. Then, out of the blue, he asked, 'Which room is it you said Regan stays in when he's here?' He was trying to trick me. I had never said he stayed there, because he never did. I had already told the police that.

The next morning saw an influx of people arrive. It was a Metropolitan Police investigation, but it fell under the jurisdiction of the Devon and Cornwall Police. This was their dig. A van of what looked like riot police, minus their shields, arrived. They were dressed in black, trousers tucked into their boots – more SAS than Gucci, but it wasn't a bad look. These were the forensic boys. Among others there was a scene-of-crime officer, a pathologist and an archaeologist. It seemed that the circus had come to town. I was concerned about the press being alerted to my house. If this digging came to nothing, then was it not possible for the police to do it and then leave quietly? Andy assured me that they would not be telling the press anything at this stage. I was relieved. It would all be over in a few hours and I could go and collect the children from school. They were expecting me back from work today.

Spencer, a local lad whom the police had hired to operate the digger, arrived. There was just one small problem: where were the keys? A digger with no keys was of no use to anyone. Someone was dispatched to fetch them and I took the opportunity to make tea and bacon sandwiches for those that wanted them. By the end of the week, I thought nothing of making seventeen cups of tea in one sitting, and bacon sandwiches I could make with my eyes shut. Spencer scraped the stone off the ditch in much the same manner as it had been done a week previously by Regan and his crew. Slowly he scraped away the earth. 'Stop!' someone shouted suddenly.

Immediately, I knew something was wrong. Why were the pipes

such a short distance from the surface? If they only needed to be there, why had Regan ordered the entire pit to be dug out? It didn't make sense. The digging continued under the careful instruction of the archaeologist. There was another shout to stop. What looked like charred remains of some jewellery were found. I asked to have a closer look and was told I couldn't.

I spoke to Tony and Russell and explained that it could have been something that belonged to the kids. Surely it would be prudent to find out now rather than later. They asked for me to be shown the item and I definitely did not recognise it. They also took it to show my neighbour Chris and she verified that it wasn't hers either. A few more items were taken out of the ground and bagged by the forensic team, and then a halt was called to proceedings. This needed to be a fingertip search and further arrangements had to be made.

Over the next few hours, the police came and went. A marquee was needed to protect the site and roadblocks were set up. No one could come and go without someone checking who they were. This would definitely get the community talking and I was concerned about my children. It was impossible to say how long the police would be here. Greg, a local detective, arrived with an army of policemen. He organised dustbins to sift the soil into, large garden-type sieves of differing gradients, tables and somehow or another a Portaloo miraculously appeared next to my stables. The troops had moved in and they looked set to stay a while.

Meanwhile, at Dover, and unbeknown to me, Regan and Bill were boarding a ferry and heading for France. I don't know if the police were aware of their departure, but at that time I don't suppose they had any reason to detain them. Bournemouth Police had found a body floating in the sea a couple of weeks previously. Thinking it was a local man, they didn't bother checking the national missing-persons files. It wasn't until the next day that the grisly truth was revealed: the body was that of Neil Chohan.

The children were due home that evening, but I didn't want them there. What if the police found a corpse? I spoke to Indiana's headmaster Nick Folland and explained the situation. He said that he had heard nothing about it at the school, but agreed it was probably only a matter of time. He would make sure Indy was taken care of. He even offered to let her stay with his family. I felt totally reassured. He let me speak to her and I told her that I would come to the school the next day and talk to her. She seemed fine. Montana took it well and gave me a list of things that she wanted me to bring her. She could board or stay with friends, but she wanted to know if I was OK. I said I was fine and would come and see her tomorrow.

I didn't sleep at all that night. Tony and Russell remained outside in the car. Every time I closed my eyes, I had visions of two small children being dug out of my field. When I eventually got up, my house did not seem like my own and the view from my window was of a white tent, a mass of police vehicles and all the paraphernalia that goes with a forensic site. I made breakfast for Tony and Russell. It was strange eating a meal with two people who were basically strangers to me but with whom, because of the circumstances, I felt a great affinity. They probably viewed me as just another witness. At least, that was what I thought. It was a few days before I realised that they actually viewed me as a suspect.

Tony's pager beeped and he went outside to make a phone call. He came back and informed me that he needed to take a statement from me and that I would have to accompany them to Tiverton Police Station. As we made the short journey through the roadblocks and then on to the main road, my mobile rang. It was Regan. I indicated to Russell that it was him. I undid my seat belt, leaned through the gap between the seats and allowed Russell to listen in on the conversation. Regan was in a phone box – I could hear the sound of the coins dropping. I told him I was on my way to the supermarket and that the police were about to dig up my field. He said he was abroad and that he would be back soon. He promised me 'a thousand million per cent' that there was nothing in my field. I was pretty sure of that – whatever had been there he had come back for and taken away. He said he wasn't going to get into trouble for a lorry driver's wage and that I was not to worry. He would call me soon. I never heard from him again.

The room in the police station was small, stuffy and totally devoid of natural light. Tony wanted me to tell him what had happened two months previously when I had found men digging in my field, and then what had happened when they had returned. All of this was time-consuming and tedious. He asked me if I knew the digger-driver or if I knew his name. For some unknown reason, probably nerves, I got a fit of the giggles. It took me a few minutes to control myself and when I looked up there were two very bemused police officers staring at me in disbelief. When he repeated if I knew his name, I started laughing again. I could see I was pushing my luck. I tried to control myself and said that I did not know his name, but if I saw him again I would recognise him because he looked to me like the Missing Link. I think Russell thought I had taken leave of my senses. Then I remembered something. When I had asked Bill if he wanted tea, he had shouted to the digger-driver to see if he took sugar in his tea and I think he had called him Pete. I told Tony this but I said I couldn't be sure that was his name. I would definitely recognise him, though.

It was getting late, and it was decided that we would resume the interview the following day. Tony then informed me that they had found and identified Neil's body. I started to cry. This was not possible. Why had Regan dug up my field a second time and then not taken the bodies? Tony apologised for not having made himself clear: Neil had not been found on my property; he had been found in the sea. For some reason, I felt a bit better about that, but the poor man had still been murdered, and that did not bode well for the rest of his family.

The story broke on the news and I knew it would not take long for the press to hear of the digging on my land. It had now taken on a whole new dimension. I needed to see my children. I wanted them to know I was safe and for them to hear the news first-hand. But I was too late – the news had reached them and they sounded worried. One kid told my daughter that the reason she was boarding was because her mother was wanted for murder and had gone on the run. I assured them that nothing could be further from the truth. Yes, the police were with me, but they were looking after me. They did not sound convinced and wanted to come home, but there was no way I wanted them to see the house in what to my mind was a state of siege. Tony and Russell were very understanding and agreed to go and speak to my children and reassure them. I was very appreciative of that, and I know it alleviated a lot of their concerns.

Tony and Russell were relieved of sentry duty, as the local police had now taken over that job and the roadblocks helped make things more secure. It would be their first full night in a proper bed for over two days. I hoped they would sleep well. Standing alone in my house with the police on a constant vigil outside, I wondered how this had happened to me. It was my own fault. I should never have allowed Regan to worm his way into my life. Lots of people would – and did – say 'I told you so'. Well, if anyone *could* have told me that five people would have been buried in my field, why the hell *didn't* they?

The following day, I felt exhausted. I managed to snatch a few hours' sleep. Tony and Russell wanted to press on with my statement and so, after seven hours in that windowless room in the basement of Tiverton Police Station, the task was finally finished. I needed something to eat and, much more importantly, I needed a drink. A strong margarita would do the trick. I had tried to explain to Tony and Russell how gossip started and how news travels fast in a small community. I don't think they realised quite what I meant, but they were about to find out.

We went to the Rackenford Club for a drink. It had been a long day on top of two days of hardly any sleep. My cigarette intake had doubled and I looked ten years older. When we entered the club, one of the locals was explaining to the others at the bar that the police had found the van that Regan had hired and that the owner, when it was returned, had said that in all the years he'd been in business or had lived in the country he'd never smelled anything like it. Russell and Tony had spent the day locked away with me in the police station and now it seemed that everyone else was better informed than they were. I think it gave them an insight into rural life. They were, after all, city cops.

It is strange spending a lot of time with people and not being able to discuss what is going on around you. I couldn't ask them questions – well, I could, but I never got an answer so it became rather boring after a while. I liked Tony and Russell, though, and was glad I was not stuck with some of the grumpy policemen I had encountered. We left the club late. If the only way I was going to get any sleep was by drinking tequila, then that was precisely what I would do. The boys drove me home and Russell asked me if I was worried for my safety. 'No,' I said, 'but I might change my mind if Regan returns from abroad.'

The last thing I wanted to do was move. There had been enough upheaval for an entire lifetime without adding to it. I had to sign a piece of paper exonerating the police of any responsibility for my refusal to move. While Russell was writing this, I mentioned the conversation we had heard in the club. 'It's odd,' I mused, 'because the digger smelled really bad as well. I normally leave my bedroom window open, but I had to close it so that I could sleep.'

Russell looked at me like I had dropped a brick on his head. 'Why didn't you mention this before?'

I shrugged. 'I hadn't really thought about it.' After all, I hadn't really been thinking in terms of dead bodies. It smelled similar to a rotting badger that my dog had once brought home. As a result of my little revelation, I had to give yet another statement at some ungodly hour.

It was the start of the May bank holiday weekend and Tony and Russell would be leaving later for London. They had been in Devon for five days, so they must have been delighted at the thought of going home to their families. My girls were also coming home for the weekend, but not until after the press conference that had been arranged for the Saturday morning. Detective Chief Inspector Norman McKinlay, the head honcho of the group, arrived early, accompanied by my least favourite detective, Graham. They took over my living room for their meeting and once more I was reduced to making the tea. DCI McKinlay was polite but curt. He definitely viewed me as a suspect, but then I think he thought that of everyone. It was agreed that I would not be at the house when the press arrived. I would go and get my children from school. The press would be brought up in convoy and allowed to take pictures. DCI McKinlay would do his piece to camera and then I would return safely.

The children arrived and wanted to leave immediately. They didn't like having the police in the drive, and they certainly didn't like the marquee in the field. They wanted to go and stay with their father. I was devastated. My elder daughter started to cry. She was angry with me. 'No one else's mother would be involved in something like this,' she said, and apparently I had no idea what they had endured that week at school. Monty had seen the police press conference in which they had named Regan and described him as highly dangerous. She couldn't understand how I had allowed someone like that into our lives. I felt terrible, and maybe she had a point. Both girls insisted they wanted to be anywhere except the house or school. In fact, they wanted to be as far away from Devon as possible. I said I would see how they felt the next day and, if the feeling was still the same, I saw no reason why they couldn't go to London. They went to bed early and barely spoke to me.

I sat on the sofa and sobbed. The phone rang and it was Mel, my friend and hairdresser extraordinaire. She was phoning to check I was all right, and she could tell from my voice that I obviously wasn't. It was nine o'clock at night. 'Sit tight,' she said, 'I'm on my way.'

By eleven o'clock, I gave up and went to bed. I was tired for the first time in days and was asleep in minutes. I woke at two in the morning to the sound of banging on the front door. What on earth had happened now? It was Mel and a friend of hers, Emma. They were drunk. Actually, they were rat-arsed. All I wanted to do was crawl back under my duvet. Mel said some nice policeman had let them through the roadblock. What on earth had they thought of these two mad women, I wondered. I went back up to bed and Mel appeared with a bottle of tequila from my kitchen and an ashtray. I was insistent that I did not wish to drink alcohol at that time of might; Mel was adamant I had to. She then demanded to see the 'Rampant Rabbit' vibrator that one of my sisters had given me. I told her it was in the top drawer of a chest of drawers under some socks. 'What on earth is it doing there?' she asked, as if she was half-expecting me to produce it from under my pillow. I told her I was worried that if the police searched my house they might find it. As I was speaking, I realised how stupid it sounded – as if they wouldn't have looked through my chest of drawers! As it happened, I had practically the entire Ann Summers catalogue hidden in there, much to the hilarity of Mel, who emptied the contents on to the bed.

Eventually, we all went to sleep. Mel's husband Anton came the next day to pick them up; she apologised for turning up late and drunk and said she would call me later. I lit a fire to make the house feel cosier, thinking it might encourage the children to stay, but they were adamant they wanted to go to London. I removed some dry-cleaning from the back of the car, and dropped the wire hangers, which I never use, by the front door. I helped them pack their bags and we left for the train station. I had every intention of coming straight home.

My girls were very subdued on the way to the station and Montana insisted that she did not to wish to return home or to school until this whole thing was over. It was definitely a murder investigation now – the police had a body – and it wasn't going to be over for a long time. There was nothing I could say to alleviate her sadness and now I also had other worries to contend with. Would I still have a job? How would I pay the mortgage? If I tried to sell the house, would anyone actually want it after this? I felt like a very bewildered little girl, and it all seemed too much for one little girl to deal with.

The train was delayed. As we stood on the platform, Monty started to cry, which made me cry, which in turn made Indiana cry. How would I ever make it up to them? They got on the train and Indy had her tear-stained face pressed against the glass. 'Don't be sad, Mum,' she mouthed. 'I love you.'

The train pulled out of the station and I wondered when they would be coming home. I sat on a nearby bench and sobbed.

Mel called to say she was coming straight over – at least this time she was sober. I told her not to bother as I wasn't there and she persuaded me to come to her house. Maybe it wasn't such a bad idea after all. I could do without seeing any more policemen, and being in that house alone again would not make me any happier, so I made my way to Mel and Anton's.

We had a lovely evening and I went to bed around midnight. I woke early the next morning and, while everyone else was still asleep, I walked along the river and decided I had to stop feeling sorry for myself, pull myself together, work out what needed to be done and get on with it. I would go back to work on Wednesday, the day after tomorrow. Mike Parr had no authority to fire me – it certainly wasn't his company and I wasn't going to be bullied by him. At least I was being positive, and I felt better. I couldn't help wonder what had happened to Neil's wife and family and I hoped that they were safe; but, after two months and no sightings and with Neil murdered, it was a very slim hope.

I got back to hear Mel and Anton stirring upstairs. It was nine o'clock. I picked up my mobile which I had left on charge. The screen told me I had seventeen missed calls. Seventeen missed calls? That was not possible. No one ever rang me either this early in the morning or that many times. Not even my bank! I also had numerous text messages. They were from Tony Bishop. He had been calling me since seven o'clock. More bad news, I thought. I called his mobile from Mel's house phone.

'Where are you?' he asked.

'At a friend's house in Exeter,' I told him.

'What's the number there?'

'It should have come up on your phone.'

'I'll call you right back,' he said.

When he called back, he wanted Mel's name and address. I checked with Mel that she didn't mind, and then Tony said he would have to send a policeman to verify my whereabouts. This I objected to.

'I'm on my way home anyway. What's the problem?'

It transpired that when I had taken the children to the train station, I had left the television on, the fire burning and the front door wide open. At some point much later, the police on duty at my house had become suspicious and said I had been seen leaving the house with suitcases. They thought, incorrectly, that I had fled the scene, never to return. They thought I might resurface later, sunning myself somewhere with Regan on the Costa del Crime.

I told Tony I was leaving Mel's now and I was going straight home; I had animals to look after. He made me give him my word. I couldn't believe what I was hearing.

On the journey home, I realised that I was obviously a suspect in this crime. I had been naively thinking the police were being pleasant to me because I was trying to help them; in fact, they just wanted to keep me within range. I was quite offended. I pulled into my drive and rang Tony immediately and told him I was home. Most likely he knew already – the police had probably radioed ahead saying the bird has returned to her nest, or whatever ridiculous codes they use. I was pissed off. I had never been asked to verify my movements with anybody, and I didn't realise I could not come and go from my house as I pleased. Being angry suited me much better than feeling sorry for myself.

I noticed the pink slip on the doormat as soon as I entered. It was a search warrant. It stated that the house had been searched at 4.30 a.m., and that the search had been executed 'to save life and limb'. When the police entered and saw the coat hangers thrown by the front door, it looked as if I had left in a hurry. That and the fact that I had not turned off the television or lights meant all hell had broken loose. 'Brewin has flown the coop,' said DCI McKinlay as he woke Tony Bishop, who was instructed to try and get hold of me. Well, it was over now. I was home, and at least I had a better idea of what the police were thinking of me. It wasn't just Graham – he was just the most vociferous.

I walked into my bedroom and suddenly thought, Oh my God, how embarrassing. By the side of the bed were a bottle of tequila and three shot glasses, and half a sex shop was strewn across the unmade bed. I wished the ground would swallow me up.

It is always best to face your fears so, rather than skulk around inside my own house hiding behind my own mortification, I ventured out to the police car in the drive. I apologised to the officers for causing them any trouble the evening before and said I didn't realise I should have informed them if I was not returning. 'Was it you who searched the house?' I asked them.

They looked at each other. 'No,' replied one of them rather cheekily, 'but don't worry – we all know.' He started to chuckle.

I had to laugh with them, which was slightly disconcerting as they were definitely laughing at me, and not with me.

I drove into London in the early hours of 7 May and arrived at CIBA at eight o'clock. Mike Parr had been busy in my absence: my desk had been cleared and was now taken by somebody he had appointed. I had only been there a few minutes when I was informed by one of the staff that Parr was now in the position of power. He was coming in to see me and had forbidden me from going to my desk or even to that floor of the building. He took me into the boardroom and said he could not believe that I had the cheek to come into the office after what I had done. What I had done?

He asked me about the police investigation and Regan and Bill. I said I had seen them in the lane at my house. He asked me how I could have passed them in the lane when they are so narrow. How the hell did he know that? As far as I knew, he had never been to my house. He also asked why Regan would have gone there knowing that the police were there. I said to him I had no idea and perhaps the next time he spoke to Regan he should ask him himself. He said that he would.

He took my arm and physically escorted me off the premises. A few days later, I got a letter informing me of my dismissal from the company. It was backdated, which was an interesting way of getting fired. Frankly, I was glad to see the back of him. Life's too short. Look at poor Neil.

I picked the girls up from their father's house and we headed back to Devon. So much for a quiet life. I was back at square one but with twice the number of problems. The coming months would prove to be testing, but we had each other and I had to remind myself on a daily basis that I was a survivor. I sure didn't feel like one. Russell had called to tell me that the marquee had finally been taken down and the ditch filled. I had asked him previously if it would be possible to remove the stone and reseed the field. I did not want it reinstated as it was. I had never liked it and I didn't wish it to remain as testimony to Regan's bloody handiwork. The police agreed and a dumper and yet another swing-shovel had been ordered for the weekend. Webbie and his son Ryan agreed to do the work for me. Soon my field would look like a field again.

Russell and another detective Damian arrived shortly after the girls and I got home. Another team of detectives would be arriving the following day to carry out a forensic search of my house. Apparently, during an interview with Regan at CIBA, he had been asked whether, if the police were to go to my house, they would find hair there belonging to Neil. 'Yes,' Regan had replied. This was news to me: as far as I knew Neil had never been to my house. Regan's reason for this bizarre answer was that I had sat on Neil's chair and there was a possibility that I might have picked some up from that. The police weren't convinced. Neither was I; it sounded very sinister.

The kids would have to board again, and I had only just got them home. But it didn't feel like home any more, and for Montana it never would. It was the beginning of the end of my idyllic life there.

The two officers arrived and certainly did not seem to be happy with the task before them. It would take them months to do a detailed forensic search of my house. A video was made of every room and they left in much the same manner as they had arrived – grumpily.

I prayed on a daily basis that they would catch Regan. It would certainly go a long way to alleviating my daughters' fear of staying in the house. A week later, there was good news. The Missing Link had been arrested. He had been on the run for a couple of weeks and had threatened to give himself up at a police station but mysteriously hadn't. It was on the news and my memory had served me well: his name was Peter. Peter Rees. One down, two to go. I always maintained I would recognise him again if I saw him, and so on Friday, 16 May at Hammersmith Police Station I correctly identified him as the man I saw on my field operating the digger on both occasions – first, when the three of them had buried the bodies, and then when they exhumed them.

All that remained of the police dig were a few dustbins and the Portaloo; I hoped that would be picked up soon. The field looked like a field again, and now I had to sell my house. The situation was worse than before; would anybody want to live in the house after this? The estate agents were divided and the valuations varied. I woke most mornings feeling sick with worry. The only people with a definite view of the situation were the bank. Pay or we repossess. It was as simple as that. My girlfriends rallied round and without them I might have gone mad. Mel Waldron (not the hairdresser Mel!) spent a lot of time dragging me out of my depression and having Indiana to stay. She was always full of practical advice and suggested I come and live in her barn. Did she mean the one with the chickens? I really wasn't sure. Corinna paid for my car to be serviced and Andy gave me lots of hugs in the school car park. Diana brought me Chinese food and we wiled away many an evening watching *Crime Scene Investigation* – as if I hadn't had enough of it in real life. Sue let me flirt with her husband Rick, and they were a source of great comfort to me and I am eternally grateful to them both. My dear friends Rose and Linda rang me on a daily basis. It was comforting to know that since moving I had made so many genuinely good friends.

The absence of police was short-lived. Charlie King called – they were coming back and they were bringing dogs. Charlie arrived on Monday, 2 June with Tony Bishop and a female detective, Sue. She seemed to be from the same mould as Graham – we were not going to get along and I objected to being treated so ambivalently in my own home. If you want to be rude, do it in a police station or your own home, but not in mine. First impressions are not always right, though, and I soon changed my mind.

The police had been busy since our last meeting and there were things that they had discovered that made them question some of the things I had previously said. I am sure that was what accounted for her scepticism about me.

Charlie produced a map of the area they wished to search. I informed them that I did not own all the land in question, but that I did know the owners. All of them gave the police permission to take the dogs across their land. All of them, that is, except my neighbours. Lyn Williams insisted that the police 'invoke the full due process of the law' and get a warrant. I was shocked. Why would you not want to help the police? One man was known to be murdered and his family were missing. Everyone is entitled to their own views, but I didn't understand their attitude at all. What if it had been their family missing, or someone local?

I spent the next two days giving Charlie and Sue a detailed statement of my meetings with Regan and Neil. Both of them were very brusque with me. Charlie, in particular, felt I had 'bewitched and beguiled' some of his officers, and informed me that half of his team wanted to have me arrested. He had yet to make up his mind, but it really upset me and it made me cry. It transpired that Regan had been at my house at times when I was not there including, crucially, the day that Neil disappeared. I could verify that I had been in London then and nowhere near Devon. Charlie said they wished to bring the dogs through my house, and I thought he was going to tell me that they had reason to believe that Neil had been murdered there. I couldn't bear it and started to cry again. Sue got up from the table and put her arm around me. I wasn't sure how much more I could take.

Why had Regan made a mortgage application in our joint names, asked Charlie. I didn't know he had, and was baffled as well as horrified. Why had passport photos of me been found at Regan's house with passport photos of him? I explained that when I had first started working at CIBA, both Regan and I had gone to a photo booth to get these done. I had given mine to Neil's cousin who worked at CIBA, as I needed to have a proper photo ID for security. I had never been given one and I had no idea where the photos had gone until now. With Regan's penchant for a forged passport, it must have been very suspicious. We worked until seven o'clock, and finally I had covered everything they asked me. Charlie then took my laptop computer and said that they would return it in due course. The canine crew finished for the day and said they would be back tomorrow; they had not finished searching the Williamses' land. Charlie and his mob left for the night and would also return the following day – my birthday. Some bloody birthday that was going to be.

Charlie and the other police officers arrived in a particularly sombre mood. So much for thinking they might bring me champagne and make me breakfast. Didn't anybody know or care that it was my birthday? Apparently, the statement I had made the day before could not be true. They had possession of information that made what I said happened on 13 February impossible. I maintained I was correct. I hadn't lied. I knew I hadn't. What I said had happened happened. Then, after much thought, I realised I had got the days muddled up. What I had said happened on 13 February had actually happened on 12 February; and, anyway, I had spent the afternoon of 13 February at Mayfair Audi picking up a new car, and not with Neil as I had said. That was a relief to everybody, and especially me – being arrested on my birthday was not quite what I had in mind.

There was another setback. Lyn Williams was again refusing to allow the police to set foot on his property. They had a warrant; what was his problem? It would seem that the warrant was 'for one use and one use only' and, according to Lyn, that had been used the day before. If they wanted to resume the search, they would have to get another warrant. I did not understand his attitude. I also did not understand why his wife Chris refused to give a statement to the police. She refused to verify anything I had said, even though she had witnessed Regan arrive at my house unannounced and had seen some of the letters that he had written me. She had even seen them on my land digging and had rung me in London to inform me. Even when I was being treated as a suspect, she would not confirm what I said was true. I was amazed; I had thought we were friends.

Charlie and Tony were dispatched to Exeter to get another warrant. It was a complete waste of their time and even the judge who granted it could not believe that two people who were not involved in the murders would hinder the police in this way. Lyn made an official complaint about Charlie King. I spoke to Chrissy and she was quite aggressive with me and told me that Charlie had been rude to her. I wasn't there so I can't say. Personally I cannot imagine Charlie behaving in any way except totally professionally and courteously. A better police officer with such a good understanding of the witnesses he dealt with would be hard to find. After the murders, the Williamses barely spoke to me. It made me very sad. Life was bad enough as it was.

The search was finished that day. The dogs found nothing in my house and the police left, but not for long. Charlie, Russell and two other detectives arrived back two weeks later. They needed to interview Montana and it had to be videoed. I picked her up from school and drove her to Exeter Police Station. I said she did not have to give a statement, but she was adamant she wanted to, especially if it would help the police put Regan in jail. I was very proud of her. We were taken to a residential house which was fully equipped for the task in hand. The house is used for child abuse and rape victims and the atmosphere is much more relaxed than that of a police station. I was introduced to Martin Ludlow. He was going to conduct the interview. I was very impressed with him and he put Monty at her ease. It was she who remembered Regan wearing the borrowed blue overalls. After she had finished and we had said our goodbyes, I took her for a pizza. She asked me if the police would be coming back and I said I wasn't sure. We went home, and Monty, as both my daughters had done since the murders, slept in my bed; it was the only place they felt safe.

Six weeks later on 21 July, a body was trawled off the bottom of the sea near Poole Harbour. It was the body of Neil's wife Nancy. She had been murdered five months previously. All I could think of were those poor children, and I hoped Nancy had not watched them die. A reporter told me that Nancy's skull had been smashed. Charlie King refused to confirm this and wanted to know who had given me the information; he would be giving them a formal warning to stay away from witnesses. He did promise me that as soon as either Regan or Bill was arrested he would inform me.

I prayed for that call. It would come, he said. Just be patient.

# CHAPTER THIRTEEN

The house went on the market and my girls could not wait to leave. Montana spent more time seeking solace in the comfort of her friends. She said I didn't understand how she felt, but isn't that what all teenagers say to their parents? The sad thing was she was right. I didn't have any idea of what she was going through, and three months after the police had finished digging it came home to me in such a way that I knew we had to move, and soon.

It was 19 July 2003. I had friends staying and we had gone to the Rackenford Club for a drink. I got a phone call from Monty asking me if we would be long. We had only just arrived and no one had ordered a drink yet. A little while later, the club phone rang. Rose answered it. It was Montana, but Rose couldn't understand a word that she said. She was hysterical. I tried to get some sense out of her and she managed to tell me that someone was outside the house. The poor kid sounded terrified. I left immediately, accompanied by two members of the club who on the way out picked up two pieces of timber to protect themselves.

The front door was bolted from the inside, as were all the other doors. The shutters covered the windows and no amount of banging and shouting would bring Montana to the front door. I smashed a back window and got into the house that way. Monty had barricaded herself into the living room and was now so hysterical that even when I said it was me she would not move the sofa from across the door. Nothing I could do would console her; she was convinced there was someone out there and they were coming for her.

There was an easy explanation. A bullock had been put in the yard next to my stables and it triggered the sensor lights. Monty thought that there was someone walking up and down the lane. When she called out to see who was there, no one answered. Bullocks cough and they sound remarkably human, so it is easy to see how her imagination ran wild: with Regan still on the run, she thought it was him. I never left her alone again. I couldn't. Even a trip to the supermarket became an expedition.

I spoke to Charlie King the next morning and asked if there was anything he could suggest to help. As it was a Sunday and he was at home, I was very grateful to him for even returning my call. He promised he would deal with it as soon as he got into the office the next day. Sure enough, Tony Bishop called on Monday morning. He had arranged for a special counsellor to come and see Monty, and a policeman would call to fit panic buttons in the house. I doubted they would ever be used but, if it made Monty feel better, I was all for it. The panic buttons arrived and were nothing like what I imagined. They were neither buttons, nor were they red, nor did they have the word 'panic' printed on them. It was connected to the phone line and looked and worked like a TV remote control. If the two buttons were pressed together it would alert the 999 centre and the local police stations.

Things calmed down, but the children still insisted on sleeping in my bed. I had a seven-bedroom house but I may as well have been living in a bedsit.

A week later, the electricity went out in the house. Monty was frightened. I rang the electricity board and they said there appeared to be no reason for us to be cut off. The girls and I went to bed by candlelight, and at three o'clock in the morning I heard a van pull up in the lane. Two men got out. They were dressed in black and were carrying torches. I wasn't going to hang around. I pressed the button and the police arrived very quickly. The men were from the electricity board. How was I to know? I had never heard of anyone coming out at that time of night or that quickly. I felt a bit stupid. The police were very understanding and the electricity board apologised for scaring the living daylights out of all of us.

Monday, 4 August started like most Monday mornings in our house: slowly. Then my mobile bleeped. It was a text message from Charlie King and it said, 'I have just made your day.' I knew exactly what that meant; Regan had been arrested. I burst into tears – I was so happy and so relieved. He was in Belgium and would fight extradition, but he was behind bars. The children and I jumped up and down, hugging each other in the kitchen. It was a great day in our household and I thought maybe, just maybe, I might get the bed to myself one day soon. We went into Exeter and I took the girls out for lunch. We toasted the fact that Regan was in jail and we all hoped – and still do – that he would never, ever, ever be released. It took the police months to get him back on English soil, but they did. Charlie King arrested and charged him. Tony was there and it must have given them a lot of satisfaction after all the effort that they and the rest of the team had put in. Regan was charged with five murders, kidnap, false imprisonment and preventing a lawful burial.

Bill Horncy was arrested a month later, again by Charlie King and Tony Bishop. He was stopped coming back into England at the same port he had sneaked out of all those weeks before. Apparently, Tony drove from London at breakneck speed to get there. Events seemed to be coming to a close. All three men were in custody. A trial date was set and all I had to do was wait. The nearer we got to the date, the more trepidation I felt, and I wondered what the defence would say to try and discredit me. Frankly, as long as they sent those three men to jail for the rest of their natural lives, I could handle the insults.

The house sale was going well. I had found a buyer and we would be out by Christmas. Then the bombshell fell. They would not buy the house because of 'the problem'. No, not the murders – the neighbours. My neighbours? I didn't understand. I had never had any problem with my neighbours, although I had learned since moving to Devon that the people whom I had bought the house from did not get on particularly well with the Williamses. So, having got rid of one problem, I inherited another through no fault of my own. Not only did they not get on, but they also had a constant running battle which had become increasingly bitter over time. Three years later, I was going to have to carry the can for an argument that wasn't mine.

I was thinking of taking legal action. Had the vendors informed me, I probably would not have bought the house knowing there had been disputes with neighbours. The Williamses did not want to get involved, which was understandable. I saw no reason why I should suffer again, but by this time nothing that people did surprised me. I lost the sale and then two more after that for the same reason. I asked the prospective buyers to explain their reasons in a letter and they all said the murders were not a problem – the bodies were not discovered there, after all – but no one wanted to live next door to neighbours with whom there would possibly be problems. From then on, whenever I had a prospective buyer, I would tell them before they walked in the door first, about the murders and then that I had never had a problem with the neighbours, but the previous owners had. If they then wished to look around the house, I was only too happy to oblige, but I'd had enough of time-wasters. I sold it eventually in June 2004, and I couldn't be bothered to sue the vendors.

In spite of everything, I was very sad to move. It had been a disaster from start to finish but I still loved the place. It was time to move on – even if I had won the lottery, my children would not have stayed there. I rented a house, moved my horse, paid the school fees and settled in. Charlie King was moved to a different department, Andy Rowell was promoted, and Tony and Russell also moved on. I would always be grateful to them for getting us all through the ordeal – and more to the point for not arresting me. New detectives who had not been there since the start were brought in. I never saw the sense in it. They could not have been expected to have had the same understanding of the case, or of the witnesses involved, but I suppose that, as long as the police got a conviction, that was all that mattered.

With the trial only about five weeks away, a couple of things happened that were significant. A body that had been washed up on the Isle of Wight had been identified through DNA matching as that of the Chohan grandmother. I knew her body had been found some months before, but there was concern that the forensic scientists would not be able to culture enough DNA to prove it was her, so when I heard on the radio that they had, I was delighted. This meant that Regan could not pretend that the children were somewhere in India with her and that the police were just unable to locate them. He would be tried for all five murders, two counts of which would be the murdering of infants.

Later that day, with the thoughts of those poor children still fresh in my mind, I was required to attend an identity parade at Tiverton Police Station. Montana was also required to come, and my dear friend Diana Breitmeyer accompanied her as an 'appropriate adult'. It's not that I'm inappropriate – although I am sure that there are a few people who would disagree – but, as I was a witness, I could not be seen to influence her in any way. It was easy. I identified both Regan and Horncy. Montana recognised Regan but was unsure of Horncy. She did narrow him down to one of two, but she could not be 100 per cent positive.

One of the strangest emotions I felt while waiting for the trial to start was when I thought of the Chohan children. I became worried that something awful could happen to my own children, and the thought would wake me at night and make me cry. I had terrible nightmares. How would I ever live, knowing the pain they would have gone through and the sheer terror that they would have suffered? What if they called for me and I was not there to help them? One night I cried so loudly in my sleep, it woke my daughter who then had to wake me up. It was ridiculous: I had to stop thinking like that. I wondered how Andy Rowell and Charlie King went home to their families and ever let them go out, knowing the level of violence they come across on a daily basis and the things that happen to people. Then I would think about Nancy, the children's mother, and I was glad that she had been spared the pain of living with the knowledge that her children had been murdered.

I also encountered enormous feelings of guilt. How is it possible that five bodies lay in my field for months and I walked over them and never realised? I pray that Nancy died first so she never had to die knowing her children were dead or, worse still, watch them die. It drove me mad for months, and my only consolation was that at least they were all together and with God. I asked Paula to go and see them and tell them how sorry I was, that I was a good person and that I would do whatever I could to make sure justice was served.

I started to receive threatening emails, which the police investigated. The first one came on 1 December, about ten days before I was due to give evidence. The email address given was 'hellmarsh', which was bizarre, as the defendants were being held in Belmarsh. The email read:

> *Purgery [sic] is an offence punishable by a custodial sentence. The SP here is that this lot are itching to get you on the stand. They are confident they now have nough [sic] information to prove purgery and so rip the case wide open with you a co-defendant. Big money has been spent for information. BEWARE*

The police investigated and traced it to a computer shop in South Kensington. A statement was taken from the owner of the shop but unfortunately he didn't have any CCTV footage. There was also no evidence to suggest that the emails came from or were instigated by the defendants.

But there was no question in my mind of not going to court: I owed it to the murdered Chohan family and to two detectives in particular – Charlie King and Tony Bishop – who, along with many other officers, had so diligently investigated the case. Not all the detectives seemed to have as much faith in me as they did, so I hope I didn't let either of them down.

The case was delayed, and then delayed again. When it eventually started on 11 November, the estimated duration of the trial had gone up from three months to six months. There was some press coverage of prosecutor Richard Horwell's opening statements, and my blood ran cold when I read what had been said: Neil Chohan had been bound and gagged and he had hidden a clue in his sock to identify his killer. The poor man must have been terrified, not only for himself but also for his family, his children, his newborn son. Such wickedness is beyond comprehension. He had been forced to sign pages and pages of blank pieces of paper before being murdered by suffocation. Somehow or other, he had the presence of mind to hide a letter in his sock that was addressed to Regan and his father. It was from their mortgage company and sent to their home address where Neil had been held hostage prior to being killed. Richard Horwell said that the contents of the letter were unimportant but the date of the letter – 12 February – was very significant because it was the day before Mr Chohan disappeared. He also went on to say, 'It is not just, of course, the fact that in folding the letter and placing it in his sock, Mr Chohan had intended to leave a clue as to the identity of his captors and the place of his incarceration. It also means that Mr Chohan had known that he was going to be murdered.'

Even as I write these words it sends a chill right through me.

The next day had been Valentine's Day. Neil Chohan would never again be able to tell his wife he loved her or send her roses. The next time she would get any flowers, they would be on her coffin.

I was informed that it was highly unlikely I would be called before Christmas. I organised an early family celebration that took place on 12 December, as everyone had other plans. I was looking forward to it and it gave me something else to think about. So, when the phone rang one Tuesday morning, I thought it would be one of my sisters asking me if they could bring anything down at the weekend, or help in any way. In fact, it was the police. I needed to be at the Old Bailey on Wednesday, 8 December. It seemed my number had come up. I felt sick. It didn't seem logical: I had been expecting this call for over a year and yet when it came it was as if it was a bolt from the blue.

I organised for the children to be taken care of and my brother Tobey and his girlfriend Alex said I could stay with them in

London. They were two minutes' walk from the Bailey and, as the days went on, I came to appreciate their offer more and more. Detective Inspector Teresa Defanis called. I had met her at my house with Paul Abbott many months before, when Charlie King had come down to introduce me to the detectives who would be taking over the investigation now he was moving departments. On our first meeting, I had thought she was very abrupt and I wasn't impressed – but then I hadn't been too enamoured of Charlie when I had first met him, as he had made me cry, so I should have learned not to be so hasty in my judgement of those I didn't know. But it would seem I wasn't the only one guilty of that crime. Criticism of me amongst some of the Murder Squad seemed to be in abundance. I asked Teresa if I could come and look at the court before being called the next day, as I did not want it to come as a surprise. I wanted to know where everything was and where everyone was sitting and then I would be able to concentrate on what I had to do and nothing else. I wished Charlie or Tony had been there.

My dear friend Mark Cook called me. He had been a great friend of Paula's too and is the most fantastic make-up artist. He had been with Take That and has worked with many people in the music and fashion industry. He had booked the week off and was going to come and support me every morning. He is extremely wicked and I knew that he would do everything possible to quell my nerves. Mark would be at my brother's at 9 a.m. the next day. Catherine Mayer also called to wish me luck and to tell me that she was thinking of me. She too took time off work to come and sit with me at the Old Bailey. It was very much appreciated.

The police had sent me my statements and transcripts the day before – all 347 pages of them. How on earth did they expect me to read all that in one day? I needn't have worried: I woke at 4 a.m. and could not go back to sleep, so I sat up reading. To make matters worse, I was worried about my ex-boyfriend, the one who had left me two years previously. He wanted to know if we could meet for a drink. I told him that I had pages and pages of statements to read, and anyway I certainly did not want to go out drinking while in court. I wanted a clear head. I thought he understood and left it at that. Later that night, I got a text saying,

'If it's war you want, it's war you've got,' and then he said he would see me in court. He had been acting a little unbalanced of late and I certainly did not want him appearing at the Old Bailey. I rang him and asked him to stay away from me and stay away from the Old Bailey. I think he told me to go fuck myself, and he may even have added the word bitch. This was all I needed – as if I wasn't stressed enough, now I was going to have to contend with his behaviour.

Mark and I made our way from my brother's apartment. I felt like it was my first day at a new school and my stomach was on the spin cycle on my washing machine. I hoped I wouldn't throw up. We made it through security and were met by a detective with the smart title of witness liaison officer. He was a terribly dour chap. I was shown to the witness room; Mark had to leave, but he said he would be back later. He asked the detective how he would get back in again and then asked if he could be put on the guest list, which cracked me up, but still the detective did not smile. I had to point out to Mark that there were no backstage passes – we weren't at Wembley Stadium, we were at the Old Bailey.

I was told to stay where I was and that the detective would be back shortly to tell me what was going on. So I sat and I waited, and I waited, and then I waited some more. I literally chain-smoked – it was disgusting. I had been up since 4 a.m. and had not eaten a thing. It was now 12.30. I was starving. I knew the courts broke for lunch at 1 p.m. so I waited some more.

At a quarter to two, a court official came into the room and told me that I was due in court in fifteen minutes. I explained I was hungry and that I would have to eat something. I didn't think I was up to two and a half hours of questioning on an empty stomach. He asked me if my witness liaison officer had been to see me. No, he hadn't, and when I left a message on his phone I received a text back to say he had been too busy working to come and see me, and that there was a canteen on the floor I was on. Too busy? How could he have been too busy, and what work was he doing that couldn't wait until I was giving evidence. I was the only witness appearing for days and it was his job to make sure I was all right.

I was not happy.

At 2 p.m. on 8 February 2005, I entered Court Six of the Old Bailey. The room was heaving with men in wigs. I saw Regan, Horncy and Rees sitting in the dock behind the bullet-proof glass screen. Regan stared at me for a long time. It made me feel uncomfortable but also more determined to make sure that the screen he now sat behind was replaced by bars. Horncy had the audacity to laugh at me. Rees barely looked up.

I started gingerly and with obvious nerves. There were photographs of my house and my field, and charts of telephone calls between the three defendants, Mike Parr, CIBA and myself. It was all too much to take in. The charts showed which telephone masts serviced each call so it was easy to see to the nearest few miles where each person was when the calls were made. It also showed how long each call was and to whom it was made. It was difficult months later even to remember the call, never mind what was said.

Richard Horwell took me through my statements, how I had originally met Regan and how I had come to be in contact with him after his release from prison. I also explained my financial situation, Regan bringing the furniture to my house and the conversation that day about the mud in my field and his recommendation that I should build a drainage ditch. He also took me through the chain of events that led to me working at CIBA, and my meetings with the planning people regarding a change of usage on the land Regan claimed to own. Throughout, I was adamant that Regan had always maintained that he was the owner of not only the freight company but also the house and the land near Hatton Cross.

Once I had got the first day over with, I didn't feel so bad. Perhaps it had been the fear of the unknown that had made me feel nervous. After a good long bath and supper, I felt very tired and was about to go to bed when I got a text message. It was from my ex and it pertained to evidence that I had given that day in court. I had told Mr Horwell that I needed Regan's furniture as, when my ex had left, he had taken all his things. We looked like we were camping and, as I was trying to sell the house, it was not a good look. My ex disputed this statement; in fact, even today there are still a couple of boxes of his things in the garage, but as far as I was concerned they were totally insignificant. Not to him though. He sent me numerous threatening texts throughout the evening, which I ignored, and then he sent me one saying, 'For a woman telling a pack of lies you are very brave,' and went on to say that he would be going to the court the next day to tell the judge I was a liar.

I knew that I did not want to go through this daily ridiculous torrent of abusive text messages while giving evidence, and I did not like the idea of my ex even being in the court. God knows what he might do. When you are in the witness box, the public gallery is behind you and you cannot see who is in it, but now I knew he was there it would feel like he was breathing down my neck and I couldn't have that. I was here to give evidence and that was all I wanted to think about. So I rang Detective Inspector Charlie King.

Charlie sounded more than a little surprised to hear my voice, and informed me that I should speak to an officer on the case. I said my problem was not directly to do with the case and, as he was the only officer, as far as I knew, who had ever met my ex, he was the only one, as far as I was concerned, I could have spoken to. Also, I knew he would at least be polite enough to listen. He understood why I was upset and I asked him if I could have my ex removed from the public gallery. He told me not to worry about anything. I asked him if he would deal with the situation. I trusted him and if he said it would be done I knew it would be. I went to bed feeling very relieved. I had warned my ex time and time again to stay away from me and the court, but he would not listen so now he only had himself to blame for what happened next.

The next morning, I was to resume giving evidence and I made my way with Mark to the Old Bailey. As we went through security, I saw Charlie King enter the court through the revolving doors. I felt better already. I wasn't able to speak to him but I did smile and nod as an acknowledgement of my thanks. I sat in the witness suite, had my obligatory cigarette and headed down to the courtroom. On my arrival, there seemed to be a flurry of activity. The prosecution counsel were outside talking to Charlie King, Richard Langdon – a police officer who had once come to my house in Devon – and another police officer whom I had seen a couple of times with Teresa Defanis. I gathered later he was the man now in charge of the case.

I sat at a respectable distance and strained to hear what was being said. I heard Richard Horwell say, 'He must be removed.' Presumably they were talking about my ex, and I was glad that the situation was being taken seriously. I was grateful to Charlie for dealing with it. My ex was stopped at the entrance to the court and asked about the text messages he had sent me. He was taken before the judge, who told him to stay away from me and the court while I was giving evidence. That was all I had wanted in the first place; it seemed a shame that I had to go to so much trouble just to achieve it.

Richard Horwell continued to guide me through my statement. It was hard remembering some things, such as who arrived at my house in which vehicle and at what time. There had been three separate days and trying to be factual about each one when they seemed to blend into each other was difficult. Other things were easier to recall, but the call from Regan saying that the police were about to arrest Neil Chohan, the man he had murdered two months previously, stuck vividly in my mind.

When Mr Horwell said we would resume on Monday, it seemed like I had been there an awfully long time. I was reminded by the judge not to speak to anyone about the case or my evidence, and I assured him I would not. It was the last thing I wanted to do. I was going to a drinks party that night and there would be no mention of the Old Bailey. Finally I could have a drink!

I drove back to Devon on Saturday and had my Christmas lunch with the family and the Breitmeyers. In no time, it seemed to be Sunday evening and I was kissing the girls goodbye, taking my dog back to Rose and Trevor's and heading off back to London. I woke on the Monday morning, again at some ungodly hour and could not get back to sleep. I felt more nervous than I had the last few days and actually thought I was going to be sick. I think it was because I knew that today at some point I would be cross-examined, and it was not something I was looking forward to. I had seen the way the three barristers looked at me while I was giving my evidence: Regan and his henchmen had spent an inordinate amount of time writing messages to their legal teams about certain aspects of my evidence. It seemed a little theatrical for me and I didn't think the jury were buying it either.

I arrived in court to be met by my witness protection officer David Chalmers. I didn't find him particularly friendly. Driven by my nerves, I walked over to him and bluntly told him I didn't think he was civil and that he might as well not say anything at all to me. To my surprise, he agreed not to. I might have over-reacted, but you could have knocked me over with a feather. I burst into tears and told him he could fuck off. I also said I wasn't going to go into court and rather dramatically walked off.

I got halfway across the hall before I realised that I couldn't go anywhere. Mark came over to see if I was OK and, like a little spoiled child, I handed him a tissue and asked – well, demanded – that he made sure I hadn't ruined my make-up. Once I started crying, I couldn't stop. The court usher came out to call me in, but I was in no fit state to give evidence and I was now on my high horse and wasn't getting off.

Another police officer, Paul Zaleski, appeared from the court and tried to placate me and stop me crying. I said I wanted someone else to look after me. Paul probably just wanted to slap me and tell me not to be such a prima donna and get in that courtroom and get on with it, but he was very charming and said that everything would be taken care of and I was not to worry. So I wiped my eyes, blew my nose and walked into court all teary-eyed and red-faced.

I found it hard to concentrate on what was being said to me, and I still felt that at any moment I would burst into tears. There was one point when the judge seemed a little irritated and was asking me to be a bit clearer – normally, it would not have bothered me, but I was obviously feeling more than a little sensitive and started crying again. The court broke for lunch and I knew I had to pull myself together. I had answered questions when I had barely heard what was being asked of me and it was the defence's turn this afternoon. I went for a walk, bought a sandwich and felt a lot better. DI Teresa Defanis came up to the witness room to check on me, and after speaking with her I felt fine and wondered why I had reacted quite so badly to some grumpy police officer. I was over it, thank God.

On the afternoon of Monday, 13 December 2004, at 2.32 p.m., Mr Mendelle appearing for the defence on behalf of Regan stood and wished me good afternoon. It was the first time I had heard him speak: his manner was pleasant and he seemed affable enough. In fact, he was quite charming. He informed me that he had good news for me and bad news: the bad news was that his questioning would probably take the rest of the day (as it happens, it went on over two days); the good news was that not much of what he had to say was 'going to be controversial'.

'That would be nice,' I replied. 'Thank you.'

He then mentioned this book – proofs of which had been shown to the prosecution and defence – and said that I had written that I expected to be given a hard time by the defence counsel. I agreed with him, and explained that I did feel that would be the case, as I was not here for his benefit but for the benefit of the police and the Crown. Mr Mendelle went over Regan's feelings for me and I could not stress strongly enough to him that these feelings were not reciprocated, nor were they encouraged.

The bundle of papers that Regan had given me relating to the land that he was hoping to get a change of use on was the subject of discussion. Mr Mendelle suggested, 'Mr Regan made no secret of the fact that this was land that he and Mr Chohan were interested in getting planning permission for.' I knew that to be wholly untrue. Regan had always maintained it was his – there was never any mention of Neil Chohan. Mr Mendelle gave me the bundle of papers that I had taken to the planning office. Out of 300 pages – none of which I had read – he asked me to look at four. These particular letters were addressed to Amarjit Chohan. It was suggested that I knew full well it was Mr Chohan's land, but for a start I only knew Mr Chohan as Neil and at that point I had never even met him. Also, the letters were addressed to the General Manager of CIBA, so why would I have thought he was the owner from four pieces of paper that I had never read. I stood my ground: I knew what had been said to me and I knew I was right.

Then Mr Mendelle moved on to discuss two emails that Regan

had sent to Neil Chohan and had also copied to me. In one of them, Regan had written 'your site' and the defence asked me what I thought 'your site' meant. They maintained Regan was being perfectly open about the fact that this was not his land. I agreed that was what was written, but that Regan had never been open: he had lied to me for months. It also said that Neil would get a percentage of the profits – if it was his land, why would he only get a percentage and not the whole lot? In any case, this was only a five-line email sent to me on one day; it certainly didn't negate the months of conversations I had had with Regan where we had discussed *his* land, *his* property, *his* business and *his* house. Obviously, since Neil's murder, things that had seemed irrelevant before became very important. Regan had never been open and honest about any aspect of the Chohan family's disappearance; why now, when he was in court accused of five murders, should it be any different? He would continue to lie and twist things to his benefit, but I don't think it worked. I for one wasn't convinced.

The mud was an obvious line of questioning that, along with everything else, Mr Mendelle and I could not agree on. At one stage, he tried to make a joke by saying that the two of us seemed to be stuck in the mud. I was a little tempted to be flippant and say, 'Well, at least we're not buried in it,' but was glad that I resisted. He quite rightly pointed out that I had told the police that Regan went on about the mud at my house, which was true, but we had one conversation, and I would be hard pushed even to refer to it as that, about the mud in my field. On 23 October, when the furniture was delivered in trucks supplied by 'his company' CIBA, Regan stated I needed a drainage ditch and that was it. I didn't even bother to comment. The rest of the time he just moaned about the mud in the lane, the mud by the stream and wherever else there was mud that day. Mr Mendelle, whose job it was to undermine my evidence, insisted that we had discussed the site where the drainage ditch should be. Again, I stood my ground; as I knew my version was correct, it was an easy position to maintain.

Another interesting but totally untrue point that the defence raised was that I had met Neil Chohan prior to our meeting on 12 February 2003. After Neil disappeared, Regan told me that, when

I had been to CIBA before starting work there, when he had
wanted to show me his 'empire', Neil had been there. I didn't think
he had, and I certainly never remembered meeting him, but I did
tell the police what Regan had said. If I had any doubt in my mind
that Neil Chohan might have been at CIBA that day, it was
instantly quashed by Mr Mendelle's line of questioning. First, in
my mind, how could Regan have pretended to me that the
company was his if the rightful owner had been there that day?
But, much more to the point, the defence was maintaining that not
only was Neil there but also that I had had a conversation with
him. Not just any conversation, but one about my car. My
Mitsubishi Evolution VII, which I love almost as much as my
children. It just didn't happen. That was a total lie and I knew it.
I would have recalled any conversation about my car: it would
have been very animated and a long discussion on brake
horsepower and torque would have ensued. The defence
maintained that Neil had remarked that my car was an expensive
car. I agreed it was expensive, but that Neil Chohan had not been
there and that he never said that to me. I asked him where he was
getting his information from, but of course I knew it was from the
lying, murdering bastard in the dock.

The subject of my ludicrous salary came under scrutiny, and
how odd it was that someone as unqualified as myself would be
paid such a large amount of money. I agreed. Well, he was right –
I was totally unsuitable for the job. Naively, I thought I had been
paid just so Regan could see me. That might have been part of it
but much more importantly he would be able to control my
movements while he buried an entire family in my field. The
defence were trying to infer that perhaps that sum had been paid
to me for my compliance. It didn't bother me – I knew it to be
untrue and I was expecting that line of attack. What else could
they say?

Eventually, we got round to the day of the meeting between
Regan, myself and Neil Chohan in the boardroom at CIBA – the
day before he disappeared and shortly before he was murdered.
The defence maintained that the meeting was mainly about what I
had discussed with Jane Gleeson regarding the change in usage of

the land at Hatton Cross. I maintained – and I was there so I should know – that it related to Regan paying Neil Chohan £3 million for his share of the company. At the very end of the meeting, Regan said that I had been talking to some solicitors and that he was working on a plan for the land. When the meeting had finished, Neil Chohan, Regan and I went back into the office and then upstairs to the accounting department where Mr Chohan introduced me as the new managing director of the company so the accountant Lionel De Silva could prepare the documents confirming me as a director. Mr Mendelle then reminded me of something that I had forgotten. He asked me if I had photocopied the letter from Jane Gleeson and given a copy to Mr Chohan. I had – Regan had asked me to and I either handed it to him or to Lionel. It had completely slipped my mind. The defence said that the whole point of us going upstairs was for this purpose and this purpose only. He was adamant he was right; I was adamant I was right. Another impasse. Then I remembered: why would we have gone upstairs to photocopy a document when the photocopier was downstairs? That ended those questions.

My surprise arrival at my home was covered. Who had I told that I was going home? How long did it take me to get back home and what happened on my arrival? There was, as Mr Mendelle said, not too much that was controversial there.

Another bone of contention was the trench, or rather my lack of accuracy in describing its dimensions. At one point, I had said it was only eighteen inches wide, which was ludicrous. Another time, I had described it as six to eight feet deep, and in yet another police interview as being four to six feet deep. I explained that my eye for judging distance was blatantly flawed and that my descriptive powers were also suspect and, although I had been incapable of describing one of the defendants, the Missing Link, I had been able to identify him correctly. I felt it was the same here. I had not described the trench accurately but it was the same size the first and second time the defendants had dug it up and was the exact same dimensions as the hole left by the police after their excavations. It was impossible for it to have been only eighteen inches wide as I had seen Horncy standing in it – there was plenty of room either side of him and the trench came up to chest height. I was adamant that it was a big trench and that it was certainly big enough. We left that subject and moved on.

Mr Mendelle then discussed some points that I had not made in my statements to the police but had written in this book. 'I just want to ask you one or two questions about Michael Parr.'

'OK,' I said and smiled.

'Although you smiled when I mentioned his name,' he continued, 'it is not, generally speaking, a name that fills you with feelings of warmth, is it?'

'No. I think he is a very unpleasant chap, actually.'

Mr Mendelle said that I described Mike Parr as 'a pit bull terrier, not my type, a most unpleasant fellow'. I did describe him as such. The judge, Sir Stephen Mitchell, then interrupted the proceedings and asked what relevance this line of questioning had and what my opinion of Parr had to do with anything. The defence maintained that, as I had had dealings with him, it was very relevant. I didn't see why it was important but I would find out soon enough. They were overruled, and then asked a couple more questions pertaining to Parr, one of which was whether I had told him at some point when he escorted me from the CIBA offices on 7 May 2003 that he was a prime suspect in the murders. I hadn't and, more to the point, had never even thought it.

Finally, Mr Mendelle said, 'Miss Brewin, thank you. That is all I ask.'

I thanked him and that was the end of my cross-examination by Regan's defence team. It really hadn't been as bad as I had been expecting.

Mr Horwell rose to make a point. 'Again, so that there is no misunderstanding, it is therefore not disputed that Regan and Parr asked this witness to give an affidavit to the effect that Parr owned 50 per cent of CIBA.'

Mr Mendelle stated that fact was not in dispute and then added, 'Whatever has not been challenged is accepted.'

Once that had been cleared up, Mr Arlidge QC, acting on behalf of Bill Horncy, stood up and faced me.

He was exactly what I expected. He looked like a mean old fox and I found his manner very abrasive, but he was good at his job. He was, I felt, a little sarcastic and patronising, but his client was looking at spending the rest of his natural life in jail so he was bound to use every trick in the book. He started by asking me if I remembered saying to Regan's defence barrister that I was 'here not for Mr Regan's benefit but for the benefit of the police'.

'I certainly do, yes,' I replied. 'I meant I was a prosecution witness.'

'And you have told us,' he said, and then in a rather demeaning tone he added as an aside, as though he were bored of the subject already, 'and we have heard more than once about it, about an autobiography you have written, which you decided to write after these events had occurred.'

I agreed, but pointed out that the events formed a very small part of the book.

'Did you decide to write this book after these events had occurred?'

'Yes, I did.'

'And you intend to include them in your book?'

'Yes.'

'As a selling point?' He asked the question rather haughtily, as if 'selling' was a dirty word and had no place coming out of his mouth.

I replied as politely as I knew how. 'I think there are many other things in my life that would contribute to that, but I'm sure it would be one of them.'

I wasn't sure where he was going with this veiled attack, but the next question left me in no doubt whatsoever. 'Have either of those factors in any way affected the evidence that you have given?'

'Absolutely not,' I replied.

He raised his eyebrows as if in disbelief. 'There is no element of exaggeration resulting from either of those?'

To which I replied the same. 'Absolutely not.'

He went on to state that the reason for asking me these questions was because I had told the court that, when I went down to Devon on 20 February 2003 and found Mr Horncy there digging my field, I went 'ballistic'. 'I am going to suggest that you did not,' he continued, before saying that in my police statements I had not mentioned the word ballistic, I had just said that I was 'not happy'. I assured him that I was furious and so much so that

his client, Mr Horncy, had told Regan of my displeasure and
Regan had bothered to mention it the next day and told me how
ungrateful I was. I also explained that there was a lot more
intonation and emphasis than he had placed on the words 'not
happy'. Mr Arlidge had spoken them very nonchalantly and yet
when I said them to the police it was as if they were in capital
letters and underlined in red. I agreed that in black and white the
words looked ineffectual, but if he were to listen to the tape
recording of the interview he would hear the emphasis in my
voice and then there would be no misunderstanding of the level
of my unhappiness.

According to Mr Arlidge, I was quite happy with the work that
had been done in the field – I just 'had the hump about the
bonfire'.

'No,' I told him, 'that is absolutely not true and literally
everybody who lived near me will know how much I complained
about my field, and I was very angry with Mr Horncy. If they were
going to have a bonfire, why hadn't they had it in the same
position I'd had one?' Because then it would have been difficult to
scrape away and bury what they had burned there.

The subject then turned to the arrival of the trucks with the
stones. In my original statement to the police, which I corrected
the next day, I said that Horncy and Rees started filling the
trench, but that was wrong – they did not fill the trench until the
next day when Regan arrived. The other thing that I had
forgotten was that I had been concerned about my horses falling
into the trench overnight and I checked on them the next
morning. The trucks delivering the stone did not arrive until after
4 p.m. and by the time it had all been dumped in the field it was
getting dark. As there was no lighting on the field, it would have
been impossible to have done any work. Mr Arlidge thought
differently: he suggested that I was 'as it were, reconstructing
things in your mind'.

'No,' I replied firmly, 'I am not reconstructing anything at all. I
know that the trench was not filled because I was concerned about
my horses and the three of them arrived and then it was filled.'

The next point related to the Easter weekend when the three

men came back and dug up the bodies. After they had got what they came for, they left the digger in my drive right under my bedroom window. I always sleep with my window open, but that night I closed it because of a terrible smell. I thought nothing of it at the time and, in fact, thought nothing of it until months later when the police arrived. After I had been interviewed for hours at Tiverton Police Station and was told that Neil Chohan's body had been found, I went for a drink at the Rackenford Club. The police had impounded the van that Regan had hired and, apparently, the owner of the van had told police about the appalling smell in the back of it. News travels fast in a small rural community. When I heard this, I said to Russell Ferris, one of the detectives who had conducted the interview with me that day, that I too had smelled an appalling smell and had closed my bedroom window. He took a statement from me to that effect: it was now the third statement I had given the police. Mr Arlidge quoted to me some of what I said to the police: 'I did not identify where the smell in my bedroom was coming from and until last night made no connection between the smell and the digger under my window. The following day the digger was still under my window but I was no longer aware of the unpleasant smell.'

I agreed that this was correct, and Horncy's defence questioned whether both statements were correct. He then went on to say, 'What I am asking you is you did not on the night when this happened, when you got the smell, relate the smell to the digger?'

'No,' I replied, 'but then I also didn't think that five people had been buried in my field, so why would I think that smell came from the digger.'

Mr Arlidge continued that the only other 'matter of fact' that he wanted to ask me about was in relation to the overalls that Regan, Horncy and Rees had left behind. 'I again suggest, so far as he was concerned – that is, Mr Horncy – that he did not leave any overalls with you.'

This was untrue. I had lent them three overalls and I got three overalls back. I had even seen Horncy standing in the trench wearing them. I hung them back in my workshop and they remained there until the police came and collected them, thanks to my daughter's recollection of them being worn.

Horncy's defence team then started asking me details about my family and whether any members of my family had ever had tea with the Queen Mother, trying to establish that my family was well connected. The judge asked him if he was going to make his position clear and Mr Arlidge said that he was. 'Various things are relayed to Mr Horncy about this lady and her relationship with Regan and I am just trying to find out whether they are accurate, whether there is something behind them. That is all.'

He went on to mention some of my friends, including Paula. I was not sure of the point of this line of questioning, and the talk of Paula and her death made me start to cry. I was given a tissue and one of the women on the jury, who looked nice and friendly with lots of curly hair, sitting in the front row, looked at me as if to say, Are you all right? She smiled at me and it made me feel better. Horncy's team continued and mentioned me living in Holland Park, being an ex-Chelsea girl, then talked about my car, my house and my horses. I pointed out that the trappings might have been there, but that I had no money. He said he understood that, but to an outsider it would look pretty impressive. I could see where he was coming from but he should have felt it from the inside – it didn't feel at all impressive from where I was sitting. Most days I was scared out of my wits, wondering where I would find the money for the mortgage and the kids' school fees.

Mr Arlidge continued and asked me what I knew about Regan going to jail and about the amount of money he used to have with him; he went on to ask how much money I would get if the land deal had come into fruition. He said that I was 'plainly hoping to get a substantial reward at the end of the day'.

I didn't think of it so much as a reward as payment for a job I would have done, but I did say, 'It would have been great for everybody. Had it been his [Regan's] land in the first place, it would have been a perfectly feasible and legal, legitimate business deal.'

Mr Arlidge continued in what I perceived to be quite a derogatory tone and I wondered if he spoke to everyone in that voice or he just saved it for work. He then stated that there came a time 'when you were offered this job in credit control and as managing director'.

'Yes.'

'It was a very good deal for you?'

'It was an extremely good deal.'

'It was a fantastic deal,' he said with more than a hint of incredulity in his voice.

I certainly wasn't going to let him dig a hole and push me in it, so I said, 'Yes. We would all like to work two days a week for that amount of money.'

'Absolutely,' came his reply.

I couldn't resist it. 'You probably do,' I said. It made me smile, and I know it made one or two on the jury smile too.

'And particularly,' he retaliated, 'in a job for which we had no qualifications.'

'Yes,' I had to reply, 'even better.'

I hoped his questioning wasn't going to go on much longer and, luckily, it didn't, though he could not resist referring to my book for his last few questions. He asked me if I had felt I was a suspect in the murders. I replied that initially I had not felt that, but, as time progressed, and after not coming home one night and then being hounded by phone calls from Detective Sergeant Tony Bishop as to my whereabouts, yes, I had. I explained that I could understand the point of view of the police. 'They've got a document saying I own 50 per cent of CIBA and it's my land. If I was a policeman, I would think that I was a suspect as well.'

He gave a slight grin as if he had suddenly snared me in his trap. 'Indeed, one of the policemen told you that he thought that half of the squad wanted you arrested.' I agreed he was correct, that was exactly what DI King had said. Thanks, Charlie! On that note he begrudgingly thanked me and sat down. Two down, one to go.

We broke for lunch and I went to find my daughter Montana who had come to London the night before with my friend Diana Breitmeyer and her daughter Alice. It was now Thursday, 16 December, exactly a week since I first took the stand. Montana was due to give evidence, via video link, after me, and had been waiting in the witness room since 9.30 a.m. She looked so bored. She wanted to go home – didn't we all? Mark had sat with her most of the morning, but he had to leave in the afternoon. Someone had to sit with her and Paul Zaleski, the police officer who had dealt with my histrionics, obliged. Monty told me afterwards that he was 'very cool and easy to speak to'. Perhaps I should get some parenting tips from him.

I told her I didn't have much more to do. What could Mr Gledhill QC really ask me? I didn't even know Peter Rees, and had never even had a conversation with him. So I told her to be patient and that we would stop by Harrods on the way home and get some Krispy Kreme doughnuts and go shopping. I was trying to make a day at the Old Bailey a little more palatable for an extremely bored and nervous teenager. It was working: the idea of spending money perked her up no end.

I returned to court and Mr Gledhill introduced himself. He was a welcome change from the less-than-charming Mr Arlidge. We covered much the same ground as I had with the other barristers, but from the perspective of his client. Mr Gledhill referred to my calling Rees the Missing Link. I did say, 'I apologise now for being so rude,' though I did not mean it. Anybody who helps bury bodies and then digs them up deserves nothing, and certainly not an apology for hurting his feelings. I explained that I never spoke to the man, although he would have been only too aware of my displeasure with himself and Horncy when I arrived unexpectedly back at my house. The next day, Rees arrived with his son who must have been five or six. I gave the child some sweets and crisps – he seemed like a nice kid, shame about his father. I was asked if Rees and the child left at any time that day. I said that I had never heard them leave and the cars were parked at the front of the house on the gravel drive – if they had left, I was sure I would have heard it. There was more discussion on the dimensions of the trench and whether or not Rees had been wearing rubber gloves. I said that as he was in the digger most of the time I did not see his hands, and as for the overalls I had no idea if he was wearing them. All I knew was that I had lent Regan three pairs and I got three back.

At least Mr Gledhill had a sense of humour, which seemed to be totally lacking in Mr Arlidge, although I would imagine his would be politely referred to as acerbic wit. For some unknown reason, Rees's defence asked me how long it would take to get from Portsmouth to my house. I have never been to Portsmouth, so why on earth would I know something like that? It didn't seem to matter – he still supplied me with a map. He asked me how long I thought the journey would take, and I asked him if he meant in *my* car or normally. 'We don't admit to criminal offences in this court,' he said, smiling, to which I was sorely tempted to reply, I can see that – but I restrained myself.

Mr Gledhill suggested, 'One of the other reasons for describing [Rees] as the missing link was the way he walked when he was not on the digger, do you remember that? Do you remember that he obviously had problems with his back?'

'I don't remember that at all, no, not at all. In fact, definitely not. He seemed perfectly able to me.' I presume Mr Gledhill was trying to imply that Rees could have played no part in burying or digging up the bodies because he was unable to lift anything heavy. That was certainly not the case. He seemed perfectly agile when he was trying to push the trailer holding the digger up the hill when it had got stuck. I wished I had remembered to say that in court.

At 2.37 p.m., Mr Gledhill QC thanked me, and that concluded my cross-examination.

The chief prosecutor, Richard Horwell, got to his feet. For a moment, I wondered what he was doing. I had forgotten that he was entitled to go over questions and issues raised by the defence. It wasn't quite over. The first week at CIBA seemed important. At what point did I realise that Regan would be away? I knew he was not going to be there that first week and because of that I had to work an extra day, though it wasn't until the morning of 19 February, my first day at work, that he told me he was in Birmingham. Yet again, my inability to judge distances came into question. Mr Horwell asked me what I had meant when I had said to Regan's barrister that the trench 'was a big trench, it was big enough'.

'If you were going to put three adult bodies and two children's bodies in it,' I replied, 'there was plenty of room for that.' One or two of the jurors immediately turned to look at the defendants: it certainly struck a chord.

He smiled at me and said, 'That is all I ask. Thank you.'

The judge also thanked me and, at 2.56 p.m., a week after I had entered the court, I left.

My job was nearly done here. Montana was to give her evidence next and then it would be back to my brother's to thank him, pack our things, go to Harrods, get doughnuts and head home. Montana had waited six hours to give evidence, and all she wanted to do was get it over with and leave. But there was a problem. The video link to the courtroom was not working. Detective Constable Richard Langdon came to the witness suite. He explained the situation to us and said that it might be tomorrow before it could be fixed. Monty was fed up – there was a birthday party she wanted to attend in Devon that evening, and she didn't want to hang around. She asked if there was any other way that she could give evidence. DC Langdon said no, unless she was to give evidence live in court, which would mean seeing Regan and standing in the witness box. She said she was happy to do that. Richard asked me what my feelings on the matter were. I knew that, if Monty had not wanted to do it, no amount of coaxing from the police would have influenced her. If she said it was fine, then it was fine with me. They allowed me into court with her and I thought she did very well and was very brave. I was proud of her.

She was asked about taking tea out to the men in the field, what she knew about Regan and why she had described him as 'weird' in her statement. Monty was in court for an hour and, when we left, we ran down the street of the Old Bailey and I felt as light as a feather. I bought Monty a T-shirt in Harrods that said 'I shagged the drummer' and we bought a dozen Krispy Kreme doughnuts. As I hit the M4 and headed home, Monty fell asleep and I started to cry – just little tears that rolled down my cheek and splashed on my lap. I was so relieved.

I prayed that Regan would die a miserable death in jail.

# CHAPTER FOURTEEN

Christmas came and went. I spent lunch with the Breitmeyers and a rather drunken but very jolly evening with the Knowleses, where we drank far too much tequila and John Knowles broke a very expensive present that his children had given him only a few hours earlier. It always ends in tears! My children spent Christmas with their father and, for the first time in twelve years, did not spent it in Thailand. As I saw the first broadcast pictures of the tsunami on Boxing Day, I was so relieved. That would have finished off my life, not just my year. My sister Julia was on the island of Phi Phi when the wave struck and was unaccounted for: eventually, we got the news that she, unlike many others in the region, was safe and well. I thanked God.

The holidays came to a close. For me, New Year was very subdued, but I knew that life had to get better and was hoping for a speedy conclusion to the trial. As the weeks turned into months, I knew that was hoping for a lot. The police seemed pleased with the evidence I had given and the way I had presented myself in court. I was glad and hoped that it would go some way to ensuring that Regan would die in prison. Obviously, I still took some interest in the trial and, whenever I found myself in London, I would go to the Old Bailey and sit in the public gallery. Most of it was very dull and extremely slow. I felt for the jury. My appearance in the public gallery seemed to cause consternation among the defendants, and both Regan and Horncy made ridiculous gestures to me that were no doubt supposed to unnerve me. They didn't, but my first visit to the public gallery did. It was probably just the unknown and the fact that the last time I had attended court I had the protection of knowing I was a prosecution witness.

I queued up with everyone else, and was duly searched by a female officer, Kim, who on future visits would chat to me while I was waiting for whatever legal argument was going on at the time to finish. No mobile phones were allowed: if you had taken one, the friendly Spar shop across the road, for the princely sum of a pound, would look after it for you. The staircase reminded me of a prison: grey, dingy and institutional. I waited on the landing until the court opened and was then called through by one of the court staff. Horncy noticed me first and nudged Regan, who in turn looked up at the gallery. On my second visit, Rees nudged Horncy and he looked up at me and sneered. What was the point? Surely the jury would not miss that? He could sneer all he liked – a bit of remorse would have been more the order of the day.

One of the things that I was really shocked to learn after giving evidence was Regan's line of defence. It was quite astounding, but I suppose that, if you can kill five people, making up a story to cover it up must be the easy part. Apparently, he had not killed Neil: that deed was allegedly committed by associates of an alleged drug dealer who drove a Lamborghini. According to Regan's fantastic imagination, Neil had got himself involved in some drug deal that had gone hideously wrong and he was then murdered. Regan maintained that he had been coerced, by the Lamborghini-driving drug dealer, into disposing of Neil's body under threats to his beloved father's life. Was he kidding? His beloved father? Regan loathed and detested the man. I never heard him say a nice word about his father – even when he was ill, he would say he hoped the bastard would hurry up and die. I never met the man and he died shortly after Regan went on the run. At least the last few weeks of his life were peaceful and he would not have had to endure the abuse and ridicule he suffered daily at the hands of his son.

Many mornings at CIBA, Regan would make himself a cup of tea and, after patting his ample belly and telling me how much weight he had lost, he would descend into a vitriolic diatribe about his aging father – how bad he smelled, how he was a dirty, filthy, disgusting human being and really how much he hated him. Regan's insistence that he buried Neil's body in my field to save the life of his beloved father was an absolute, bare-faced lie. And it goes without saying that Regan maintained he knew nothing of the murdered women and children. The audacity of the man was beyond comprehension.

I wished I could go back to court and tell the jury that what Regan was saying was just not true, but I am sure the police must have covered that angle and found someone who could dispute his claims of being the loving, caring son, because it was such a blatant lie. I don't suppose that the police knew what his line of defence was going to be right up until the end, but I would have thought that the prosecution counsel might have asked me if I had any inkling of the kind of relationship they had. Maybe it wasn't necessary.

Mr Mendelle put to Mike Parr that, 'To deflect attention from yourself, you said to Ken Regan he must move the bodies and dump them at sea.' He went on to say that an agreement was made between Parr and Regan that the latter would exhume the bodies, get the boat and deliver it to the drug dealer's people and that Parr was the go-between. It followed that Chohan was killed by associates of the drug dealer, 'who you, too, were associated with.'

'You are talking rubbish,' Mike Parr replied.

However, Parr said in court that Neil had given him half of the company and made him a partner, though there was never anything written down. Parr had hoped to make £1.5 million when the firm was sold and, after Neil's disappearance, he went to the High Court to have Neil's assets frozen. Mr Mendelle maintained that Parr had also helped Regan compose a letter that was allegedly written by Neil Chohan and posted from Calais after he had disappeared. Regan's defence went on to say that the letter would have been beneficial for Mr Parr in his High Court action. Mike Parr replied that he was not relying on the letter and that he did not compose it. He also said that he knew Mr Chohan did not write the typed letter as he never used a keyboard. Parr did, however, admit that he did not tell the police of his suspicions immediately. Mr Mendelle stated that this was because, 'When it comes to money, you are completely unscrupulous.' Parr, of course, disagreed.

Another audacious act on Regan's part was to give Mike Parr a letter, handwritten by Neil Chohan, and the keys to Neil's family home in Sutton Road. In the letter, Parr stated that Neil had said he 'had got into some trouble and was going to run away'. According to Parr, he 'was obviously concerned that the family were not at Sutton Road' and had tried ringing the house on numerous occasions but there was no answer. Parr decided, along with Neil's nephew who worked at CIBA, to visit the house. Regan, on hearing of this imminent visit, 'tagged along'. 'No one asked him to go,' said Parr.

On arrival at the house, they found the back-door key in the outside lock, food in the fridge, washing in the washing machine and the child's buggy was there. No clothes had been taken, and Regan, who showed them round the house, said, 'The clothes are still there so they must have left in a hurry.' An outrageous affront, you would think, but then, before the family vanished, he had told Mike Parr to tell Nancy to 'stop fussing' about her husband's disappearance and then arrived later that evening at Sutton Road with a tape-recorded message, which he had forced Neil to make, and played it to his wife to appease her worries. Having been capable of actions such as these, nothing that he did to cover up his crime comes as much surprise. The message on his mobile from Neil, according to Parr, 'was along the lines of "Don't panic. I'll be home tomorrow."' Parr said that Neil 'sounded OK – quite chirpy' and he then went on to say, 'Nancy calmed right down. You could see the relief in her face.' I doubt she stayed calm for long: the poor woman was about to be murdered.

What I was most interested in hearing was the evidence of certain police officers in relation to what had happened in and around my house, and what exactly was found in my field. As the trial was running well over schedule, it was difficult to get the timing right and usually I ended up listening to evidence that I didn't really want to hear. Keith Luxton, to whom I had leased my land for his cattle, was called to the Bailey, and so was Stephen Paine, another local farmer. When asked what my reaction to the drainage ditch was, Stephen said I had gone ballistic.

The next person to give evidence after the Christmas break was Webbie. I was going to London that day and had a meeting so I said I would give him a lift. I picked him up at 5 a.m. He had been drinking in the club until gone 2 a.m. I was not impressed. Each to their own, I suppose, but I thought a shave wouldn't have gone amiss. I didn't really see the point of him turning up, because it certainly didn't do the prosecution any favours. I listened to him give evidence and he said that one day he had heard myself and Regan have a heated argument in my kitchen. When asked by counsel about the nature of that discussion, he said he didn't know as he had gone outside. I was gobsmacked. I had heard him tell the same story numerous times in the pub and he had said I was furious that Regan had arrived unannounced and that I had told him, basically, to fuck off out of my house and who the hell did he think he was to keep turning up unannounced. Why didn't he say that? Perhaps he forgot it under the stress of giving evidence. He also failed to mention how Regan had stopped him from entering the field while they were exhuming the bodies and had distracted his attention elsewhere. I felt it had been a wasted effort.

Just before the break for lunch, a note that Regan had written to his barrister was passed to the prosecution and Richard Howell stood and suggested that it would be best if Mr Webb did not discuss the case with anyone or have lunch with Miss Brewin. There was absolutely no danger of that happening – I would probably have slapped him.

Once he had finished giving evidence and my meeting was over, we made our way back to Devon. He asked how he had done. What could I say? I said I was sure it was fine. He slept the whole way back, much to my relief.

On one of the occasions that I attended the Old Bailey to listen to a specific police officer, I ended up listening to the evidence of a Mr Mountain, an officer with Bournemouth Police who was on duty when Neil's body was found by a canoeist in the sea. He described how Neil's head had been bound with packing tape from the neck upwards. It was horrible to imagine how he must have felt as the tape was wrapped round his neck, his face, his mouth and his eyes, over and over again. He had been sedated and I could only hope that it at least numbed some of the terror that must have enveloped him. The police officer then went on to describe how they had tried to fingerprint him to try and confirm his identity. It had been a very difficult job: he had been buried in my field for nearly three months and had been at sea for a while, so his skin had come away from the bone. 'De-gloving' was a term that was used. I felt sick.

There was, of course, mention of the items of clothing that had been removed from Neil's body. Mr Mountain explained that, as they were wet, they were placed in brown paper bags, unsealed, and taken to a secure drying unit. This allowed the air to circulate. Obviously, the greatest interest was in the sock that the hidden letter was discovered in months later. Mr Mendelle asked if Mr Mountain knew any of the Metropolitan Police officers involved in the case. Mr Mountain stated that he did not.

One witness who was a neighbour of Regan's described how one morning when going to put his rubbish out he noticed a white van outside the house. The neighbour said it was February and it was 'in the early hours. It was just after seven in the morning.' He said that Regan said hello to him and that the 'white van was backed up to the garden gate on one side of the bungalow'. He also went on to say that the garden path behind the van 'looked wet, as though it had been washed. It hadn't rained.' An hour later, he noticed the van had gone.

Richard Horwell then went on to explain to the court that, around that time, Regan had replaced the flooring in the front room of the house with a remnant of carpet from Carpetright in Salisbury. Regan had told the woman in the shop that he wanted something that would not show stains as his father was 'a dirty old man'. Surely Regan wasn't describing the same man whom he claimed to love more than any other living being? Having dealt with the flooring, Regan then went to Courts in Salisbury and purchased a three-piece suite, including a reclining chair. Interestingly enough, there was a defect in the reclining mechanism of the chair. The saleswoman said that Regan 'didn't care. He didn't ask for a discount.' When the suite was eventually delivered, the delivery man noted that the room was bare and there was no sign of the old furniture. The room had also been recently decorated.

Regan's father, Roy Avery, had given a statement to the police regarding these events in early May. He died on 19 May 2003; Regan did not attend his funeral. How could he? He was on the run somewhere in Europe, though he must have been delighted: finally, the filthy bastard was dead. Roy told the police, 'One day I went out of the house and when I returned Ken was in the house and the carpet was missing. I had only been out for about two hours … Ken said he was in the money and decided to change the carpet and the sofa. About two weeks later, the sofa and chair arrived.' Roy also maintained that Regan claimed to be working for a company importing fruit into the country and that the owner of the company was an 'Indian man who owed money to the tax man and had done a midnight flit'.

I never did get to listen to any of the forensic evidence that had been collected from my field, though I did see an article in a local paper describing some jewellery that had been found. One of the things unearthed was an anklet that, according to Nancy's cousin, was 'definitely of Indian origin. Nancy used to wear one of these.' She also stated that she was 80 per cent sure that a choker chain that was found in my field was the sort of thing that Nancy would have worn. There were other items of jewellery that also fitted the sort of pieces that Nancy had. Remnants of burned children's clothing were found, as well as hair from Neil Chohan. Clothing and a watch believed to be Neil's were also unearthed and for sure these were not transported by me carrying them from Neil's office chair, whatever Regan wanted everyone to believe.

No wonder Regan eventually had to admit to disposing of Neil's body: he didn't really have any other choice. The forensic evidence was too great, even for a sociopath like him to ignore. I hoped that he felt a little like Neil had: suffocated, buried by the mountain of evidence that would ensure his days were spent locked up with sex offenders and paedophiles, watching his back, waiting for someone to slash him with a razor blade at any given opportunity. The price of being a double child murderer and a police informer in prison would hopefully scar him for life, and I don't mean metaphorically.

When geoscientist Professor Kenneth Pye entered the witness box, he only confirmed more of the same: Neil Chohan had been buried in my field. Professor Pye explained to the court that he had recovered tiny stones from tape used to gag Neil Chohan and he had also recovered soil from his clothes and his shoes. 'The particles were indistinguishable in terms of colour and appearance from several samples taken from the trench site.' He also went on to say that a reddish-brown stain on Neil's jeans matched the soil found on my land. The other damning factor was that the 'red soil' was also found in the boat that had been used to dump the bodies in the sea and, much more to the point, on a spade found outside Regan's house. Professor Pye said the red soil on the spade did not match the soil in Regan's garden.

The case, though slow, seemed to me to be progressing well. Chinks seemed to be appearing in the solidarity of the defendants, which came as no surprise really. Why would anyone take responsibility for five murders if they had not committed them? Why would anyone want to protect Regan, who really was beyond redemption? Horncy and Rees's only option was to scramble around and point the finger of blame, though in my mind they were equally guilty: they buried them, they dug them up and, when given the opportunity to help the police, neither of them ever did. Hopefully, they would pay a very heavy penalty.

On one of my visits to the Bailey, I got to hear the end of Tony Bishop's cross-examination. Tony and Russell Ferris were the two police officers I had spent hours with, holed up in Tiverton Police Station, giving lengthy statements at the beginning of the investigation at my home. I hadn't seen Tony since then, apart from a brief meeting at Chelsea Police Station when I had handed over photographs of paved driveways that Regan had once given me to show me the kind of work that he could do. I thought he came across very well in court. He was very coherent and, I thought, rather dapper in his pink shirt and dark suit – a far cry from the borrowed Wellington boots I had seen him wearing in Devon. I stayed a bit longer before heading back to my brother's.

While walking up Ludgate Hill, I bumped into Graham Thurlow – the officer whom I had initially met with Andy Rowell in the Carlton Towers and who had accused me of lying and made me cry. Unbeknown to him, at this point, he had been promoted quite heavily in the ranks of my affections. We actually exchanged pleasantries and shook hands. He said he was on his way to the court and I remember being shocked at how he looked. I assumed he was working undercover. He looked unshaven and his clothes were a bit dishevelled. I was far too polite to comment and we wished each other well and departed. It made me smile remembering how much I had disliked him. How times change!

The trial continued slowly and eventually, on 17 March, the prosecution case came to a close. It had taken a long time to get there, but finally it was the turn of the defence. The court broke for two weeks over Easter and, on 4 April, Regan's defence began. There was a slight variation on the theme of his defence. He added the fact that, if he had not helped this fictitious gang of Asian drug dealers dispose of Neil Chohan's body, then I and my two girls would also be murdered along with his father. The news that Regan would not be taking the stand came as no surprise to me or, I am sure, to the police. There would be far too many questions that he did not want to be asked, never mind have to answer. He was used to informing on people and hiding his crimes behind those of others; but on this one he had no bargaining chips or leverage. There was no defence for his actions: he had cold-bloodedly murdered an entire family.

I learned that Regan's co-defendant and lackey Bill Horncy would be going into the witness box. I simply had to listen to his excuses. I left home at 3.30 a.m. on Monday, 11 April. I took my seat in the public gallery – nothing much had changed except Regan looked older, fatter and more and more like the broken man I hoped he would become. The first witness in the box that morning was a man brought into CIBA by Mike Parr to act as director. He was an independent man who was an excellent troubleshooter. This witness mainly dealt with the money that Neil Chohan had siphoned off from the company. He mentioned three cheques, amounting to £50,000, that had gone through Neil's personal account instead of the business account. In fact, I had discovered this anomaly and had contacted Barclays Bank fraud department to try and ascertain which account these cheques had been cleared through, but there was no point in splitting hairs. However, I must have either nodded in agreement or shaken my head in disbelief at some of his evidence. Mr Arlidge QC, the wily old fox, didn't miss a thing. He brought my presence in the public gallery to the attention of the judge, who cautioned me to remain 'as solid as a rock'. I said I would, so under a caution I managed to keep my seat. Thank God, because what was about to unfold became absolutely riveting and unmissable.

Horncy entered the witness box at 3.32 p.m. He spoke in practically inaudible tones and it was almost impossible to hear what he said. The only thing that you could tell was that he was lying. He was totally unbelievable and the more ludicrous the story got the more his voice faltered and the quieter he spoke. He obviously couldn't bear to listen to his own lies. I wanted to laugh but was too nervous even to cross my legs for fear of alerting anyone's attention. Mr Arlidge took Horncy through his obviously self-rehearsed but totally incredible version of events. They started with his criminal record – two counts of violence, so he was well qualified to progress to murder, and then of course the passport fraud that he had committed to help Regan's heroin business. Horncy stated that Regan had given a statement against him when Regan had turned supergrass in his own trial, and this had lead to his conviction. Horncy was not happy and was not too keen to renew contact with Regan when he got out of prison, though foolishly he did. I bet as he stood in that witness box he wished he had never set eyes on him again; but he did, and he helped him murder five people, and now he was going to have to pay.

The two became friends again and Regan told Horncy that he had managed, somehow or other, to siphon off £2 million into a bank account abroad, although he could not touch it until October

2004 when his parole travel restrictions would be lifted. Regan discussed the land that he 'owned' and said that he was 'now back in the freight business with Mike Parr'. Interestingly enough, he also told Horncy that he was 'back with Belinda again'. It was the 'again' bit I found interesting – he'd certainly kept that fantasy going in his head the whole time he had been in prison. Regan then went on to tell Horncy that in January 2003 he had 'got me a wife'. So, I was now apparently married and, of all people, I chose Regan – a fat, ugly, old bloke who would end up being a serial killer. I'd made a few mistakes in my life, but that would have been the worst. Again, I wanted to laugh – the audacity of the man was almost incomprehensible. Then, when I heard he had been saying that not only were we married but also that he had adopted my children as his own, I felt enraged. But still I sat there stony-faced. Regan, on the other hand, sat with his head down, picking imaginary bits of fluff off his trousers; gone were the glares that I used to get.

There was some talk of a car that Horncy had bought from Peter Rees: it was causing Horncy some problems so he left it at Regan's house and Rees was going to go there and fix it. Mr Arlidge then turned to the days running up to Neil Chohan's disappearance. On Tuesday, 13 February, the day after I had the meeting with Neil Chohan and Regan to discuss the sale of the company and the actual day that Neil disappeared, Horncy arrived at CIBA. His excuse for this visit was to discuss putting in a mezzanine floor in the warehouse to create more storage space. Nothing happened and neither Mike Parr nor Regan discussed this with him. Apparently, he was furious about this and so returned the next day, Valentine's Day, to have this meeting. I was there at the office having had a meeting with Regan and the accountant. I left shortly afterwards and headed home where I found the Valentine's card that Regan had said took him an hour to choose. Obviously planning and committing five murders was not the full-time job I would have expected it to be. Horncy remembered meeting me that day but I did not remember him. Regan and Horncy left later that afternoon and headed down to Regan's father's house in Sailsbury. There they stayed the night, and this is where the story becomes complicated.

On Saturday, 15 February, two days after Neil Chohan disappeared, according to Horncy's version of events, he and Regan went to a pub called the Master Robert. The pub was located approximately a quarter of a mile from Neil Chohan's house. The house was near CIBA and close to Heathrow Airport. Horncy stated in his evidence that the reason for this was that there were some drugs at CIBA that Regan wanted to get rid of. Apparently, the drugs were not his and had been shipped in by Neil Chohan for someone he knew. Horncy said he was not interested in helping Regan as he disliked drugs, had never been involved with drugs and believed that they ruined people's lives. It was unbelievable – drugs were a no-go area, but murder was no problem. He wasn't convincing me with this newfound Christian resolve. Once Regan explained that the drugs were not illegal in England, though they were in America, Horncy agreed to help. So, according to Horncy's version of events, these perfectly legal drugs that were in the warehouse in CIBA were transported to some pub car park and then handed over to someone else.

This job needed to be finished the next day, and so, on Sunday morning, the two men yet again drove to the Master Robert, and arrived around ten o'clock. Horncy maintained that, shortly after they arrived at the pub, a red 4 x 4 turned up, the same vehicle he had seen the day before. There were approximately thirty boxes in this vehicle: these were unloaded into the back of Peter Rees's car, which Horncy had borrowed as his car still had not been fixed, and also into Regan's car. When the red car left, a white van arrived and the boxes were unloaded from the cars into the van. This happened a couple of times, and the man in the red 4 x 4, who was Asian, as was the driver of the other vehicle, said that this process was too slow and asked why they couldn't borrow the other man's white van – I'm not sure how he was supposed to have known about it as, according to Horncy's evidence, the red car was gone before the white van turned up. Regan apparently agreed to ask the van driver to lend him the van, but the next time the van driver appeared he was in a blue people carrier.

For a pub that was closed, there was a hell of a lot of activity going on in the car park – it's incredible that not one person spotted them there loading and unloading the boxes.

Regan then apparently had a conversation with the Asian man in the blue people carrier and the two went off together, only to return shortly afterwards with a hired transit van. Then the red 4 x 4 came back with two people in it, and one of them took away the white van. I hope you are keeping up with this – it's getting to be a little like Spaghetti Junction, and we are only in a quiet suburb of London on a lazy Sunday afternoon! Horncy, still mumbling, stated that Regan and he then went to a café where Regan ate though he didn't. Then Regan decided to go for a drive. Horncy explained that, at the time, there were terrorist threats and the airport was heavily patrolled and armed. I think the press dubbed it the 'ring of steel'. They saw the armed police and, after driving around for an hour, they returned to the Master Robert. I suppose, if you are about to transport dead bodies in the back of a transit van, it would be a good idea to avoid the police and any checkpoints, so I understand the point of that little afternoon jaunt. It was, to my mind, possibly the only truthful event he related to the court that day.

When they returned to the pub, the white van and the red 4 x 4 were there. The white van remained and the red car left. Then the blue people carrier arrived with two people in it, and one of them drove the white van away. Regan told Horncy to wait there as there were still ten more boxes of drugs to come. He left in his car, but told Horncy to wait until 5 p.m. and, if no one came back, to leave then. Horncy apparently waited until 5.15 and then left.

Neil's twenty-five-year-old wife Nancy, her mother Charanjit Kaur and the two Chohan children, eighteen-month-old Devinder and eight-week-old Ravinder, were never seen again. The white transit van that Regan had hired, when eventually found and impounded by the police, was found to contain blood belonging to Neil Chohan.

Why this elaborate and obviously untrue story? They had to think of something. The police had traced all the calls that had been made from their mobile phones and, by working out which satellites had been used, they could place Regan and Horncy in the vicinity of Sutton Road where the Chohans lived, so they had to think of a story. What better excuse than they were doing a drug deal? I watched the jury while Horncy was in the witness box and I got the impression that they thought it was just one lie after another. When Horncy's barrister asked him if he had anything to do with the kidnapping and murder of the Chohan family, he replied, 'Definitely not.' At that point three of the jury rolled their eyes and looked up at the ceiling as if in disbelief. One of them even turned round to his fellow jurors in the back row and shrugged. I was delighted: hopefully Horncy would hang himself and Regan.

The following day, Horncy alleged that he had arrived at Regan's house to see if his car had been fixed. The hired transit van was in Regan's drive. Regan said that he wanted the drainage ditch dug on my land – apparently, the two of them had discussed this work back in January. Regan, who now had five bodies on his hands, needed somewhere to put them all. It would be dug the next day, Tuesday, 18 February. Horncy went to Tiverton to hire a digger. He was unsuccessful. Regan hired one in Salisbury, and the following day, Wednesday, 19 February, Rees and Horncy picked up the digger from the garden centre and took it down to my house on a trailer.

Horncy stated in court that Regan drove the transit van and that, when the three of them arrived at my house, they unloaded the digger and Rees took it on to the field and started the trench. Horncy was moving large stones off the field, and Regan, unaided, took the furniture out of the back of the van, along with numerous bin liners. He then set fire to them. The flames were fuelled by the diesel that Regan poured on the sofa and bags: they rose to about twenty feet and were very fierce. No wonder my fence post was almost burned through and all the surrounding trees and bushes scorched. When the trench was about four and a half feet deep, Regan sent Rees to get some burgers in the local town. Horncy said that he and Rees left shortly after that and Regan stayed to await the delivery of stones that had been ordered. Early that evening, Horncy spoke to Regan who informed him that the stones had not arrived but should be there first thing in the morning and asked if Horncy could be there to take delivery of them. Horncy agreed to do this. He also agreed to pick up the ten boxes of drugs that had now mysteriously appeared in Regan's garage and drop them off in London. This gave Horncy the perfect excuse for giving Regan a lift, as Regan now needed to return the van he had transported the bodies in, so he asked Horncy to pick him up after delivering the drugs. Horncy then drove Regan back to Salisbury.

According to Horncy, he arrived at my house the following day, Thursday, at around 8 a.m., as he was expecting the stone to be delivered early that morning; Rees arrived about an hour later. Horncy stated that the trench was exactly as it had been left the day before – it was still four to four and a half feet deep. Rees and Horncy waited around all morning but, instead of the stones arriving, I did. Shortly after my arrival, the three trucks carrying the base stone and the chippings turned up. Not feeling well, but having voiced my displeasure with what I had found, I went to bed. The next day, Regan arrived and they filled the trench.

That was what Horncy stated under oath in court happened. He knew nothing of any body or bodies being buried, and his barrister asked him again if he had anything to do with the kidnapping or murder of the Chohan family. Horncy maintained he did not.

The story didn't end there; Horncy still had plenty more to say. Shortly after this alleged drug deal and the digging on my land, Regan gave Horncy a suitcase to look after. According to Horncy's evidence, this suitcase had been given to Regan by Michael Parr and it belonged to Neil Chohan and held his personal effects. Neil wanted it kept safe so he could pick it up later. Horncy said he could not take it home because, if he had told his girlfriend that it belonged to someone who was on the run from the police, he 'did not know which one would be thrown out first', him or the suitcase. Because of this, he took it to a friend's house. Apparently, this man gave a statement to the police stating that Horncy came by about a week later saying that he needed to get something out of it. Horncy says he didn't get anything out of it, he just wanted to check it was the same combination on it and that his mate had not touched it. It was in this suitcase that the police found the blank sheets of paper that Neil Chohan had been forced to sign while being held against his will. The sheets of paper were in a plastic file which had the fingerprints of Horncy on it.

In the period shortly before Regan decided to dig the bodies up and dump them at sea, Horncy helped him buy a boat. Apparently, the purpose of this boat was to take Neil Chohan and his family out to a larger vessel that did not want to come into shore and incur charges, thus affording them safe passage out of the country. To divert police attention away from CIBA, which was supposedly hindering business, Regan asked Horncy, on behalf of himself and allegedly – though untruthfully – Michael Parr, to meet with the police and tell them that he had met with Neil Chohan on 13 February and then again in mid-March, and that they had discussed Horncy getting the family fake passports. Horncy met DI Andy Rowell and DC Graham Thurlow at CIBA. He stated that he met with Parr before the meeting with the police and Parr asked him what he was going to say to them. He told Parr what he had in mind, and Parr allegedly nodded in agreement as if he already knew what he was going to say. Horncy told Andy Rowell about the meeting that was going to take place in Wales with himself and Neil Chohan. This was the wild goose chase thought up to divert attention from my house in Devon so that Regan, Horncy and Rees could return and exhume the bodies before the police found them. Of course, the murdered Mr Chohan did not turn up.

The questioning continued, and with each explanation Horncy sounded less and less credible. Mr Arlidge moved to events of 19 April 2003. Regan and Horncy arrived in Tiverton driving Peter Rees's car; having already ordered a digger and some stones in the name of J Brewin, which happened to be the same name they had bought the boat in. At one point, Horncy made this elaborate show to the jury that made me cringe by saying, 'Ladies and gentleman, this happens nationwide. In every building site in the country you will find that no one signs for things in their own name.'

For some reason, I felt embarrassed for him. It would have been so much less painless if he had just admitted to murder right there and then.

Once Regan and Horncy were in Tiverton, they went to Travis

Perkins and bought some concrete pipes, which Horncy refused to allow in Rees's car for fear of ruining it. Regan went and hired another transit van. By some miracle, on Regan's return, they realised that they did not need the concrete pipes and bought a length of plastic pipe, which they then cut up. The judge asked if these pipes could have gone into the car, to which Horncy replied they could.

Horncy maintained that, when the two of them arrived at my home, Regan then started the digging. He said Rees was not there. This is not true. I saw all three of them there in the morning and that was the day that Regan borrowed the three overalls. When I made tea in the morning, Rees was in the digger, but according to Horncy he did not arrive until the afternoon – a blatant lie. According to Horncy, Regan dug out the trench until it got to about three foot and then he got out of the digger and came over to him and told him not to panic. Regan told him that Neil Chohan's body was in the trench. Horncy said he felt sick and didn't know what to do. Regan went on to explain that he had been forced to dispose of the body otherwise the Asians would have been murdered me and my children. Horncy described Neil Chohan as looking like a 'Christmas cracker' – not a great analogy, but it was the one he gave. He was wrapped up in a dark drape knotted at each end. Horncy said he reluctantly helped place the body in the back of the transit van and apparently I appeared about five minutes later. I remember that Regan led me away from the gate towards the stable and Rees was in the digger. Horncy then says Rees turned up in his car to help them level out the stones. Regan told Horncy that Mike Parr had asked him to deliver the body and the boat back to the Asians. Horncy said he felt so sick by what he had just done that he could not tell Rees what had happened. He said he left with Rees, leaving Regan with the body.

It was a lot to take in and I felt sick at the thought that these men, who now looked so pathetic, had walked round my property with such nonchalance while burying and digging up bodies on my land. Regan had even castigated me for my ingratitude for what he was doing. I felt overwhelmed and was glad that the day had come to an end. I went to a nearby bar, ordered a drink and wrote up notes on what I had heard. It brought back the terrible sadness of those times and the unhappiness that the girls and I had been through. Retribution for Regan, Horncy and Rees was getting closer.

The next day brought new levels of disbelief. Horncy sounded less believable with every passing minute, the explanations for his actions more outrageous. He and Regan had been given the telephone data that the police had gathered months before the trial started, and they had weaved a web of deceit and duplicity around it. According to Horncy's testimony, he and Regan had met by the Ringwood roundabout near Bournemouth. The day after the bodies were exhumed, Regan went to fetch the boat and instructed Horncy to wait for the Transit van. Not long after Regan left, the van appeared with two men in it – apparently, the driver was white and his passenger Asian. Regan had asked Horncy to take them to the Little Chef that was just up the road. The reason that Horncy gave for this was that Regan had wanted to catch the two men in the van on video as he had no telephone numbers for them and did not know who they were. As it happened, only the vehicles were caught on film, not the occupants, and it was the police who found the CCTV footage. Horncy said he drove into the Little Chef and then left almost immediately. They went down a little side street by a post-office shop, as the two men in the van wanted to get something to eat and needed cigarettes. When asked why they did not get something to eat in the Little Chef or buy cigarettes at the garage, Horncy pathetically replied that he thought they were Muslims.

According to his version of events, he then left these two men near the post office and went to find Regan who had gone to pick up the boat. He passed Regan on the road, flashed his lights at him and Regan pulled over. Horncy turned around and the two returned in convoy with the boat. They then left the car and the boat with the two men in the white van, Regan got into Horncy's car and the two of them departed, returning to the Ringwood roundabout to retrieve Regan's car. It was Rees's car that was being used to pull the boat, and Regan told Horncy he had left a phone in it so that the two men could contact Rees to give him his car back. Horncy protested that he was not happy with that arrangement and suggested that Regan went back and retrieved the phone. The judge then interjected and enquired as to why Horncy thought the car would still be there. Horncy could not give a reason. He said he then went home.

The next day, Horncy went to Regan's house in Salisbury to give him a lift to Tiverton to return the van, which had been mysteriously returned to Regan's house by 'the Asians'; on the following day, knowing that Neil Chohan was already dead, he went to this spurious meeting in Wales that he arranged with the police. Horncy's reasons for helping Regan dispose of Neil Chohan's body was that the bank scam was still an ongoing proposition and he wanted his money.

Nine days after the bodies had been exhumed, the police arrived at my house. I had met with Andy Rowell and Graham Thurlow on the morning of 28 April and informed them that Regan had specifically asked me not to mention he had been digging on my land. They went that day to my house and, the following day, just after the helicopters had left, I bumped into Regan and Horncy in my lane. According to Horncy, Regan had wanted to come and say hello to me. Later that day, the two of them left the country – though Horncy maintained that their departure bore no relevance to the police activity at my house. They left in connection with the bank scam that had so inextricably tied them together.

Horncy then waffled on for another hour about where the two of them travelled, and how, having fled the country, he had learned a few days later that he was wanted in connection with the murder of Mr Chohan and that his body had been found. Horncy said he wanted to come back to England and sort the problem out, but he was concerned about being arrested. I think that might have been the understatement of the year. Horncy remained on the run in Europe for some five months. One of the more ridiculous reasons he gave for not coming back 'to sort it out' was that he wanted to get back into England without being arrested. I'm sure he did! He said that he and Regan had even caught a boat from northern Spain that was supposed to dock secretly in Falmouth, but it was intercepted by the French

Customs. Horncy and Regan left the boat in France, leaving their bags and possessions aboard, and headed back to Spain. Horncy said that Regan had bought a recording device and wanted to get Mike Parr on tape admitting it was him who had asked Regan to dispose of Neil Chohan's body. This, of course, was untrue and it never happened because Regan was arrested and Horncy remained on the run until some time in September.

At no point during his evidence was there any mention of the Chohan women and children: no one, it seemed, had any idea of what happened to them. It was so sad and utterly shocking.

Horncy's cross-examination started with questions from Mr Mendelle, Regan's barrister. I was not expecting any major revelations, as it was unlikely that Mr Mendelle would wish to be too harsh on Horncy for fear that he might implicate his client further. Mr Mendelle suggested to Horncy that he had known about the body of Mr Chohan in February 2003 and not April 2003 as he maintained, because Regan had told him and he had helped Regan to bury Mr Chohan; much to my surprise and that of everyone else in the court, Horncy agreed. I was stunned, as, it seemed, was the judge, who asked him if he had meant to say yes. To which Horncy said he had. So one of the very first questions from one of the defence barristers suddenly negated the evidence that Horncy had given over the last three days. The jury seemed as perplexed as the rest of us. Horncy then went on to give his second, and this time supposedly 'true', version of events. It was almost farcical – his second version did not last long, and he had to amend that with a third version. It was difficult to keep up with his explanations.

When Mr Gledhill QC, the barrister for Peter Rees, asked Horncy why he had suddenly had this 'road to Damascus experience', Horncy stood pathetically in the witness box with his head down and muttered, 'Well, because it's bloody serious.'

Bloody serious? Was he kidding? Five murders and nearly two years later he had only just realised that. It made me angry. As if that was not insulting enough, he then added that he was 'sick of the lies' and that he 'owed it to the Chohan family' to tell the truth. I couldn't believe it – he had done nothing before his arrest or since to alleviate the pain of that family or that of Nancy's brother; now he was using them in his defence. Personally, I couldn't listen to much more of it.

When Mr Horwell for the prosecution stood up, I was not sure if Horncy would survive the onslaught. Mr Horwell asked him if he had ever visited Regan's house before 13 February, and Horncy admitted that he hadn't. But over the next five days he was there every day and spent, by his own admission, at least two nights there. These were the days that Neil Chohan was held against his will before being murdered. And, by some strange coincidence, he was stuck at Regan's address because his car was not working, and even odder was the fact that Rees was also there on a daily basis trying to fix his car.

On the weekend that Neil Chohan's wife, mother-in-law and two tiny children were murdered, Horncy originally maintained that the drug he had helped move was 'khat'. I had never heard of 'khat' but apparently it is a leaf, similar to coca leaves, chewed mainly by Somalians, and a mild stimulant. At first, Horncy maintained that the Lamborghini driver was involved. All of a sudden, the drug that he and Regan moved while at the Master Robert pub, just 600 metres from the Chohan home, was, of all things, cocaine. It just didn't make sense. Horncy maintained that he and Regan moved 200 boxes, weighing approximately 20 pounds each, full of cocaine. This, according to the prosecution, amounted to millions of pounds' worth of drugs being moved in broad daylight in a pub car park, from one vehicle to another over a period of many hours: it just could not be true. No one who ran an operation of that magnitude would do it like that, especially with Regan, a supergrass, as the pivotal pin. Why did they change their story again? Presumably it was more believable for the family to have been murdered for that amount of cocaine rather than boxes of leaves that barely anyone in this country had ever heard of. Personally, I didn't really understand how they thought anyone would believe them.

Mr Horwell continued his questioning. He asked Horncy about the day that Neil Chohan was dug up and he said that no doubt Horncy wanted to get it over and done with as quickly as possible.

Horncy agreed. The pipes had only been bought in order to deceive me. Horncy admitted that he and Regan had buried Neil Chohan's body at one end of the long trench, but instead of just digging at that end they excavated the entire trench. Mr Horwell suggested that this was because they had to exhume the rest of the bodies as well. Horncy maintained it was in order to put the pipes in – pipes that were, in the end, thrown into an almost full trench. They had been laid up against the hedge and forgotten about and were haphazardly strewn in the trench just to get them out of the way. I saw the trench when it was dug out and I will never believe that there were fewer than five bodies in my field. Mr Horwell insisted that the five bodies had been exhumed that day. Horncy scratched his head, drank water and said, 'No, no, no,' numerous times. I wondered if he thought that, by admitting to lying earlier, the jury would believe that what he was saying now was the truth.

Horncy still stuck to his story that Rees did not arrive on the day of the exhumation until some time in the afternoon and only helped level the stone across the field. This was just not true: he had arrived with Regan and Horncy at around 9.30 a.m. and operated the digger all day. I hoped the jury would believe my evidence. Mr Horwell, though, was relentless, and he asked Horncy why this alleged Asian drug gang that had asked Regan, a man who had turned Queen's evidence in his last trial, to dispose of the bodies. Why would anyone ask a man to commit such a crime who so obviously could not be trusted? Mr Horwell asked why, if the gang had not wanted to dispose of the bodies in the first place, would they want to do so now? Horncy did not give an adequate or believable reply to any of the questions.

Throughout Horncy's evidence, Regan never looked up once, not at Horncy or the jury – although the jury often looked over at him. By now, he must have worn a hole in his trousers from the amount of imaginary fluff he had picked off them. He had put on a lot of weight since the start of the trial and, although he was now wearing a shirt and jacket instead of the usual tracksuit, it had not improved his appearance. Occasionally, as he was led to and from the dock to the cells below, he would glance up at the public gallery and I would always hold his stare; it never lasted long – he would put his head down and shuffle off. Peter Rees seemed to doodle on a pad of paper, but invariably he held his head in his hands. The two of them looked a sorry sight.

Horncy finally finished giving evidence and returned to the dock, where he slumped down in his seat and proceeded to roll himself a cigarette. For one awful moment, I thought he was going to light it in court, but he restrained himself. The next person on the stand would be Rees. I listened to a little bit of his evidence but by this stage I was in no mood to hear him regurgitate the same lies and cover-up that Horncy had put us all through for days on end. I left and headed home to Devon. I felt like I had been away for weeks. It was good to get back and the girls were thrilled to see me. Montana was horrified to hear that Regan had said he had adopted her; she laughed when I told her that he had pretended we had got married.

Mr Horwell's cross-examination of Horncy had been as thorough as it was persistent; his cross-examination of Rees was equally relentless. Rees's defence centred mainly on Horncy's broken-down car: like Horncy, he claimed it was his reason for being at Regan's house. Rees, like Horncy, had missed spending Valentine's Day at home with his girlfriend. He was a self-confessed family man, but spent most of the five days from 13 February, the day Neil Chohan disappeared, until 17 February at Regan's home. Very strange behaviour for a man who maintained he couldn't stand Regan and referred to him as a 'cunt'. He did, however, return home on the Easter Saturday after he had helped exhume the bodies from my field (which he denied any knowledge of). The following day he had received a call at 4.49 a.m. from Horncy, presumably a wake-up call as it was an important day in their calendar. To most people, it was Easter Sunday, a day that you would normally spend with your family, but not for Regan, Horncy and Rees. Why spend time with your family when you can dump the bodies of another family into the sea, which is exactly what they did.

On Thursday, 13 February, Rees maintained he drove Horncy the two-hour journey from his house to Regan's, as Horncy's car was broken down there. But, amazingly enough, when he got there not only did he not fix it, but he didn't even look at it. Under cross-examination, he told Mr Horwell that he didn't have a lot to do that day and, as Horncy owed him nearly £3,000 for cars that he had given him over the years, and according to him Regan was going to give him the money, he didn't mind the four-hour round trip. Bizarrely enough, a little while later he said he was too busy that day to fix the car and that he was not in his work clothes and didn't want to get the clothes he was wearing dirty. Rees went on to explain to Mr Horwell that he worked differently to him – I'm sure Mr Horwell was delighted to hear that! He said that he worked when he wanted to, and if he didn't feel like working then he wouldn't.

So, having made the journey to Regan's house on the Thursday, not only did he not get his money, but also the car remained unfixed. Having spent all day there, Rees returned home and then arrived back on Valentine's Day at 8 a.m. in the morning. Still the car remained unfixed. The prosecution were adamant that the reason for his early return that morning was to guard Neil Chohan while Regan and Horncy went to CIBA. Later, Rees returned home, and the next day he repeated the two-hour journey back to Regan's house. Still the car remained unfixed. Rees's time, according to his evidence, seems to have been spent waiting for money and getting drunk in nearby pubs. On the Saturday night, he says he had a lot to drink and was incapable of driving home, but did not want to spend the night at Regan's so apparently made enquiries about local hotels. Mr Horwell was having none of it: he repeatedly asked him for the names of hotels he had tried and who he had spoken to. Rees said that he spoke to a man in the pub.

When Mr Horwell told him that on the night in question there were two empty rooms available at that particular pub, Rees had no response.

Rees also spent the whole of Sunday at Regan's house and finally he managed to fix Horncy's car, but he could not remember where he had bought the spare parts that he said were needed for it or, in fact really explain what was wrong with it. After four days of the car being broken down outside Regan's house, Rees certainly never told Horncy what the matter was with it, nor did Horncy ask what had been wrong with his car. It was the prosecution's case that on Sunday evening, after Neil Chohan was forced to make a phone call to the home of the CIBA accountant at around 8 p.m. to tell him that it was OK for me to sign the company cheques, he was murdered. Now no one had to guard Neil Chohan – he was dead – and, while Regan and Horncy had gone to Sutton Road on the Saturday and Sunday to murder Neil's wife, children and mother-in-law, Rees had assisted in holding hostage the man who would have strained every sinew in his body to protect them.

Rees followed Horncy's story and maintained he knew nothing of either the burial or exhumation of the bodies. He said he was not there. He was. At one point, he tried to argue with Mr Horwell: it was a mistake – he was never going to win. Mr Horwell asked him why he had spent so much time away from his family over the two weekends when the bodies were moved. Rees said that he probably spent more time with his family than Mr Horwell did with his. 'Let's not make this personal,' Mr Horwell replied. It was a foolish move on Rees's behalf, and I wished I had not apologised for calling him the Missing Link because he really was stupid. Whether he murdered the Chohans is, in my mind, doubtful, but he certainly was instrumental in helping Regan and Horncy do the job and at no time did he show any remorse or assist the police in any way. In my opinion, he may as well have murdered them – he was no better than the two men who had and who sat next to him in the dock.

On 25 April, things took a more sinister turn. I remember the day well – it was my daughter's birthday. My mobile phone rang as I was fiddling with candles on a birthday cake and I asked Montana to answer it for me. She spoke and then looked confused and told the person on the other end of the phone to wait. I took the phone and asked who was speaking. An Indian-sounding man answered. 'We know where you are, we know where your children are and we are going to come and kill you.'

'Who is this? Who's speaking?' I replied.

'Stay away from the courts. This is a message from …' – I was unable to hear what he said before he hung up. Naturally, I was shocked, and I rang the police. The number had come up on the phone and I noted it down along with the time of the call. I was surprised, but certainly not in fear of my life. The call came at the time that the defence were presenting their case, and central to Regan's case was the fact that the fictitious Asian drug gang had killed the Chohans and were then going to kill me and my girls if Regan did not help. I knew this was a ploy to add weight to his farcical story, and I for one did not want to aid his defence in any way. I explained to the Metropolitan Police that I felt this call had been arranged by Regan, though there was no evidence that this was the case.

A few people told me to be careful, that they were worried about me; but I had every faith in the police. It concerned me slightly to think that it was a possibility that he could get anyone to make the call, but it didn't come as any great shock and, after all, there wasn't any proof that he had been behind it.

The defence case rested on Wednesday, 27 April. It had been a long time coming and, as I left the court that day, I felt an enormous sense of relief. There was still a long way to go – the summing up would take weeks – but there would be no more witnesses and no more evidence. There seemed to be light at the end of the tunnel and with my luck I prayed it wouldn't be an oncoming train. I headed home: the long Bank Holiday would bring a welcome respite, and I'm sure my brother Tobey and his girlfriend Alex probably felt the same. The two of them had put up with me staying with them for weeks on end. They never moaned, not even when I came home a little drunk one night and mistook their bedroom for mine. I would always be grateful to them.

As I drove home, I thought not only about them, but about all the people who had gone out of their way for me over the last two years. It was incredible to think that it had been just over two years ago that the Met boys had pitched up at my house; some days it felt like they had never left! I had had some very low moments during that period, but it was now coming to a close. I was grateful for my friends in Devon, particularly Rose and Trevor who had been solid in their support of me, as had all of the Breakfast Club girls, and the idea of seeing them all again made me want to get home quicker. I felt like I had been away for months rather than weeks. I thought about some of the people I had met who under normal circumstances I would never have encountered. They were mainly Metropolitan Police officers: Charlie King and Tony Bishop, Andy Rowell, Russell Ferris and Dick Langdon – who turned out to be a charming man and not the grumpy bastard he had seemed when I first met him. Even Graham Thurlow got the odd affectionate thought! I hoped that once the trial was completely over we would be friends.

Maybe I really should have called this book *Punctuated by Policemen*!

# CHAPTER FIFTEEN

The final leg of the journey began at 10.30 a.m. on 3 May 2005, exactly two years and four days after the police had arrived to dig my field. Richard Horwell stood and faced the jury for his summing-up. It had been one of the most expensive murder hunts and the longest murder trial in the history of the Old Bailey and the Metropolitan Police and Mr Horwell sounded clear and confident. The jury looked attentive as he reiterated the main points of the Crown's case. He said it was significant that Regan would not travel the short distance from the dock to the witness box to answer the charges laid against him, and then he added that Horncy probably wished he hadn't made that journey. I'm sure he was right – Horncy had not done himself, or his co-defendants, any favours in the witness box, and Mr Horwell's comments brought a wry smile to my face and to the faces of one or two of the jurors.

I was surprised to learn that Regan had attempted to order a stun gun on the Internet only a few days before the abduction and murder of Neil Chohan. Regan's defence had argued that the reason for this was that Regan was in fear of his life, having turned Queen's evidence in his earlier trial for the thirty-five kilograms of heroin. Mr Horwell dismissed this claim out of hand: Regan had lived for seven months at his father's home, where he could have been easily traced, and had never expressed any concern for his safety to his police handler; he had even refused to go into the witness protection programme, saying it was unnecessary and he was not in fear of his life.

The other fact that I learned was that Nancy Chohan's body had been found in a sailing bag. They are rather like body bags but intended to hold sails, so they are large, waterproof and waxed. This, Mr Horwell explained, was one of the reasons why no DNA apart from that of Neil Chohan, who had been wrapped in fabric, was found in my field. Obviously, Regan maintained that the women and children were not buried there; but, as Mr Horwell asked the jury in his summing-up, what was the likelihood that there were two burial sites and that this fictitious Asian drug gang would really dispose of four bodies and not want to dispose of another? 'As a rule,' he told the jury, 'criminals do not bury people unless they themselves have killed them. If you have the resources and the will to kill five people, you have the resources and the will to dispose of them.' For a start, two burial sites doubled the risk of being caught. Moreover, if all the bodies had been dumped in the sea together, surely they must have been buried together? The defence teams again argued this point and the fact that when the grandmother was found she was not in a sailing bag. They felt that negated the prosecution's argument. Personally, I didn't agree. I felt it was more than plausible for her to have been in a bag. When she was eventually found washed up on a beach on the Isle of Wight, the poor woman was nothing more than a battered torso. Her lower limbs were missing and so was her head. She had been buried for months in my field and had then been in the sea for a year. The bag would have ripped or rotted.

Rejecting Regan's argument that it was Mike Parr who had asked him to bury Neil Chohan's body and then dig him up again and return him to the 'Asians', he quoted some of my evidence. Mr Horwell reminded the jury of how deferential I had said that Parr was to Regan, and that, when Parr had wanted to fire me from my job, Regan had stated that it was not his decision to make and that if Parr did not do what he was told he would 'give him a slap'. It was, as I had always maintained, Regan who was in control.

Regan had, from the very beginning, always claimed that the company and the land were his. That point was underlined by Mr Horwell, who described me as an intelligent woman and my testimony as being precise. He also asked the jury to consider how thoroughly many of the witnesses had been cross-examined, and that my cross-examination had not thrown up any anomalies – but then, it's hard to argue with the truth.

At one point, Mr Horwell was describing Regan and Horncy's use of their mobile phones, and both men gave a derisory snort, almost laughing. I was stunned. Mr Horwell turned to the dock and pointed out to the jury the obvious amusement that these men felt. There was no remorse, and it would seem they had a blatant disregard for the seriousness of the crimes they were charged with.

Mr Horwell went on to describe Regan as a fantasist, mentioning the fact that he had pretended I was his girlfriend and that we were married. No doubt he thought he was in love with me, Mr Horwell said, but it was not reciprocated in any way; this pretend love life that he had also extended its way into his so-called business life. When Regan had gone to jail for his part in the drugs case, he had owned a share in a bonded warehouse called Superior. He had told me he owned the entire company. Mike Parr had worked for him there and, after going to jail, Parr then went on to work for Neil Chohan. Regan was apparently furious with the police that, even after helping to convict many people with his evidence, he still got an eight-year jail term – in fact, he should have received at least twenty years. So, when he had a confiscation order placed against him and his house and assets were taken, he felt that he had been done an injustice. According to Mr Horwell, Regan felt he was perfectly within his rights to come out of jail and take what he felt was rightfully his. The opportunity to return to the big houses, flash cars and suitcases full of money presented itself to him in the form of Neil Chohan. The problem was that Regan did not have the money to buy the company, nor even a tiny percentage of it, so Neil Chohan was going to have to die. Then Regan could have what he felt should never have been taken from him in the first place. Mr Horwell also confirmed the Crown's belief that both Horncy and Rees had been crucial in the execution of Regan's plot to appropriate CIBA by murdering Neil Chohan and his family.

He took a day and a half to sum up his case, and he did an excellent and convincing job. Mr Horwell stressed to the jury that 'to be present at the time of the disappearance of one section of the family may be said to be unfortunate. But to be present in an entirely different place at the time of the disappearance of the remaining members of the family may be seen to be consistent only with guilt, and any other explanation is revealed as the nonsense that it is.'

I was very interested to hear what Mr Mendelle would say in support of his client when he rose and faced the jury. He was more quietly spoken than Mr Horwell and, from my seat in the public gallery, it was sometimes difficult to catch every word. He started by saying that it would not take him a day and a half to sum up the case, but probably only an hour and a half. Well, there was not a lot to say in defence of his client. Although Mr Mendelle maintained that there was 'not a scrap of evidence' that convicted his client of the murders of the Chohan family, I was already unconvinced, not just by the tone in his voice, but by his arguments. When he described Regan as a very brave man, I wanted to laugh. According to Regan's defence team, there was a contract out on him and he was in fear of his life, even though he had moved around freely, lived at his father's address, had never asked for help from his police handler and, until going on the run after murdering Neil Chohan and his family, had never mentioned threats or the fact that someone might want to kill him.

Quite incredibly, Mr Mendelle maintained that, because of this, Regan would rather go to jail for five murders that he did not commit than give evidence: prison would guarantee his safety and therefore his life. He also maintained that Regan had been forced to dispose of Neil's body because of the threat to the life of myself and my children. How dare he use my children and me as an excuse for his murderous behaviour? It made me sick. Mr Mendelle continued to say that the Crown was asking the jury to speculate and that there was not one eyewitness to the murders. Well, that was true, but it certainly could not negate the enormous amount of circumstantial evidence and the huge number of witnesses that were called, or the fact that he told me right from the beginning, four months before he murdered the family, that the business was his, or that he had dug a mass grave in my field. After an hour and a half, Mr Mendelle sat down. He hadn't saved his client. How could he? He had nothing to work with.

Whereas Mr Mendelle had spoken about me in nice tones, I was not expecting the same from Mr Arlidge QC. Listening to him, I felt I should have been sitting in the dock with the rest of the defendants. His opening few sentences were excellent and quite amusing. What do you do, he asked, when everything you have based your case on turns out to be a pack of lies? What do you do when your client admits to lying in the witness box? What can you say after that has happened? 'I went home,' he said, 'had a stiff drink, contemplated it overnight and I thought about it.' He got out of that quite well, I thought, and with some humour.

He then went on to talk about lies and the varying degrees in which we all tell them and for what reasons. His closing speech, though biased and obviously viewed from his client's perspective and definitely through rose-tinted spectacles, was a job well done. He described me as 'vulnerable' and in desperate need of a job and some money. He went on to state that most of the case against his client was based on his mobile-phone records. He said it was interesting to note that, on the crucial day of Neil Chohan's disappearance, his client had made three phone calls to Regan but I had made six. His argument was that, if they could build a wholly circumstantial case against his client, as I had made twice as many calls that day, then they had double the evidence against me. He omitted, of course, to point out that I had spent days in the witness box explaining these calls, and anyway it wasn't the *number* of calls that was important but *where* each person was when the calls were made. He observed that his client was not working at CIBA, as I was; that his name did not appear on any of the alleged documents relating to the sale of CIBA, as mine had; and that his client was definitely not getting paid a ludicrous salary for a job he was not qualified to do, as I was. 'And lo and behold, whose land is Neil Chohan's body buried on, but Miss Brewin's.'

It was quite an impressive attack, and well executed, though flawed in its argument. The implication was that, if I had been lucky enough to escape justice when I was so heavily involved, surely Horncy shouldn't be in the dock either. I wondered what the police made of it. It was as if, after nearly two years of a very thorough investigation, Mr Arlidge was suggesting that these points had been overlooked by them. I can assure you they were not – the hours and hours of interviews that I gave are testimony to that, never mind all the weeks of investigations that I knew nothing about. I know for a fact that they didn't just take my word on these matters. Mr Arlidge also stated, 'There is no one they can call who can give direct eyewitness evidence of the commission of the crime,' as if the fact that no one saw the murders meant they didn't happen.

At around lunchtime, Mr Arlidge finished his assassination of my character and evidence and the courts broke for lunch. I had a couple of appointments that afternoon and was supposed to be going back to Devon that evening. I was annoyed that I could not go back to court – I certainly didn't want anyone to think that a couple of bad comments had scared me off – so I cancelled the trip home and returned to court the next morning.

I found the defence's closing speeches slightly nauseating. Mr Arlidge, as Mr Mendelle had, tried to place some of the blame at the feet of Mike Parr. Whatever my feelings about the man were, he wasn't in the dock with these three, so it was an easy shot to make to deflect the blame from the defendants – as easy as throwing mud at me and hoping it would stick. When Mr Arlidge finished, it was the turn of Mr Gledhill QC, who defended Rees. By the time he stood up, I was bored of listening to the excuses and, after an hour of hearing how if Regan had managed to dupe me – an intelligent woman – that the court could surely understand how someone as thick as Rees had been conned, I'd had enough and wanted to get home to the children, ride my horse and breathe some fresh air. There was nothing to keep me in London.

The judge summed up for three weeks. He went through the entire case in chronological order. He explained to the jury what each witness had said in relation to the movement and actions of the defendants on each day. I am sure that after eight months the jury might have needed to be reminded of certain evidence, but at times it must have been tedious. On 14 June at 10.57 a.m., after directions from the judge on what charges to consider first, the jury rose to consider their verdict.

I decided to drive to London the next day. I wanted to hear the jury come back with their verdict. I knew it would be a lot of waiting around, but it didn't matter. I had waited long enough for it to get to this point. I wouldn't miss it for the world. When I heard the news, I lit yet another Marlboro and wondered if I would manage to give up smoking after the verdict – I had tried numerous times during the trial but had never managed it. I wondered if Regan would find someone else to threaten me, or worse still, do harm to me or my children. He was a desperate man and there was always that possibility, but he hadn't scared me the last time and I certainly wouldn't allow him to control my life from jail. So, with the events of the last two years running yet again around my head, I started another journey, one of yet more waiting.

For the first time in a long time, I made a wish – I wished that no one I ever knew would die in any way apart from peacefully, and hopefully in their sleep. Not like Michael, not like Paula and certainly nothing like the Chohan family.

The waiting was almost unbearable, as days turned into weeks. I spent thirteen days within walking distance of the Old Bailey. I read a lot of books, basked in the glorious weather that London was having and hoped that each day would be the final day. When the jury had been out for ten days, the judge called them back into court after discussions with the barristers on whether he should instruct the jury on majority verdicts. The judge was reluctant to go down that road, especially after such a short amount of deliberating, the length of the trial and the number of counts that the jury had to consider. The judge asked them if they would be able to come to unanimous verdicts on all counts, to which the foreman replied that they would be able to do so. Please hurry, I thought. The suspense was palpable.

It really had been a long journey and I desperately wanted to see Regan's face when the verdicts were announced. It was worth the wait. On Friday, 1 July, as I sat down to lunch with my friend Catherine Mayer, I said to her, 'Knowing my luck, I'll order the food and the phone will ring telling me the jury have reached a decision and are coming back with a verdict.'

We ordered our food, it arrived and the phone rang. The jury were coming back. Catherine and I left the food on the table, told the waiter we would be back to pay later and the two of us ran the 200 yards to the Old Bailey. It was strange that Catherine had been with me at the start of the trial and that she would now be with me at the end of it. I was glad and when the verdicts were read out: Guilty, Guilty, Guilty. I kissed her and could not have been happier. I was happy that justice had been done and that maybe the Chohan family could get some measure of comfort from knowing these men would be spending an incredibly long time behind bars. Hopefully, Regan would never get out. I was pleased for the Metropolitan Police officers who initially worked on the case, they had been diligent in their pursuit and investigation of Regan, Horncy and Rees and it was a credit to them that these men were convicted.

Regan was found guilty on all charges. Five charges of murder, two of them charges of murdering children (an eight-week-old baby and a seventeen-month-old toddler). He was also guilty of false imprisonment and unlawful burial. Horncy was guilty on the same charges, and Rees was found guilty of murdering Neil Chohan and assisting an offender on the other charges of murder against the two women and the two young children. Regan showed neither emotion nor remorse. Horncy did his usual pathetic shaking of the head and Rees looked down at the floor. Sir Stephen Mitchell said he would pass sentence on Tuesday, 5 July at 10.30.

On Tuesday, 5 July at 10.25am, I entered the Old Bailey for what I hoped would be the last time in my life. My bag was searched and I was instructed to go to Court Eleven. There were a lot of people wanting to get into the public gallery. One of the court staff took me through and I stood by the public gallery along with numerous police officers. Some I recognised from the investigation, like Tony Bishop, Teresa Defanis and Paul Abbott. It was nice to see Tony, as it had been a long time. The courtroom was packed. I sat in the front row where I had a good view of Regan who, for the first time ever, did not look up at the public gallery. In fact, he barely moved at all – he still showed no emotion and certainly no remorse. I was shaking. The judge outlined the law and then spoke to the defendants. He said, 'Your characters are as despicable as your crimes. Each of you is a practised, resourceful and manipulative liar.' He then went on to describe the cold-blooded murders saying that they 'provide a chilling insight into the utterly perverted standards by which you have lived your lives'.

I actually felt sick and I hoped that the judge would impose a sentence whereby life meant life, but I was unsure if there was such a thing. So when I heard him pass a 'whole life sentence' on both Regan and Horncy, I had to check that what I had heard was correct and had to stop myself from kissing the officer sitting next to me. I heard the judge state quite clearly that neither man would ever be released from jail. Sir Stephen Mitchell said he was aware that Horncy was not involved in the initial planning to take over CIBA and that he had only become involved with Regan a few weeks before the disappearance of the family, but he said he had involved himself very heavily in an extremely heinous crime, that he had lied continually in the witness box and had even, as I had noted previously, tried to gain the sympathy of the court by saying he was telling the truth because he owed it to the Chohan family. It was utterly shocking and then of course he got caught lying. When he finally uttered the words 'Take them down', I watched Regan shuffle off, head bent. Hopefully, it would be the last time I ever saw him and he would never see the light of day again.

Rees was alone in the dock. He, too, stood with his head bent and the judge sentenced him to a minimum of twenty-three years in jail. This was a prime example of misplaced loyalty. He could have helped both himself and the police if he had been co-operative instead of insisting on saying, 'No comment.' Rees had spent two weeks on the run and, when he eventually stood in the witness box all those months later, he too had lied and had tried to cover up the crimes that he and the other defendants had committed. He would now have twenty-three years to think about whether he had made the right decision. I doubt it would take him twenty-three hours, let alone years, to realise the mistake he had made!

As for Horncy, he will have the rest of his life to rue the day he ever allowed Regan, a man who had turned Queen's evidence against him and therefore led to his previous conviction, to re-enter his life. Personally, I felt the sentences were deserved. I couldn't wait to telephone my daughters with the news.

With the defendants now sentenced, the judge thanked DCI Norman McKinlay QPM (Queen's Police Medal), the officer in charge of the investigation at the outset. He also thanked Dick Langdon and Paul Zaleski, the two officers who had been in court for the duration of the trial. They both deserved it and, as I left court that day, I hoped I would be able to buy them a drink in appreciation of everything they had done for me and Montana.

When I got to the pub, it was crowded and full of police officers, most of whom I didn't know and a few faces that I did recognise. The legal teams were there but most of them looked different without their wigs and gowns. I said 'Hello' and one of the barristers commented on my book and told me he thought that I had very much got the measure of Regan. It was nice to really be able to celebrate, but it was nicer still to wake up the next morning (even with a monumental hangover) and drive home to Devon, to my children and my friends knowing that this nightmare and the Old Bailey were now part of my past. Life would never be the same again, but at least the girls and I had each other. As one detective commented, it was as if, for the last two years, I had been running towards the edge of a cliff and now I was finally there. It did feel a bit like that, but I knew for sure I wasn't going to jump. I would just have to rebuild a life that seemed to have lost its sense of direction. I hope it is going to be fun trying to find it again.